Real Food Microwave

Other Cookbooks by Donovan Jon Fandre:

More Time for Lovin', Since I Got My Microwave Oven, 1979

Microwaves Are for Cooking, 1983

The Microwave Master, 1988

Real Food
MICROWAVE

400 Recipes from Television's "Microwave Master" That Taste As If They Were Made the Old-Fashioned Way

Donovan Jon Fandre

William Morrow and Company, Inc.
New York

Library of Congress Cataloging-in-Publication Data

Fandre, Donovan Jon.
   Real food microwave / by Donovan Jon Fandre.
     p.   cm.
   ISBN 0-688-09115-6
   1. Microwave cookery. I. Title.
TX832.F363 1991
641.5'882—dc20
                                          91-612
                                          CIP

Printed in the United States of America

First Edition

1 2 3 4 5 6 7 8 9 10

BOOK DESIGN BY RICHARD ORIOLO

To my mother, Ada,
the first great cook in my life

Acknowledgments

I often reflect on how lucky I am to be able to make a living doing something that I really enjoy. A large part of that enjoyment comes from the people I work with when spreading the gospel of modern cooking. For this book I especially want to thank . . .

My wife, Doris, for tolerating me in the kitchen and insisting on the ''R'' word.

My children Sarah, her husband, Don, and Andrew for reluctantly yet obediently trying my new recipes.

My children Thomas and Jessica for their moral support from afar.

The dogs in my life: Great Danes, Lucille and Mollie, and Cocker, Peter, for eating my test recipes with relish and sometimes mixed with dog food.

All of the radio and TV talk shows who have repeatedly allowed me to do my thing and especially to the *Live with Regis and Kathie Lee* show for letting me do my ''schtick.''

Bill Adler, my agent, who watched the Regis and Kathie Lee show and liked what he saw.

Maria Guarnaschelli, my editor at William Morrow, who made it easy and who soon will love her little zapper.

Liz Portland, my editor's assistant, for all her wonderful help along the way.

Irv and Patricia Hamilton, associates and friends.

Al and Ann Castin, fellow hedonists always in search of a great recipe.

Arthur and Merle Friedman for opening the door.

Dore and Betsy Schwab for providing haven for this microwave maven.

Contents

Introduction

One very important point—to cook successfully with a microwave oven you must WANT to cook by microwave. Most of the objections voiced by cooking professionals and food writers are based on prejudice and negativism. The same objections were voiced when food processors came on the market and now you can't find a person in the cooking profession who doesn't own one. If Julia Child and Pierre Franey and Craig Claiborne and Paul Prudhomme and Marian Burros and Merle Ellis and Irma Rombauer and Wolfgang Puck and Carlo Middione and Martin Yan and Alice Waters and Jacques Pépin and Ken Hom and Martha Stewart and the thousands that I haven't mentioned cooked by microwave, believe me, they would come out with fantastic recipes and probably cookbooks. The same applies to you. If you want to, you WILL cook beautifully with your microwave oven.

Microwave cooking is a lot like marriage. You can talk to friends about it, you can attend classes about it, you can watch television shows about it, and you can read books about it, but until you actually do it yourself you'll never know what it's all about. This book is designed as a guide to help you enter into the realm of microwave cooking and gain the confidence to not only cook the recipes here but also to use your own talent to create new recipes or to convert conventional recipes, either in part or totally, to microwave. You must enter into this with an open heart and without prejudice. You must anticipate the joys of producing great meals and also be aware of the possibilities of less than perfect results. Microwave cooking is not the panacea to cooking woes. It is just another way to apply heat to food. In most cases it is easier and cleaner than conventional cooking. After you learn to use your microwave oven as a tool within the whole spectrum of kitchen appliances and acknowledge that YOU are the cook and not the machine, you will realize the advantages and disadvantages of microwave cooking. The truth of the matter, sweethearts, is that if you're a good cook, you'll be just as good using a microwave; however, if you're a lousy cook, it'll only make you a faster lousy cook!

Learning to cook with a microwave oven compared to cooking conventionally is just like learning to write with a word processor compared to writing with a typewriter. It takes a little effort to learn, but once you do it it's almost impossible to go back to the other way. It's just so much easier and more efficient using a microwave or a word processor.

Let me tell you a little story of how this book came about. One day I did a couple of microwave tips for the Regis and Kathie Lee television show in New York City. Upon returning to my home, I found a message on my answer phone to please call Bill Adler in New York. I called and Adler explained that he had seen my act, had liked what he saw, and would I be interested in writing a cookbook for a major publisher with him acting as agent.

Eventually, I hooked up with William Morrow and my editor is Maria Guarnaschelli. After our first meeting, I knew that I could have fun with this book because she agreed with my philosophy that cooking and eating should be enjoyable and fun. We should look forward to exciting and nourishing meals without the fear of food that now seems to pervade most expressions about cooking and eating. I still hold to the expression eat, drink, and be merry! Life's too short to eat, drink, and be miserable. If you've got a healthy body, ENJOY! If not, enjoy with moderation.

Understanding Cooking

To be successful in any kind of cooking, you should understand a little about heat. In simplest terms, heat is the movement of molecules within a substance. This is called kinetic energy.

The faster they move, the hotter the substance; the slower they move, the colder the substance. At absolute zero (-460° Fahrenheit), molecular activity ceases. As things get hotter and molecular activity becomes greater, the form of the substance can change. Perhaps the easiest example to illustrate is temperature associated with water. When water is very cold and its molecules are moving slowly it becomes solid in the form of ice. As you heat the ice, the molecules move faster and the ice again becomes water, and if you continue to heat it the molecules move so fast and far apart that the water turns to gas in the form of steam.

Now you must acknowledge that cooking is just the application of heat to raw foods. Heat can be applied three ways: by conduction, convection, and radiation. **Conduction cooking** occurs when the food is in direct contact with a hot surface. Stove top cooking is a prime example of conductive cooking. You heat the utensil and it heats the food. **Convective cooking** occurs when air is heated and the hot air comes in contact with the food to be cooked. Baking and oven cooking are prime examples of convection cooking. **Radiant cooking** occurs when energy is transferred from the source to the food without any intermediate medium. Broiling, toasting, charcoal grilling, and microwave are prime examples of radiant cooking. Isn't it interesting that early man's first cooking refinement was from conductive cooking, where he cooked his leg of dinosaur right in the fire and had to pick and scrape the cinders off before he could eat the meat, to radiant cooking, where he learned to just place the meat alongside or over the fire and it cooked just as well but without the mess. Here I am today, in this modern day and age, trying to convince you to graduate from primitive cooking, where foods can burn and scorch in hot pots, to cool, clean, modern, radiant cooking.

Also remember that in cooking, no matter how heat is applied—conduction, convection, or radiation—only the surface of the food is affected. The remaining mass is always cooked by conduction of the heat created on the surface to the center of the item being cooked. I mention this here because there's an old myth that microwaves cook the food from the inside to the outside. In fact, the majority of microwaves penetrate food only slightly, depending on its density; about 1/2 inch or so into a roast and several inches into bread or cake. A fraction of the total microwave energy does extend farther into the food, but it's of little consequence in cooking. I always found it amusing that the same people who insisted that microwaves cooked from the inside to the outside would also complain that the chickens they mircrowaved were bloody rare around the joints when the chicken appeared to be done on the outside.

When cooking you are increasing and decreasing the movement of the molecules in food to change taste and texture to your specifications. When you sear a steak you increase the movement of the water molecules in the meat to the extent that they convert to steam and boil away and you get the dry, crusty surface and taste that many people like. Conversely, you dash hot vegetables and pasta into icy water to slow the molecular movement and prevent overcooking, thus preserving the al dente texture. Incidentally, if you burn your fingers or hand and can apply ice immediately, you will slow the molecular activity of the burn and minimize the injury.

Understanding

Microwave Cooking

Microwaves are a form of electromagnetic radiation. Electromagnetic radiation ranges from the very powerful X rays to the much less energetic radio waves and includes ordinary light, television, and radar. Microwaves fall into the radio wave category of radiation. Another form of radiation is nuclear and all too often people lump the two together and think that the microwave oven uses harmful radiation to cook food.

If only microwave manufacturers had originally referred to the power in the oven as microwave energy rather than radiation, nobody would have been concerned. Because they referred to it as microwave radiation, people thought they had a bomb in the oven and they were nuking their food and someday they would start glowing in the dark. People are so freaked by the word *radiation* that if light bulb manufacturers started calling light bulbs radiation bulbs, half the homes in America would revert back to using candles. Another fear was that microwave radiation had a residual effect on the oven and the food that was microwaved—the same as radiation contamination from nuclear and X rays. There is no residual radiation from cooking with microwaves. What started out as radio waves is converted to heat when it contacts food.

Microwaves travel at the speed of light and they are instantly on and instantly off, the same as light from a light bulb. No microwaves remain in a microwave oven or in the food being cooked after the oven has been turned off; the same as there being no light in your closet after you turn off the light bulb. I once factitiously mentioned that folks should place a shallow pan or cookie sheet under their microwave ovens so that when they opened the door the excess microwaves would flow out of the oven and into the pan and then they could collect them and throw them out of the window. Would you believe I received several requests as to where to buy these pans.

Microwaves are emitted at their source as electromagnetic radiation and convert to heat when they come into contact with food. Here's how that happens: Microwaves cause water, fat, and sugar molecules to rotate. In your microwave oven this happens at the rate of 5 billion times a second. With all those molecules bumping against each other at that rate you can see that they would cause a lot of friction, which causes heat, which cooks food. Cooking is cooking no matter how you produce the heat. You now know that anything containing water, sugar and/ or fat will get hot from microwave energy.

There are two other things you must know before you can cook successfully by microwave.

First, microwaves pass through materials such as glass, porcelain, clay, paper, rubber, plastic, ceramic, and cloth. You can use containers made of these materials for microwave cooking and only the food within will get hot from microwave energy. On my TV shows I always say that one advantage of microwave cooking is that the pots don't get hot, so it's easy to handle them when cooking. I'll usually get a few letters from viewers complaining that their pots do get hot and that they must be doing something wrong. When I say the pots don't get hot, I mean compared to cooking in a hot conventional oven where the temperature will be anywhere from 250 to 500 degrees. Microwave containers get slightly hot from the heat of the food within them. Sometimes ceramic containers will have certain minerals in their glaze or they will absorb water and then they will get very hot. I remember one time I used a beautiful hand-made ceramic pot to make a beef stew and, being used to only the slightly warm temperature of plastic pots, I reached into the oven and grabbed the ceramic pot with my bare hands. Immediately I commenced a performance of an Apache war dance from the searing of my hands on the pot. It had not been cured properly and subsequently got very, very hot.

ZAP TIP: To test a container to determine if it's microwave safe, place it in your oven with 1/4 cup of water in a glass measuring cup. Turn on the oven for 1 minute. The water should be hot and the container should be cool. If the container is hot, it's wise not to use it for cooking. Not only will it disrupt the cooking process, but it could break from the expansion of its material.

Using Metal in Microwave Cooking

Second, you must realize that microwaves cannot pass through metal and are reflected from it. This means that you cannot cook in completely enclosed metal containers, but you can use metal to shield food from overcooking and to redirect the energy for more effective cooking. For example, if you cover the top of a ham with aluminum foil, the microwaves will reflect off the foil and then reflect off the metal walls of the oven and continue to reflect off metal surfaces until the microwaves come into contact with the ham, where they are converted into heat. Using metal and microwave radiation are the two most difficult concepts for microwave cooks to understand. To help you grasp the effect of microwaves on metal, try these experiments. Radio waves and microwaves are virtually the same and neither can pass through metal. When you are in a building constructed with a lot of steel beams you'll find that radio reception is usually very poor because the radio waves from the station are disrupted by the beams before they reach your radio receiver. If you take a small transistor radio and tune it in to your favorite station and then wrap it in aluminum foil you'll see that you can't hear it anymore. The radio signal can't go through the foil to get to the receiver in your radio. If you place two potatoes, one wrapped completely in foil, in your microwave and cook them for 5 minutes, you'll find that the unwrapped potato will be cooked and the one in the foil will be totally raw. The microwave cannot pass through metal. Using this principle, you can shield foods from overcooking or drying out by placing foil over any area that you wish to protect. Take a carrot and wrap one half in foil and microwave it for 3 minutes. The unwrapped half will be cooked and the half in the foil will be raw. Interestingly, the area under the foil, where it meets the unwrapped part, will be hot because the heat has been conducted under the foil from the cooked part of the carrot.

When microwave ovens were first introduced, most cookbooks that came with the ovens showed how to heat a TV dinner in its aluminum tray. You just removed the foil on the top and heated the container for about 7 minutes. The energy could go into the top of the tray and since it was so shallow it would thoroughly heat the food within. It stands to reason that if you can heat something with metal on the bottom you can also heat it with metal on the top. When I tell people to cover their vegetables and stews and roasts and hams and whatever with foil so the food will only cook from the bottom of the dish where the moisture collects, their first response is "I thought you couldn't put metal in the microwave!" Believe me, metal is your best friend when you're trying to perfect your microwave cooking.

An early cookbook showed how to cook hard-boiled eggs in your microwave by wrapping them in foil and then immersing them in water and boiling the water in the microwave until the eggs were cooked to your specification. It's easier to do this on top of the stove without the foil, so why bother? Currently there are many "made for microwave" products on the market that are made partially from metal. The shelves or racks and the probe that come with the oven are made of metal. I once overheard a salesman, when questioned about the metal racks in a microwave oven, tell the customer that the racks were special metal designed just for microwaves. Those salespeople will tell you anything to make a sale.

The Magnawave Roaster and the Microfryer are two utensils that have metal bases and glass tops. Perhaps the greatest innovation to improve microwave cooking is a device called the MICRO-AIRE cooker that is a totally metal pot coated with a microwave-absorbing material on its surface and a fan incorporated into its design that allows you to bake, crisp, and brown all manner of foods. Browning dishes have metal components and the microwave pressure cooker has a metal band and pres-

sure valve. So, realize that you can't cook in completely enclosed metal containers but you can use metal to shield and
redirect microwave energy.

Occasionally I will read an article or hear someone talking about
arching (ARCH) when you use metal in a microwave oven. *Arching* is something associated with architecture or a pain in the
middle of your foot. Arcing (ARC) is a spark or a visible bow of
light created when electricity or electromagnetic energy jumps
between two electrodes. All of us have experienced an arc from
static electricity when we walk across a new rug and reach for
a doorknob. And we all remember the tremendous arcs pro-
duced by the Van de Graaff generator demonstrated in our high
school science classes.

When you are using metal in microwave cooking sometimes
you will leave a small gap between two pieces of metal and the
microwave will jump across the gap and you will see an arc or
spark. This can happen around the edge of aluminum foil or
between foil and the sides of the oven. When you see an arc,
just crimp the foil where it's arcing or move the dish away from
the side of the oven. Because an arc is hot it can cause problems if you have something flammable, like a paper towel or
wax paper, in the oven also. If an arc occurs on the side of the
oven, it can cause a small scorch spot. To prevent any problems from arcing, just watch the pot for a few seconds after you
start cooking and if you don't see any little flashes, relax and
enjoy.

Usually if you're cooking a sizable amount of food, all of the
microwave energy is absorbed and you'll never get an arc. If
you have some old metal trimmed dishes, they make nice arcs
until the trim burns off. Beware of twistems, those little metal
ties that come on loaves of bread. Sometimes people will freeze
bread and then thaw it in the microwave and if they don't remove the twistem the bag can catch on fire, which gives the
bread a nice color, but can be very harmful to the oven.

Read the instructions that came with your oven regarding
metal in the microwave and then follow the directions in my
recipes.

Microwave

Cooking Utensils

You can use containers made of glass, porcelain, clay, paper, rubber, plastic, ceramic, and cloth. I recommend that you get a set of made-for-microwave plastic containers for general every-day cooking and heating. They are light, easy to handle, and usually won't get hotter than you can touch with your bare hands.

Some other essential items:

Roasting and/or bacon rack. This is a plastic or glass device that elevates the food so the fat and juices will drain away to the bottom or sides of the cooking container. It works on the same principle as the broiler pan in your conventional oven.

Plastic colander. All of you now use this to drain water from salads, vegetables, and cooked pasta. It also works great in microwave cooking to cook off the fat in ground meats, meatballs, and other fatty foods. Just place it inside another larger dish. Some microwave cookware manufacturers make the colander and container as a set and it works well.

Plastic or glass or ceramic ring pan. This container is shaped like your angel food cake pan with the hollow cone in the center. Most people associate it with the baking of cakes but it is the ideal microwave container for stews, casseroles, soups, rice, or anything that requires long-duration cooking. The hollow center allows microwaves to enter the center of the dish as well as the top and sides. This gives you a very even application of heat to food and minimizes stirring and/or turning. They come in 1-, 2-, and 3-quart sizes and I recommend you get one of each. As you'll see in my recipes, I use this dish more than any other.

Muffin pan. These are plastic versions of the standard metal muffin pan. The difference, besides being made of plastic, is that they are circular in design and usually have only six cups. I personally don't like to make muffins or, for that matter, any other bread-type food in the microwave oven. But because of the design of these pans, they perform several wonderful functions in the microwave. Use them for baking potatoes. They keep the spuds perfectly separated and hold them in an upright position so you don't have to turn them over halfway through the cooking. Make ramekins and other individual servings of puréed foods in muffin pans. They are great for making hard-cooked eggs to be used for egg salad. They hold tomatoes and onions to use as cups for fillings, such as rice-filled tomato cups and peas in onion cups. Anyway, the muffin pan is very useful and inexpensive and can also be used as a cover to other pots.

Microwave pressure cooker. This device is very useful for cooking small amounts of tougher meats and stews and dried beans. It's one of those appliances that the more you use it the more things you'll find to do in it.

Vertical roasting stands. These are metal wire stands with a wide base and a narrow top. You mount poultry over them and thus cook the birds in an upright position. In a conventional oven this allows the hot air to circulate around the bird and through the cavity, which gives you faster cooking and thus juicier results. The stands are ideal for the microwave because they elevate the birds above the cooking pan and the oven floor. The pattern of microwaves is usually better in this area, so cooking is more even and you usually don't have to turn or move anything while cooking. It also keeps the bird out of and away from the juices, so you don't have to remove them either. They come in several sizes; use them for Cornish hens, chickens, ducks, and even turkeys.

Instant read thermometer. This thermometer is designed to show the temperature of anything it is inserted into almost instantly. It is invaluable for any type of cooking, but especially microwave because it's so easy to overcook foods. The thermometers are made of metal with a plastic face cover. They can be left in the microwave while cooking or can be used to check temperature periodically as the cooking progresses. Do not leave them in your conventional oven or the plastic face will melt. Just check the temperature near the end of cooking or after you've removed the food from the conventional oven.

I've found that when I'm cooking over charcoal I can use this thermometer and have the meats come out perfectly every time. No more bloody rare chicken joints or underdone pork. Since you always know the exact temperature of what you're cooking you can virtually eliminate problems of food poisoning. I remember when I was learning to cook, the head chef taught us to determine the doneness of roasts by inserting a metal skewer into the meat and then pressing it to our lips to tell the degree of doneness. With experience this is an excellent way to check temperature, but the instant read thermometers are more accurate and easier to use. You'll find that most fine restaurants have instant read thermometers in their kitchens. Incidentally, when you visit a professional kitchen, you can always tell who's the head chef by looking for the person with the blistered lips.

Ceramic and glass containers. Because you can use glass and ceramic dishes both in the microwave and conventional oven they are very useful for combination cooking. Starting the cooking in the microwave oven and finishing it off in the conventional oven is the best way to cook many foods as you'll see as you use this book. The dishes I use most are the glass bread loaf pan, glass pie plates, glass skillets, and the 9- x 13-inch glass lasagne dish.

Clay pots. These porous clay pots work very well in the microwave oven. I like them especially because they have a rustic and hearty appearance. It's nice to cook and then serve in the same dish.

Micro-Aire cooker. This is a metal pot coated with a microwave-absorbing material that when placed in your microwave oven reaches a temperature of 400 degrees in about 1 1/2 minutes. It has a fan on the top that circulates air through the cooker at a fantastic rate so the food inside is cooked by this very hot air. It allows you to convert your microwave oven into a convection oven. Anything with a crust cooks beautifully in the Micro-Aire cooker. Frozen turnovers, refrigerator breads and rolls, pizza, pot pies, frozen fruit pies, frozen precooked breaded chicken and fish and almost every convenience food can be prepared to perfection with the Micro-Aire. A soufflé for two comes out perfectly. I like to use it for foods that I've microwaved first, like Cornish game hens and small roasts, to brown and quickly crisp the outer surface. Almost all of the high-quality convenience foods available can be cooked in about one-third the time required in a conventional oven. It eliminates the need for preheating the oven and the speed at which it cooks makes it very energy efficient. It adds that quality of texture and appearance that is sometimes lacking in pure microwave cooking.

Plastic oven cooking bags. These bags are made specifically to use for cooking in the conventional or microwave oven. Do not confuse them with plastic storage bags which should never be used for cooking. They are especially useful when you want to keep the cooking liquid close to the food being cooked, as with the poached eye of round recipe in this book. Keep a supply of bags on hand and use them as needed. They also retain steam, so even if you have a microwave with "hot spots," the food cooks evenly.

Rules for Successful

Microwave Cooking

1. Always undercook. If you're a beginning microwaver or trying a new recipe, always cook it for less time than suggested. You can cook it longer if it's not done but you can't uncook it if it's overdone. This is especially true with small quantities of food and things that you want to be rare or al dente in texture.

2. Apply your conventional cooking experience and talent to microwave. After all, cooking is cooking no matter what heat source you're using. Poke, stir, test, and taste. You are the cook and the microwave is just a machine.

3. Don't be afraid to fail. The best way to learn to cook is by trial and error. You can read books, watch videos, and attend classes, but you'll never learn to cook by microwave until you actually do it. All of us burned food, overcooked it, undercooked it, seasoned it improperly, and generally made mistakes when we learned to cook conventionally, so why should it be any different when learning to cook by microwave. It's always been curious to me that when people ruin a recipe on their stove, they'll take the blame. "Oh dear, I must have left it in the oven too long!"

But if it doesn't turn out right in the microwave, they'll always blame the machine. "That microwave can't cook worth a damn!"

4. Approach microwave cooking with an open mind. Forget all of the bad things you've heard about and tasted cooked in a microwave. Remember that the microwave oven is only a machine and you are the cook. Once you learn how to use it you'll be just as good with it as you are with your conventional tools. Most cooking professionals put down microwave cooking because they haven't taken the time to learn how to do it. If they would, they would find that the microwave is as viable a tool as the food processor, which they used to ignore but now can't live without.

5. Use your microwave for what it cooks best. Use it for cooking poultry, fish and seafood, fruits and vegetables, cereals and grains, casseroles and one-dish meals, sauces, small roasts, and, of course, for defrosting and reheating.

6. Don't use your microwave for cooking foods that can be cooked better another way. Pasta cooks better on your stove top. You can fry and deep fry better on your stove top. Breads and other bakery items need hot air to cook properly. Steaks and chops are superb when broiled or pan fried, so don't compromise and cook them less than perfectly with your microwave.

7. Use your microwave combined with your other cooking tools. As you use this book, you'll find numerous examples of cooking both with the microwave and another heat source. Microwave a chicken first so it stays moist and juicy, then pop it into a hot oven to brown and crisp the skin. Microwave a roast, then sear it in a hot skillet to form a crust. Make delicious soup quickly by microwaving the meat and vegetables as you heat the stock on your stove top. Combine the two when everything is ready. In most cases, when you need a lot of water for a recipe, the microwave is less efficient than cooking with conventional heat.

8. Start thinking microwave. When you see a new recipe, analyze it to see what steps or if the whole dish can be made

better by microwave. Pretty soon it will become second nature to convert conventional recipes. But remember, it's not worth cooking easier if the result is not as good or better than conventional cooking.

Once you get a microwave you'll wonder how you ever lived without it. Even people who don't cook with their microwave admit that. With what other cooking device can you both heat your coffee in the cup and bake a beautiful ham?
ENJOY!

Convenience Items to Enhance Modern Cooking

Garlic: Available in jars in the produce department of most supermarkets. Comes either chopped, minced, or mashed. Also available in tubes at specialty food stores.

Shallots: Available, chopped, in jars.

Ginger paste: Available in tubes. The paste imparts a better flavor than powdered and is much easier to store and use than the raw root. However, it's best to have all three on hand.

Garlic and chili paste: Available at Asian specialty stores. Lasts forever, is easy to store, and I don't think most of us can make it as good from scratch. Excellent ingredient for curries and other hot dishes.

Tomato paste in tubes: Available as either pure paste or sun dried. Easy to use in small quantities, whereas the canned variety always seems to discolor and spoil unless the whole can is used.

Canned soup stocks: Less salty than the powdered and granular varieties. Keep a variety on hand.

Canned shelled beans: I always wince at the thought of the energy, water, and time wasted in drying and then reconstituting beans. In my opinion, canned beans are as good and are so much easier to use. People complain that canned beans have salt added. So how come I always see these complainers adding salt to their dried beans?

Dried herbs: Keep the whole spectrum and include parsley and chives.

Fresh herbs: Easy to grow on your windowsill in small flowerpots or egg cartons.

Cooking oils: Get a variety of olive oils and other vegetable and seed oils to add variety and subtlety to your cooking.

Frozen pie crusts: Very close in quality to homemade ones and easy to use baked or raw.

Canned tomato products: Stewed, sauce, paste, whole crushed and with chili peppers.

Miso paste: Available at health food stores, this soy-based product gives a nice meaty taste to meatless dishes. Use in soups, stews, stir fries, and so on.

Vegetable extracts: Vegemite, Savorex, and Maggi are the ones that I know and they are available at most health food stores.

Meat extracts: Bovril is the most popular. Use to enrich the flavor of stocks, soups, and stews.

Appetizers and
First Courses

For informal occassions, the appetizers we serve usually con-
sist of a platter of cheese and crackers or maybe some nachos
and dip or perhaps something convenient that comes straight
from a can or jar. However, when we entertain most of us love
to show off and present some really delicious accolade-inspiring
tidbits. The best-tasting ones, of course, are those that are salty
and fatty—rumaki, cheese puffs, spicy meatballs, cheese dips,
chicken wings, and the like. Since we're all becoming conscious
of our fat and salt intake, I've included appetizers in this book
that border on "health" foods. I've found that using lots of hot
spices gives you the satiety value normally found in fatty and
salty things.

One of the nicest things about using your microwave for entertaining is that you can prepare appetizers on serving platters
and store them in the refrigerator until you want to serve them.
Try to arrange the platters so that the majority of items are on
the periphery of the platter. Most of the energy in a microwave
oven concentrates around the edge of the cooking dish; arrang-
ing food in this manner allows for even heating.

Garlic Dipping Sauce for Beans

MICROWAVE ONLY

ENERGY LEVEL:
high, 100%

YIELD:
about 2½ cups

COMPLETE RECIPE TIME:
about 12 minutes

COOKING TIME:
about 3 minutes

MICROWAVE COOKWARE:
none

ACCESSORY EQUIPMENT:
food processor

TRIVIA:
You don't have to pierce potatoes before cooking them. If you don't believe me, place two potatoes, only one of them pierced, in your microwave and cook them until done. You'll see that there is no difference.

I discovered this recipe in a popular travel magazine. The instructions called for boiling one small potato until tender and then blending it with the other ingredients. Whenever I see instructions like that my microwave mind becomes highly agitated. Why in the world would you waste the water, energy, and time to boil a potato when you could cook it perfectly in your microwave oven in about 3 minutes? The recipe could at least give you the option of boiling or microwaving.

Also, the recipe calls for using a dried bean called gigandes, which are difficult to find at most markets. Use canned fava or butter beans instead. I prefer canned beans because they are ready to use and you don't have to waste the time, energy, and water reconstituting the dried beans. There's a tremendous variety of canned beans, and they are so easy to use.

Here's the recipe. It's a great one.

1 small potato, about 4 ounces	¾ cup olive oil
6 slices plain white bread, crusts removed	½ cup water
½ cup (4 ounces) slivered almonds or other nuts of choice	¼ cup lemon juice
	Salt and fresh ground pepper
10 cloves garlic, peeled, or 4 teaspoon puréed garlic paste	Canned fava, butter, or other large beans of choice
	Hot sauce to taste (optional)

Microwave the potato on high for about 3 minutes, or until soft. Contrary to what you may have heard, there's no need to ever pierce a potato before you cook it. I like to leave the skin on for the roughage, but you may want to remove it for aesthetic reasons.

Place the potato, bread, nuts, and garlic in your processor and process until smooth. With the processor running add the oil and water slowly until the sauce becomes the consistency of mayonnaise. Add the lemon juice and season.

Drain and rinse the beans and serve alongside the sauce. To eat, spear a bean and dredge it through the sauce.

Use the sauce also as a raw vegetable or chip dip or dilute it with some of the juices from cooked fish or meat and use it as a sauce.

Cheese-Coated Grapes

Here's another recipe that's so much easier to make using your microwave oven rather than the conventional one. The conventional recipe instructs softening the cream cheese with a mixer and browning the nuts on a cookie sheet in your oven. Both tasks are easier in the microwave.

10 ounces slivered almonds or other nuts

8 ounces cream cheese

2 to 3 ounces blue, Roquefort, Stilton, or Parmesan cheese

1 pound seedless grapes, washed, wiped dry, and stems removed

Place the nuts in a bowl and microwave on high for 4 to 8 minutes, stirring every minute or so until they start turning brown. Stop cooking at this point or you may burn them. Allow to cool and crush or process until coarsely ground.

Place cheeses in a 1-quart measuring bowl and microwave on high for 1 to 3 minutes, or until soft and smooth. Stir a couple times during the heating. If the cheese is too thick you may add a couple tablespoons milk or cream.

Drop in the grapes, a handful at a time, and stir to coat them with cheese. Spread the nuts on a piece of wax paper and roll the grapes in the nuts. Place the grapes on a cookie sheet and chill until cheese becomes firm. Spread unused cheese on crackers or use as a raw vegetable dip. You can substitute coconut for the nuts or add it to them.

MICROWAVE ONLY

ENERGY LEVEL:
high, 100%

YIELD:
about 60 to 75 grapes

COMPLETE RECIPE TIME:
about 1 hour, including chilling time

COOKING TIME:
about 5 to 11 minutes

MICROWAVE COOKWARE:
4-cup Pyrex or microwave plastic bowl or measuring cup

ACCESSORY EQUIPMENT:
food processor and cookie sheet

TRIVIA:
Some microwave cookbooks recommend that you spread nuts on a plate or platter and microwave them until they become brown and dry. It's better to do them in a cuplike container so that the mass is heated instead of the individual nuts. The contained nuts share the heat created by the microwave and thus brown more evenly and faster. Be sure to stir them several times or they may burn in the center.

Oriental Eggplant Dip and Spread

MICROWAVE ONLY

ENERGY LEVEL:
high, 100%

YIELD:
about 1½ cups

COMPLETE RECIPE TIME:
about 18 minutes

COOKING TIME:
about 15 minutes

MICROWAVE COOKWARE:
1- to 1½-quart bowl or measuring container

ACCESSORY EQUIPMENT:
food processor

COVERING:
plastic wrap or a dinner plate to contain the steam and thus shorten the cooking time

TRIVIA:
The only reason to cube the eggplant is to make it easier to put in the cooking container. Cook it whole if you prefer.

Cooked eggplant has a wonderful texture that makes it a perfect base for all manner of dips and spreads.

1 medium eggplant, cubed, with skin left on	1 tablespoon sesame oil with chiles
1 to 2 ounces soy sauce, according to taste	2 tablespoons Mirin rice wine vinegar
1 tablespoon crushed garlic	4 tablespoons sesame seeds

Place all ingredients, except the sesame seeds, in a 2-quart microwave bowl, cover with plastic wrap or a dinner plate, and microwave on high for 15 minutes, or until the eggplant has become mushy. In a food processor process until smooth. Add seeds. Use as a dip or cracker spread.

Spinach Dip

There's not much microwaving to this recipe, but it's been a very popular recipe whenever I've served it.

2 10-ounce packages frozen spinach

1½ cups mayonnaise

1 cup sour cream

1 bunch green onions, thinly sliced

4 tablespoons chopped fresh parsley

1 package dry vegetable soup mix

Hot sauce to taste (optional)

1 round loaf of bread, sourdough French preferred, top removed and hollowed out

Remove the wrappers from the spinach boxes and place the boxes on a plate. Microwave on high for 10 to 12 minutes, or until just defrosted. Squeeze out as much water as possible. Blend with the remaining ingredients, except the bread. Place in the hollowed-out bread and serve with crackers or as a dip for raw vegetables.

Note: You can use lite mayo and low-calorie sour cream to reduce the calories.

ZAP TIP: After you hollow out the bread, microwave the shell uncovered, for about 4 or 5 minutes on high and let it cool. The shell will harden and hold its shape when filled with the dip.

MICROWAVE ONLY

ENERGY LEVEL:
high, 100%

YIELD:
about 3 cups

COMPLETE RECIPE TIME:
about 15 to 18 minutes

COOKING TIME:
about 10 to 12 minutes

MICROWAVE COOKWARE:
dinner plate

ACCESSORY EQUIPMENT:
large mixing bowl or food processor

TRIVIA:
Microwaving frozen food in its package eliminates the need for extra cooking containers.

Spinach Loaf

MICROWAVE ONLY

ENERGY LEVEL:
high, 100%, and medium-high,
80%

SERVINGS:
8 as a side dish, 16 as an hors
d'oeuvre

COMPLETE RECIPE TIME:
about 30 minutes

COOKING TIME:
about 22 minutes

MICROWAVE COOKWARE:
dinner plate; 1-quart ring pan or
an 8½- 4½-× 3-inch glass or
plastic loaf pan

ACCESSORY EQUIPMENT:
food processor or large mixing
bowl

COVERING:
plastic wrap or a dinner plate to
contain the heat and assure even
cooking

TRIVIA:
A ring pan is hollow in the middle
so you never have to worry about
that area being uncooked. When
you cook in a loaf pan, always
check to be sure the center area
is done before you serve the dish.
The outer edges cook faster than
the center does.

This vegetarian pâté makes a nice hors d'oeuvre and can also serve as a side dish for a light entrée.

2 10-ounce packages frozen spinach	2 tablespoons olive oil
1 cup seasoned bread crumbs	2 tablespoons dried tarragon leaves
1 bunch green onions, thinly sliced	2 eggs, beaten
1 cup walnuts, chopped	Vegetable stock or milk

Remove the wrappers from the spinach boxes and place the boxes on a plate. Microwave on high for 10 to 12 minutes, or until just defrosted. Squeeze out the water. Mix or process with the remaining ingredients, adding just enough stock or milk to make a thick mix. Place the mixture in a 1-quart microwave ring pan or glass loaf pan. Cover with plastic wrap and microwave on medium-high 80% power, for 12 to 15 minutes, or until the mixture has set.

Slice thin and serve on crackers. Top with a spicy tomato sauce when serving as a side dish.

Variations: Use only the egg whites or an egg substitute to reduce cholesterol. Substitute ½ cup instant mashed potatoes for the bread crumbs for a smoother texture.

Easy Stuffed Mushrooms

The nice thing about mushrooms is that nature made the small ones just the right size for a one-bite snack. Fill the mushrooms with prepared, store-bought ingredients and you've got an "easy-to-make" appetizer. In all of the stuffed mushroom recipes that follow remove the stems and either chop them fine and add to the filling or freeze them and add them to soups and sauces. The mushrooms used in these recipes are brown, tan, or white supermarket mushrooms called champignons de Paris. Use ones that are tightly closed without any gill showing.

These combinations exemplify the many stuffings possible. Use your imagination to create your own favorites.

ZAP TIP: When possible, always place food around the edge of the cooking container because microwave energy is more intense there.

Sausage-rooms

10 servings

Remove the stems from 10 1½-inch diameter fresh, firm mushrooms. Take 2 spicy, hot Italian sausage links and squeeze the filling into each mushroom (similar to applying toothpaste from a tube). Place mushrooms in a glass pie pan or a 9- × 13-inch glass lasagne pan, cover with plastic wrap, and microwave on high for 2 or 3 minutes, or until the sausage is cooked.

Pizza-rooms

10 servings

Remove stems from 10 1½-inch-diameter fresh, firm mushrooms and chop finely. Place in a paper towel and squeeze to remove moisture. Mix with ¼ pound Italian bulk sausage, 2 ounces mozzarella cheese, and ¼ cup pizza sauce. Fill mushroom caps with the mixture and place them in a glass pie pan or 9- × 13-inch glass lasagne pan. Cover with plastic wrap and microwave on high for 2 or 3 minutes, or until the filling is firm and the sausage cooked.

MICROWAVE ONLY

ENERGY LEVEL:
high, 100%

SERVING:
10 to 20

COMPLETE RECIPE TIME:
about 10 minutes

COOKING TIME:
2 to 3 minutes

MICROWAVE COOKWARE:
glass pie pan or 9- × 13-inch glass lasagne pan

ACCESSORY EQUIPMENT:
mixing bowl and/or food processor

COVERING:
plastic wrap to contain heat and assure even cooking

Anchovy-rooms

10 servings

Remove the stems from 10 1½-inch-diameter fresh, firm mushrooms and place rolled anchovy fillets in the mushroom caps. Place in a glass pie pan, cover with plastic wrap or a dinner plate, and microwave on high 15 seconds per mushroom.

Pesto-rooms

10 servings

Remove the stems from 10 1½-inch-diameter fresh, firm mushrooms. You can buy *pesto* in tubes and all you have to do is squeeze it into the mushrooms. Or use commercially prepared pesto sauce and spoon it into the mushroom caps. Place the mushrooms in a glass pie pan and cover with plastic wrap or a dinner plate and microwave on high 15 seconds per mushroom.

Corned Beef Caps

20 servings

Remove the stems from 20 1½-inch-diameter fresh, firm mushrooms. Place the contents of one 12-ounce can corned beef in a 1-quart glass or plastic bowl and microwave on high about 4 minutes. Drain off the fat and blend the beef with 4 tablespoons Dijon or other good mustard of choice. Fill the mushroom caps with the mixture. Place the mushrooms in a 9- × 13-inch glass lasagne pan, cover with plastic wrap, and microwave on high 15 seconds per cap.

Sardine Caps

20 servings

Remove the stems from 20 1½-inch-diameter fresh, firm mushrooms. Mix 1 tin sardines, including the oil, with ½ cup bread crumbs and divide mixture among mushroom caps. Microwave as above. For a stronger fish taste, eliminate the bread crumbs and use only 10 caps.

Spinach Caps

20 servings

Have ready Spinach Dip (page 5). Remove the stems from 20 1½-inch-diameter fresh, firm mushrooms and chop finely. Place them in a paper towel and squeeze to remove the moisture. Add to the spinach dip. Fill the caps and microwave on high for about 15 seconds per cap.

Shrimp-rooms

10 servings

Drain 1 7-ounce can shrimp and mix with 2 tablespoons mayonnaise. Remove the stems from 10 mushrooms and fill the caps with the shrimp mixture. Microwave on high for 15 seconds per cap.

Cheese and Sausage Caps

Cut your favorite cheese into small cubes. Do the same with a cooked sausage (I like the hot wiener-type). Put a cube of cheese and a slice of sausage into each mushroom cap and microwave on high for 15 seconds per cap.

Sauerkraut Balls

MICROWAVE AND SKILLET (optional)

ENERGY LEVEL:
high, 100%

SERVINGS:
about 12

COMPLETE RECIPE TIME:
about 10 minutes

COOKING TIME:
2 to 3 minutes microwave only;
2 to 10 minutes if browned
in a skillet

MICROWAVE COOKWARE:
shallow 2-quart microwavable
casserole, a glass pie plate, or a
9- × 13-inch glass lasagne pan

ACCESSORY EQUIPMENT:
mixing bowl or food processor and
skillet for browning (optional)

COVERING:
plastic wrap to contain heat and
assure even cooking

TRIVIA:
This is an excellent recipe to
prepare ahead of time and freeze
in a microwavable container or
plastic cooking bag. Just heat on
high power when ready to serve.

All right, so you say you don't like sauerkraut. Just try these and see if they don't taste delicious. Also, they are low in fat and high in fiber.

8 ounces sauerkraut, drained
    and rinsed

⅓ cup bread crumbs

¼ cup grated Parmesan
    cheese

1 egg, beaten, or equivalent
    egg substitute

2 tablespoons flour

Thoroughly mix all the ingredients together or process until blended. Form into 1-inch balls and place in a 2-quart casserole. Cover with plastic wrap and microwave on high for 2 or 3 minutes, or until the balls are firm.

Option: Heat 1 tablespoon cooking oil in a skillet and quickly brown the balls before serving.

Sauerkraut and Sausage Balls: Mix ¼ pound bulk Italian sausage to the above recipe and cook as directed.

Sauerkraut and Corned Beef Balls: Add ¼ pound canned corned beef, chopped, to the above recipe.

Buffalo Chicken Wings (Low Fat)

How do you make chicken wings that contain less fat? Simply cook them first in your microwave, then bake them instead of deep frying them.

2 pounds chicken wings, tips removed and halved at joints

4 tablespoons margarine

⅓ cup hot sauce (I prefer Texas Pete brand.)

Store-bought blue cheese dressing

Celery sticks

Place the wings in a 3-quart casserole, cover, and microwave on high for 15 to 20 minutes, or to an internal temperature of 160 degrees. Separate fat and juices and save juice for soups or sauces.

For best results, spread the wings on a metal broiling pan and place them in your refrigerator overnight. (They will dehydrate slightly, then become very crispy when you bake them.) Bake the wings in a preheated 400 degree oven for 15 minutes, or until they are brown and crispy.

In the meantime place the margarine and hot sauce in a large glass bowl and microwave on high for 2 minutes. When the wings are baked, add them to the sauce and stir them to coat them evenly.

To serve, dip the wings in the blue cheese dressing and enjoy. Savor a celery stick to sooth your palate.

ZAP TIP: Add the juices plus the wing tips to 4 cups water and microwave on high, uncovered, for 30 minutes to make stock that can be used for soups and sauces.

MICROWAVE AND CONVENTIONAL OVEN COMBINATION

ENERGY LEVEL:
high, 100%

SERVINGS:
20 to 24 pieces

COMPLETE RECIPE TIME:
45 to 60 minutes

COOKING TIME:
microwave 15 to 20 minutes; conventional oven 15 to 20 minutes

MICROWAVE COOKWARE:
3-quart casserole

ACCESSORY EQUIPMENT:
large mixing bowl and a conventional broiling pan

COVERING:
plastic wrap or the dish cover to contain heat and assure even cooking

TRIVIA:
The wings are edible and good after just microwaving them. But if you bake them conventionally as directed the texture is even better and the skin is crispy.

Pizza

CONVENTIONAL OVEN

ENERGY LEVEL:
400 degrees

SERVINGS:
8 slices or 12 to 16 squares in
12-inch-diameter pizza

COMPLETE RECIPE TIME:
20 to 30 minutes

COOKING TIME:
15 to 20 minutes

MICROWAVE COOKWARE:
none

ACCESSORY COOKWARE:
pizza stone for baking and cookie
sheet for preparation

Pizza doesn't bake well in a microwave, but it's one of my favorite foods so I must include some recipes for it in this book. I think I could eat pizza for every meal and I have several times. In fact, I think it makes a great breakfast meal, well balanced and easy to eat.

When I was in high school I worked in a pizza joint and later owned one north of San Francisco called Pizza Europa. Our large deluxe weighed seven pounds. If we had sold it by the pound, we might have made a profit.

The more things on a pizza the more I like it. My dear wife, however, likes a barren pizza. She developed an appreciation for simple pizzas when she lived in Naples, Italy, where they make pizza with few ingredients.

I've heard people rave about how easy it is to reheat pizza in the microwave. I think it turns out badly because the microwave makes the crust soggy and I like a crisp crust.

ZAP TIP: To reheat pizza using your microwave, place several pieces on a plate and microwave them about 1 minute per slice, or until the cheese starts bubbling. In the meantime, heat a skillet on your stove top. Take the pizza from the microwave and slide it into the skillet and heat for 40 to 60 seconds, or until the crust is crisp. It'll be as good or better than the first time you served it.

It's very important to layer a pizza properly, although I'm sure I'll get some arguments regarding my technique. I believe you should always precook the crust for added crispiness. Since there are so many great prepared crusts available I buy them premade rather than going through the bother and mess of making them from scratch. Also, you can usually buy plain crusts, from your friendly, neighborhood pizzeria and freeze them to use later. If you eat a lot of pizza I recommend that you splurge and buy a pizza stone. It makes any crust so much better than when it is baked on a cookie sheet or directly on the wire oven racks.

To make pizza, start with a crust that you like and brown both sides in a preheated 400 degree oven. Brush one side with olive oil (optional) and cover with Italian tomato sauce. Add fresh herbs if available, especially basil and oregano. Spread shredded cheese over the sauce. I like mozzarella, provolone, and Parmesan. Add chopped onion and garlic and any fresh vegetables such as mushrooms (never use canned mushrooms) and sliced bell peppers. Then add cooked sausage like pepperoni and, finally, raw Italian sausage. I love anchovies and always place them on the top of the pizza so that folks who don't appreciate their wonderful fishy taste can avoid or remove them.

Bake the pie on a pizza stone or cookie sheet or the oven rack without any pan underneath for 5 to 8 minutes, or until the cheeses are bubbling and the sausage cooked. Incidentally, if you want to eliminate some of the fat in the sausage, just microwave it for a few minutes and pour off the fat before adding the sausage to your pizza.

Rome-Style Pizza

1 prebaked 10- to 12-inch
   pizza crust

Olive oil

1 cup (8 ounces) shredded
   mozzarella cheese

4 tablespoons grated Parmesan
   cheese

4 tablespoons chopped fresh
   basil

Brush the crust with the olive oil, spread the cheeses over the top, and sprinkle with the basil. Bake in a preheated 450 degree oven for 10 to 12 minutes, or until the cheese melts and starts to brown.

Wisconsin White Pizza

This recipe is a nice change from the basic tomato-sauce pizza.

1 cup prepared store-bought
   Alfredo sauce

1 prebaked 10- to 12-inch
   pizza crust

½ cup (4 ounces) shredded
   mozzarella cheese

½ cup (4 ounces) shredded
   provolone cheese

4 tablespoons shredded or
   grated Parmesan cheese

6 scallions, chopped

2 tablespoons minced garlic

Spread the Alfredo sauce over the prebaked crust and top with the remaining ingredients. Bake in a preheated 450 degree oven for 6 to 8 minutes, or until the cheese melts and starts to brown.

Top Wisconsin White Pizza with:
canned clams and/or anchovies; peeled and deveined shrimp; drained sauerkraut; sliced red, green, and yellow bell peppers (a beautiful presentation); sliced fresh mushrooms; and microwave-cooked broccoli flowerets.

Other possibilities—canned artichoke hearts; sliced green and black olives; chopped jalapeño peppers; raw ripe tomatoes; sun-dried tomatoes, and anything else that suits your taste.

Sicilian-Style Pizza

1 prebaked 10- to 12-inch
    pizza crust

1 cup prepared pizza sauce or
    basic tomato sauce

4 tablespoons capers bottled in
    brine, drained

1 tin anchovy fillets, drained

10 black olives, sliced

Spread the tomato sauce over the crust and top with the remaining ingredients. Bake in a preheated 450 degree oven for 10 to 12 minutes, or until the flavors blend and the crust is crisp.

Neapolitan-Style Pizza

1 cup prepared pizza or basic
    tomato sauce

1 prebaked 10- to 12-inch
    pizza crust

1 cup (8 ounces) shredded
    mozzarella cheese

4 tablespoons each of chopped
    fresh oregano and basil
    leaves

1 large raw ripe tomato, sliced

Spread the tomato sauce over the crust and top with the cheese, herbs, and tomato slices. Bake in a preheated 450 degree oven for 10 to 12 minutes, or until the cheese melts and starts to brown.

Garlic Pizza

1 cup prepared pizza sauce or basic tomato sauce

1 prebaked 10- to 12-inch pizza crust

8 tablespoons minced garlic

½ cup (4 ounces) shredded mozzarella cheese

½ cup (4 ounces) shredded provolone cheese

4 tablespoons shredded or grated Parmesan cheese

Spread the tomato sauce over the crust and sprinkle with the garlic. Top with the cheeses. Bake in a preheated 450 degree oven for 10 to 12 minutes, or until the cheese melts and starts to brown.

Note: For a less pungent taste, microwave the garlic in 2 tablespoons olive oil for about 2 minutes before adding to the pizza. Four tablespoons of garlic paste from a tube can also be mixed with the sauce and the result is wonderful.

ZAP TIP: Whole garlic cloves can be precooked in your microwave. Just break the heads into separate cloves and soak them in water for a couple of minutes. Wrap them in plastic wrap and microwave on high for about 10 seconds per clove, or until soft. Peel and add to the pizza.

California Vegetarian Pizza

1 cup prepared pizza or basic tomato sauce

1 prebaked 10- to 12-inch pizza crust

1 cup (8 ounces) crumbled goat cheese

Sun-dried tomatoes packed in olive oil

Canned artichoke hearts

Sliced black olives

Red bell peppers, sliced

Spread the sauce on the crust and top with the remaining ingredients. Bake in a preheated 450 degree oven for 10 to 12 minutes, or until the cheese melts and starts to brown.

Mexican Pizza

1 cup thick prepared salsa or taco sauce

1 prebaked 10- to 12-inch pizza crust

½ pound firm chorizo sausage, sliced

½ cup (4 ounces) shredded Monterey Jack cheese

½ cup (4 ounces) shredded Cheddar cheese

½ medium yellow onion, chopped

2 pickled jalapeño peppers, chopped

Spread the salsa or taco sauce over the crust and top with the remaining ingredients. Bake in a preheated 450 degree oven for 10 to 12 minutes, or until the sausage is cooked and the cheeses start to brown.

Beef

Most people are reluctant to cook beef in the microwave, probably because they have tried it once and it came out less than perfect. Or they may have eaten a roast that didn't taste as good as one that was cooked conventionally, or they tried a cut of meat that should have been cooked another way. The number-one example of this is with steak. Beef steak has to be America's favorite cut of meat. When I used to sell microwave ovens, people would take an oven home and either call me or come back to the store to relate their experience of cooking a steak in their new microwave. "Didn't brown, didn't taste right. Turned out like leather," they'd say. And I would say: "DON'T COOK STEAKS OR CHOPS IN YOUR MICROWAVE OVEN!" It's the wrong tool. You wouldn't cook turkey in a wok, so don't cook steak in your microwave. When you cook a steak, you want that charred flavor from the intense heat of a hot pan, broiler, or charcoal grill. Roasts, however, cook beautifully by microwave, as you'll see in the recipes that follow.

In the early days of microwave cooking, I tried to convince people to cook beef purely and solely by microwave. I now lean toward using combination cooking; the results are identical to conventional cooking, but it takes less time. By combination, I mean using the attributes of microwave plus those of hot cooking. For example, microwave a roast first, then transfer it to a very hot (500 degree) oven to crust the surface. Or, after microwaving, sear a roast in a hot skillet to crust the surface. By doing this, you retain the juicy quality of microwave cooking and add the searing process of hot cooking. Incidentally, searing a steak or roast doesn't help the meat retain juices as we've heard so often. It does, however, add the desirable flavor of burning and charring.

Here are the basic rules for cooking beef by microwave:

1. Cook beef roasts very slowly—50 percent power or less or on the defrost cycle. This allows the energy to be conducted to the interior of the roast gradually so that you have an even gradualism of degrees of doneness: that is, well done on the surface, to medium under the surface, to medium rare near the center, to rare in the center. If you cook a roast on high power, the surface will overcook before the heat generated by the microwaves can be conducted to the center of the meat. You get an overcooked surface and a raw center. This is not desirable unless some of your family enjoys well-done beef while others like steak tartare. It would be the same as cooking a roast in your conventional oven at 500 degrees. You would burn the surface before the inside had a chance to cook.

2. Season the roast just as you would in conventional cooking. Most microwave cookbooks advise that you not put salt on your roasts. We all should eat less salt, but I've found that adding salt to the surface of the meat tends to dry and crust the surface, which is desirable for texture and appearance.

3. Cover roasts according to the type of cooking you desire. Cover securely for moist cooking—pot roasts and stews—and leave uncovered for dry cooking—rib, sirloin, and other tender cuts of meat. Use the dish cover or plastic wrap for moist cooking; or cover with wax paper or nonstick cooking paper for dry cooking, where these papers hold in some heat and prevent juices from spattering all over the interior of your oven. Paper towels and wax paper are not necessary if you don't mind wiping out your oven after each roast.

4. One of the best ways to cook tough cuts like brisket and pot roasts is to use a glass or ceramic container and start the cooking in your microwave, then transfer the container to a preheated conventional oven. Microwave the meat 3 to 5 minutes per pound or to an internal temperature of 120 to 130 degrees. That period of cooking contributes very little to the taste and texture of the meat, so it doesn't matter how you get to that point. By doing this, a 5-pound brisket that would take 4 to 5 hours to cook conventionally takes only 2 to 2½ hours and the quality is the same.

   If you cook a tough cut totally by microwave, be sure to use a lot of liquid and cook it until it becomes tender. You can't always cook according to exact times because some meats of the same cut may be tougher than others. After cooking the recommended time, check the tenderness of the meat and cook it longer if it's still tough. Too often people will cook a stew or pot roast as directed in a recipe and find that it's hard to chew. Instead of cooking it some more they blame the microwave for not cooking properly. Good grief, I've had tough meat that my mother cooked for hours in her Dutch oven and still had to return to the pot for longer cooking. If you cook stews and pot roasts ahead of time and let them sit for a day or two they taste better. You also don't have the problem of timing your cooking to finish when you want to sit down and eat.

5. Don't microwave steaks. I have at times microwaved a steak, usually in my motel room when I'm on the road. They taste okay and they're nutritious, but if I had my choice I would broil, pan fry, or grill it. There's nothing like the seared, charred flavor of a steak cooked with hot energy. But if you microwave steaks just to get them warm, about 100 degrees, they'll cook better conventionally. Other thin cuts of beef—round steak and cutlets—can be cooked well by microwave as long as they are cooked in a sauce or with liquid.

Boneless Prime Rib Roast

MICROWAVE AND CONVENTIONAL OVEN COMBINATION

ENERGY LEVEL:
microwave, medium-low, 40%;
conventional oven, 500 degrees

SERVINGS:
6 to 8

COMPLETE RECIPE TIME:
90 minutes

COOKING TIME:
microwave, 50 to 60 minutes;
conventional oven, about
10 minutes

MICROWAVE COOKWARE:
shallow glass or ceramic
casserole large enough to
accommodate the meat; 8 inches
square or 9- × 13-inch Pyrex dish

ACCESSORY EQUIPMENT:
basting bulb and large measuring
cup to remove fat from juices

COVERING:
wax paper or other nonstick paper
to contain heat but allow moisture
to escape and to keep spatters off
oven walls

5- to 6-pound boned standing rib roast, small end

Salt and fresh ground pepper

Garlic powder to taste

Remove as much fat from the roast as possible. Season with the salt, pepper, and garlic powder. Place in an 8-inch-square or larger Pyrex or ceramic baking pan and cover with wax paper or other nonstick paper. Microwave on 40% power for about 10 minutes per pound or to an internal temperature of 120 degrees. Halfway through the cooking turn the roast over. During the last 10 minutes of microwaving, preheat conventional oven to 500 degrees. Remove the juices from the pan, discard the wax paper, and place the roast in conventional oven for about 10 minutes or to an internal temperature of 130 degrees. Let stand for 10 minutes, slice, and serve with fat-free juices.

Sirloin Tip and Cross Rib. Use the above recipe.

Gravy: I prefer to remove the fat from the juices before I make gravy (see instructions in Zap Tip 14, page 308), but you may opt to leave it in. In a 4-cup measure or other similar bowl make a paste of 4 tablespoons flour or 2 tablespoons cornstarch and an equal amount of beef juice. Gradually add the remaining beef juices while stirring with a whisk. Add canned beef broth or water to make 2 cups gravy. Microwave on high for 2 or 3 minutes, or until the gravy reaches the desired consistency.

Dry Roasted Rump Roast

3- to 4-pound rump roast **Garlic powder to taste**

Salt and fresh ground pepper

Remove the fat layer from the roast (optional). Place roast in an 8-inch-square glass baking pan or similar dish. Season with salt, pepper, and garlic powder and cover with wax paper or other nonstick paper. Microwave on medium-low, 40%, for about 10 minutes per pound or to an internal temperature of 140 degrees. During the last 10 minutes of microwaving, pre-heat conventional oven to 500 degrees. Remove the juices from the pan and discard the wax paper. Place the roast in hot oven for about 10 minutes, or until the surface is brown and crisp.

MICROWAVE AND CONVENTIONAL OVEN COMBINATION

ENERGY LEVEL:
microwave, medium-low, 40%;
conventional oven 500 degrees

SERVINGS:
about 5 to 6

COMPLETE RECIPE TIME:
50 to 60 minutes

COOKING TIME:
microwave, 30 to 40 minutes;
conventional oven, 10 minutes

MICROWAVE COOKWARE:
8-inch-square Pyrex baking pan or similar dish

ACCESSORY EQUIPMENT:
none

TIP:
Always slice rump roast across the grain, which makes it easier to chew.

Moist Roasted Rump Roast

MICROWAVE ONLY

ENERGY LEVEL:
medium, 50%

SERVINGS:
5 to 6

COMPLETE RECIPE TIME:
about 50 minutes

COOKING TIME:
about 30 to 40 minutes

MICROWAVE COOKWARE:
2-quart microwave casserole

ACCESSORY EQUIPMENT:
basting bulb and 2-cup bowl

COVERING:
plastic wrap or dish cover to
contain heat and steam and assure
even moist cooking

3- to 4-pound rump roast   Salt and fresh ground pepper

1 cup canned beef stock   Garlic powder to taste

Remove the fat from the roast. Place the roast into a 2-quart microwavable casserole and season with salt, pepper, and garlic powder. Cover with plastic wrap or the dish cover and microwave on medium, 50%, power for about 10 minutes per pound or to an internal temperature of 150 degrees.

Gravy: Place 2 tablespoons butter and 2 tablespoons flour in a 2-cup bowl or measuring cup and microwave on high for about 2 minutes. Stir and gradually add the juices from the roast. Microwave, uncovered, for 2 or 3 minutes, or until the gravy is as thick as desired.

Rump Roast with Roasted Vegetables

Use the recipe for Moist Roasted Rump Roast, but during the last 10 minutes of cooking add:

2 sliced carrots   2 large potatoes, diced

1 medium onion, chopped

Recover and cook 10 to 15 minutes longer at high power, 100%, or until the vegetables are tender. The vegetables in this recipe taste as if they were cooked separately but with just a hint of the luscious flavor of the meat. The addition of the vegetables takes energy away from the meat so when you raise the power to 100% the meat is still cooking slowly. For variety, substitute or add sliced turnips or diced rutabaga.

Pot Roast

2½-pound boneless chuck roast, fat removed

2 cloves garlic, smashed

1 medium carrot, shredded

1 medium onion, chopped

1 cup dry red wine

1 8-ounce can tomato sauce

MICROWAVE ONLY

ENERGY LEVEL:
medium, 50%

SERVINGS:
4 to 5

COMPLETE RECIPE TIME:
80 to 90 minutes

COOKING TIME:
70 to 80 minutes

MICROWAVE COOKWARE:
shallow 3-quart casserole

COVERING:
plastic wrap or the dish cover to contain heat and steam to assure even and moist cooking

Cut the meat in half and place it and remaining ingredients in a 3-quart glass or plastic casserole, about the same size as the meat. Cover with plastic wrap or the dish cover and microwave 45 minutes on medium, 50%, power. Turn the meat over so the inside edges are to the edge of the dish and bottom side up. Re-cover and microwave about 40 to 50 minutes, or until the meat is very tender.

You may want to sear the meat before you microwave it, but I've found that meat cooked as long as it is in this recipe tastes the same whether you brown it or not.

ZAP TIP: Sometimes when you microwave meat for a long time, as in this recipe, the edges will dry out and harden. If this happens with your microwave, place foil over and around the edges of the meat and then cover with plastic wrap or the dish cover. This directs the microwave energy to the bottom of the pan where the juices accumulate; thus you are actually simmering the meat, as if you were cooking it on top of your range. The meat cannot dry out. If this is confusing check the section Using Metal in Microwave Cooking.

Combination Microwave-Conventional Pot Roast

MICROWAVE AND CONVENTIONAL OVEN COMBINATION

ENERGY LEVEL:
microwave, medium, 50%;
conventional oven, 350 degrees

SERVINGS:
4 to 6

COMPLETE RECIPE TIME:
about 1 hour and 40 minutes

COOKING TIME:
about 1 hour and 30 minutes

MICROWAVE COOKWARE:
shallow 3-quart glass or ceramic casserole

COVERING:
plastic wrap or the dish cover and aluminum foil

Microwave pot roast as described in preceding recipe but be sure to cook it in a Pyrex or ceramic container. Cover with plastic wrap or the dish cover and microwave about 20 minutes on medium, 50%, power to an internal temperature of 120 degrees.

Remove the plastic wrap and replace it with foil. Roast meat in preheated 350 degree conventional oven for 1 hour, or until very tender.

Barbecued Brisket

This recipe yields more than most others in this book, but the brisket makes such great leftover meals and sandwiches that I had to include it.

4 large onions, sliced

4 tablespoons mustard seeds

2 cups barbecue or chili sauce

1 4- or 5-pound flat-cut beef brisket

In a 9- × 13-inch Pyrex lasagne pan spread half of the onions, mustard seeds, and chili sauce. Add the brisket and cover with the remaining ingredients. Cover with plastic wrap and microwave on medium-high, 80%, power for about 20 to 25 minutes or to an internal temperature of 130 degrees.

Preheat conventional oven to 350 degrees. Replace the plastic wrap with foil and bake the roast for about 2 hours, or until very tender.

MICROWAVE AND CONVENTIONAL OVEN COMBINATION

ENERGY LEVEL:
microwave, medium-high, 80%;
conventional oven, 350 degrees

SERVINGS:
about 10

COMPLETE RECIPE TIME:
about 2 hours and 45 minutes

COOKING TIME:
about 2 hours and 30 minutes

MICROWAVE COOKWARE:
9- × 13-inch Pyrex or ceramic lasagne pan

COVERING:
plastic wrap and aluminum foil

Sauerbraten

MICROWAVE ONLY

ENERGY LEVEL:
high, 100%, and medium, 50%

SERVINGS:
4 to 6

COMPLETE RECIPE TIME:
1 to 3 days for marinating time

COOKING TIME:
1 to 1¼ hours

MICROWAVE COOKWARE:
deep 3-quart casserole

COVERING:
plastic wrap or the dish cover

A favorite recipe from my childhood. It always turns out very tender when cooked by microwave.

1 3-pound rump roast	1 bay leaf
1 large onion, sliced	3 tablespoons sugar
1 cup red wine vinegar	3 cloves
1 cup water	8 gingersnap cookies, processed or crushed into fine crumbs
1 ounce gin	
5 peppercorns	

Place the meat and remaining ingredients, except the gingersnaps, in a deep 3-quart glass or plastic container. Cover and microwave on high for 10 minutes. Place in refrigerator for 1 day or up to 3 days. Turn and with a fork pierce the entire surface several times during the marinating period.

To cook, remove half of the liquid, cover with plastic wrap or the dish cover, and microwave on high for 15 minutes and on medium, 50%, power for an additional 50 to 60 minutes. Turn over once during the cooking.

Remove the meat and test for tenderness. Cook longer if necessary. If tender, set aside and add the gingersnap crumbs to the juices. Microwave for 5 minutes, or until thick. Slice the roast across the grain and serve with the sauce.

Poached Eye of the Round

This recipe is best prepared in a plastic cooking bag. If you don't have one, use a narrow steep-sided container like a glass 8½- × 3½- × 2½-inch loaf pan.

2-pound beef, eye of the round, roast

½ cup dry red wine

½ cup canned beef stock

1 teaspoon dried marjoram

2 bay leaves

4 black peppercorns, smashed

2 cloves garlic, smashed

1 medium onion, chopped

MICROWAVE AND SKILLET COMBINATION

ENERGY LEVEL:
medium, 50%

SERVINGS:
4

COMPLETE RECIPE TIME:
about 45 minutes

COOKING TIME:
about 40 minutes

MICROWAVE COOKWARE:
plastic cooking bag or glass loaf pan covered with plastic wrap

CONVENTIONAL COOKWARE:
10-inch skillet

COVERING:
plastic wrap if using loaf pan

Place all the ingredients in a plastic cooking bag and close with a rubberband or the plastic strip provided, leaving a gap in the opening about the size of your finger. Place the bag in another container and microwave on medium, 50%, power for 25 to 30 minutes or to an internal temperature of 150 degrees. Or place everything in a glass loaf pan and cover with plastic wrap. Remove the meat from the bag or pan and pat it dry with a paper towel.

Heat a skillet and sear the sides of the meat. Set the meat aside and deglaze the pan with the juices and reduce by half. Slice the roast about ¼ inch thick across the grain and pour the sauce over the slices.

Fancy Meat Loaf

MICROWAVE ONLY

ENERGY LEVEL:
medium-high, 80%

SERVINGS:
up to 8

COMPLETE RECIPE TIME:
about 40 minutes

COOKING TIME:
25 to 30 minutes

MICROWAVE COOKWARE:
2-quart plastic ring pan or glass
bread loaf pan

COVERING:
wax paper or other nonstick paper
to contain the heat but allow the
moisture to escape

This recipe makes a rather large meat loaf perfect for an informal get-together or for one meal, with leftovers.

3 pounds lean ground beef

½ pound kielbasa or other cooked smoked sausage, chopped or sliced into small pieces

2 whole large eggs, or 3 egg whites if cholesterol is a consideration

1 cup seasoned bread crumbs

½ cup grated Parmesan cheese

1 cup prepared spaghetti sauce

Mix all the ingredients, except half the spaghetti sauce, and place in a 2-quart plastic ring pan or glass loaf pan. Spread the remaining sauce over the top of the loaf. Cover with wax paper and microwave on medium-high, 80%, power for about 25 to 30 minutes or to an internal temperature of 150 to 160 degrees. Drain off the fat and juices and let stand for about 10 minutes. Slice and serve.

Option: Instead of chopping the sausage, lay whole sausages over half the meat mixture and top with the remaining meat mixture. The loaf will look very interesting when sliced.

ZAP TIP: Cut any leftover meat loaf into 1-inch slices and freeze each slice separately in a plastic bag. When you want a quick snack or a meat loaf sandwich, just microwave a slice in its bag on high power for 1 or 2 minutes, or until heated through. Defrosting is not necessary.

Meat Loaf Mexicana

I'm sure you could make as many variations on meat loaf as there are ethnic categories of cooking. In fact, that's one of the real joys of cooking: playing around with different ingredients within a basic recipe. One advantage of cooking by microwave is that you don't have to wait so long to taste the recipe before you can serve it, or include it in your pet's diet. However, this one I know you'll like.

2 pounds lean ground beef

1 cup crushed tortilla chips

1 teaspoon ground cumin

½ teaspoon dried red chili flakes

1 large egg

1 cup prepared salsa, hotness to taste

2 chorizo sausages, each about 8 inches long

1 cup shredded sharp Cheddar cheese

MICROWAVE ONLY

ENERGY LEVEL:
medium-high, 80%

SERVINGS:
4 to 6

COMPLETE RECIPE TIME:
about 30 minutes

COOKING TIME:
15 to 20 minutes

MICROWAVE COOKWARE:
glass bread loaf pan,
8½ × 4½ x 2½ inches

COVERING:
wax paper or other nonstick paper

Mix all the ingredients, except the sausages and the cheese. Place half the meat mixture in a glass bread loaf pan. Lay in the sausages about 1 inch apart. Press the remaining meat over the sausages. Cover with wax paper and microwave on medium-high, 80%, for 15 to 20 minutes. Toward the end of the cooking, remove the wax paper and spread the cheese over the top of the loaf. Finish the cooking.

Note: There are two types of chorizo sausage. One is firm; the other is soft. For this recipe use the firm ones.

(Picadillo) Cuban-Style Hash

MICROWAVE ONLY

ENERGY LEVEL:
high, 100%

SERVINGS:
4

COMPLETE RECIPE TIME:
about 25 minutes

COOKING TIME:
20 minutes

MICROWAVE COOKWARE:
2-quart glass or plastic casserole or mixing bowl

COVERING:
wax paper or other nonstick paper

Here's a very interesting recipe to add some variety to your ground beef repertoire.

1 pound lean beef, coarse ground

2 tablespoons paprika or annato oil, available at speciality food stores

1 medium onion, chopped

1 medium green bell pepper, seeded and chopped

2 cloves garlic, minced

1 teaspoon dried chili flakes, or less if desired

1 14-ounce can stewed tomatoes, drained

½ teaspoon ground cloves

⅓ cup pimiento-stuffed olives, sliced

½ cup raisins

2 tablespoons white vinegar

Place beef in a 2-quart glass or plastic casserole and microwave on high, uncovered, for 5 minutes. Pour off fat and break the beef up into small chunks. Add the remaining ingredients. Cover with wax paper and microwave on high for about 15 minutes, or until some of the water evaporates and the hash thickens slightly.

Cuban-Style Hash #2

Substitute 1 pound canned corned beef for the ground beef (cook exactly as directed in recipe above) and 1½ cups prepared salsa, hotness to personal taste, for the stewed tomatoes.

Baked Papaya with Spicy Meat Filling

MICROWAVE ONLY

ENERGY LEVEL:
high, 100%

SERVINGS:
4

COMPLETE RECIPE TIME:
about 25 minutes

COOKING TIME:
20 minutes

MICROWAVE COOKWARE:
deep 2-quart glass or plastic
casserole and a 9- × 13-inch
glass or plastic lasagne pan

COVERING:
plastic wrap to contain heat and
assure even cooking

Here's another Caribbean recipe with variations by me.

1 pound ground beef

1 medium onion, chopped

2 cloves garlic, minced

1 14-ounce can tomatoes,
   Cajun style, drained

½ teaspoon dried crushed red
   pepper or bottled hot
   sauce to taste

¼ cup grated Parmesan
   cheese

1 teaspoon allspice

½ cup slivered almonds

1 cup raisins

2 papayas, slightly green

Plain yogurt as garnish

Place the beef in a 2-quart casserole and microwave on high for 5 minutes. Pour off fat and add the remaining ingredients, except the papayas. Microwave for about 10 minutes. Cut the papayas in half, scoop out the seeds, and score the flesh in a crisscross pattern. Fill each papaya half with the beef mixture and place in a 9- × 13-inch glass or plastic dish and cover with plastic wrap. Microwave on high for about 5 minutes. Top with a dollop of yogurt and serve.

Variations: Use diced, raw chicken breast or cocktail shrimp for the beef. No need to cook off the fat.

For a meatless dish, substitute canned garbanzo or black beans, drained for the beef.

Stuffed Round Steak

MICROWAVE AND SKILLET
COMBINATION

ENERGY LEVEL:
medium, 50%

SERVINGS:
4 to 6

COMPLETE RECIPE TIME:
about 40 minutes

COOKING TIME:
about 30 minutes

MICROWAVE COOKWARE:
glass loaf pan, 8½ × 4½ × 2½

CONVENTIONAL COOKWARE:
10-inch skillet

COVERING:
plastic wrap to contain heat and
moisture

I've done a lot of presentations on the Nashville network for a popular prepared stuffing mix and have found these mixes to be very good and so much easier to use than making one from scratch.

1 large stalk celery, chopped

1 small onion, chopped

2 medium carrots, chopped

1 6-ounce package prepared stuffing mix

Dijon or other good mustard

1½ pounds round steak, butterflied and pounded with a meat bat or tenderizing mallet

1 cup canned beef stock

Place the celery, onion, and carrots in a large measuring cup, cover, and microwave on high for 3 to 5 minutes, or until the vegetables are soft. Mix the stuffing according to package directions and add the vegetables to it. Spread the mustard over the surface of the meat and spread the stuffing over the mustard. Roll up the meat and secure with toothpicks or tie with string. Place in a glass loaf pan and pour the beef stock over the meat. Cover with plastic wrap and microwave on medium, 50%, power for 20 to 25 minutes, or until the meat is tender. Remove the meat and pat dry with a paper towel. Heat a skillet until very hot and in it sear meat on all sides. Set the meat aside and deglaze the skillet with the juices. Reduce the liquid by half. Slice the meat into 1-inch rounds and serve with the sauce.

Tomato Beef Curry

When I was working for NASA in the 1960s, I was sent to India to work on a joint United States–India space venture. I developed a love and appreciation for Indian cooking and subsequently found that it cooks beautifully in the microwave.

1 pound round steak, about ¾ inch thick, fat removed and cut into ¼- × 2-inch pieces

1 tablespoon minced garlic

1 tablespoon minced raw ginger

1 tablespoon soy sauce

1 tablespoon sweet sherry

1 tablespoon curry powder

1 14½-ounce can tomato wedges, drained, or canned whole tomatoes, drained and cut into quarters.

1 tablespoon cornstarch dissolved in 1 tablespoon soy sauce

Mix all ingredients, except the tomatoes and cornstarch mixture, and place in a 1-quart microwavable casserole. Let marinate for 1 hour. Cover with the dish cover or plastic wrap and microwave on high for about 7 minutes. Stir once during the cooking. Add the tomatoes and cornstarch mixture, stir, and microwave, uncovered, 1 to 2 minutes, or until juices thicken.

Indian Steak Tartare

MICROWAVE ONLY

ENERGY LEVEL:
high, 100%

SERVINGS:
4

COMPLETE RECIPE TIME:
1 hour and 20 minutes

COOKING TIME:
about 10 minutes

MICROWAVE COOKWARE:
1-quart casserole

COVERING:
plastic wrap or the dish cover

Use 1 pound coarse ground round steak and combine with the above ingredients, except the tomatoes and cornstarch. Serve raw as a spread on crackers or Indian bread.

African Steak Strips

MICROWAVE ONLY

ENERGY LEVEL:
high, 100%

SERVINGS:
4

COMPLETE RECIPE TIME:
about 17 minutes

COOKING TIME:
about 10 minutes

MICROWAVE COOKWARE:
1-quart glass or plastic casserole or mixing bowl

COVERING:
plastic wrap or the dish cover

Here's a recipe that uses peanut butter as one of the ingredients. It creates a unique flavor and a nice consistency.

1 small onion, chopped

½ green bell pepper, chopped

1 pound round steak, about ¾ inch thick, fat removed and cut into ¼- by 2-inch pieces

4 tablespoons catsup

1 cup canned beef stock

¼ cup chunky peanut butter

½ teaspoon dried crushed red pepper or hot sauce to taste

½ teaspoon Kitchen Bouquet or other browning agent (optional)

Place the onion and pepper in a 1-quart casserole, cover with the dish cover or plastic wrap, and microwave on high for 3 minutes. Add the meat and remaining ingredients and mix thoroughly. Re-cover and microwave on high for about 7 minutes. Stir once during the cooking.

Chili

I've always been tempted to enter a chili-cooking contest using my microwave oven. I'm sure I'd get a lot of static and raised eyebrows because good chili needs long duration cooking to develop the flavors associated with the dish. Well, in microwave cooking, just as in conventional cooking, you cook the recipe as long as is necessary to tenderize the ingredients and create the consistency and flavors you desire. Cooking is cooking no matter what process you're using. Try your favorite recipe or the following and see for yourself that cooking by microwave produces results equal to or better than conventional cooking. The advantage of making chili by microwave is that you don't have to watch the pot and stir as often to prevent the ingredients from scorching or burning. Remember, the pot never gets hot in your microwave, just the food being cooked.

Dem Bones Chili

MICROWAVE ONLY

ENERGY LEVEL:
high, 100%

SERVINGS:
8

COMPLETE RECIPE TIME:
about 80 to 90 minutes

COOKING TIME:
60 to 70 minutes

MICROWAVE COOKWARE:
4-quart glass, ceramic, or plastic casserole

COVERING:
plastic wrap or the dish cover and wax paper or other nonstick paper

Cooking this recipe with the bones creates that wonderful gelatinous consistency that I love so much, especially after the chili sits overnight. This makes a large amount, but I like to have some left over so that I can freeze and reheat it for a no-cooking meal later on.

4 pounds veal shanks, cut into 1-inch slices (about 2 pounds meat and about 2 pounds bones)

2 medium yellow onions, chopped

4 tablespoons minced garlic

1 red bell pepper, seeds removed and chopped

¼ cup chili powder (Be sure it's fresh.)

1 teaspoon cayenne pepper (optional)

2 tablespoons ground cumin

1 teaspoon salt (optional)

4 10½-ounce cans stewed tomatoes

Bottled hot sauce as an accompaniment

Remove the meat from the bones and cut it into ½-inch chunks. Place all ingredients, except the tomatoes and sauce, in a 4-quart glass or plastic container, stir, and cover with plastic wrap. Microwave on high for 30 minutes, stirring after 15 minutes. Add the tomatoes, cover with wax paper, or other nonstick paper, and microwave on high for 30 to 40 minutes. Remove the bones and serve with hot sauce.

Barbecue Salad

During one of our family outings, it occurred to me that I could make a delightful salad using the typical picnic items. It can be done easily in your home using your microwave oven instead of the charcoal grill. You also have the option of cooking the meat on your stove top; it's up to you. When you mix the pan juices with the salad dressing you get a really rich, beefy taste somewhat like gravy.

1 large Russet potato

1 ear raw corn

¾ pound top sirloin or filet of beef

2 tablespoons beef extract, such as Bovril

2 tablespoons Worcestershire sauce

¼ teaspoon smoked salt seasoning

Italian-style salad dressing

½ head lettuce, broken into small pieces

1 large ripe tomato, diced

1 carrot, sliced

½ green bell pepper, seeds removed and diced

1 6-ounce jar, marinated artichokes (optional)

MICROWAVE AND SKILLET (OPTIONAL)

ENERGY LEVEL:
high, 100%, for vegetables;
medium, 50%, for meat

SERVINGS:
4

COMPLETE RECIPE TIME:
about 25 minutes

COOKING TIME:
about 17 minutes

MICROWAVE COOKWARE:
plastic cooking bag or small glass or plastic dish

ACCESSORY EQUIPMENT:
small skillet (optional)

COVERING:
plastic wrap

Microwave the potato on high 6 to 8 minutes, or until soft. Microwave the corn in the husk on high 3 minutes.

Place the meat in a plastic cooking bag or a microwave dish as close in size to the area of the meat as possible. Combine the extract, Worcestershire, and salt and pour over the meat. Fold the bag around the meat or cover the dish with plastic wrap. Microwave on medium, 50%, power for 6 or 7 minutes, or to an internal temperature of 120 degrees. Or, pan-fry the steak and deglaze the pan with the extract, Worcestershire, salt, and ¼ cup water. Drain the juices into a measuring cup and add enough salad dressing to make ½ cup liquid. Cut the potato into ½-inch dice and cut the corn from the cob and combine with the remaining vegetables. Slice the meat very thin, across the grain, and add to the salad. Serve the pan juices-dressing with the salad.

Simple Sukiyaki

MICROWAVE ONLY

ENERGY LEVEL:
high, 100%

SERVINGS:
4

COMPLETE RECIPE TIME:
about 15 minutes

COOKING TIME:
10 minutes

MICROWAVE COOKWARE:
deep 2-quart glass or plastic
casserole or ring pan

COVERING:
plastic wrap or the dish cover

The Japanese have a wonderful, healthful diet that is easily cooked by microwave, except for tempura and sashimi. This recipe can be made with or without the beef and tastes great either way.

¾ pound lean ground beef

1 medium onion, chopped

½ pound raw mushrooms, sliced

½ cup soy sauce

1 10-ounce box frozen spinach, defrosted

1 pound tofu, diced

½ cup *miso* broth, available at Asian specialty food stores

4 scallions, thinly sliced

Place the beef, onion, and mushrooms in a 2-quart microwave dish or ring pan. Cover with plastic wrap or the dish cover and microwave on high for about 5 minutes, or until the meat is barely cooked. Drain off the fat, crumble the meat, and add the soy sauce, spinach, tofu, and broth. Re-cover and microwave on high 5 minutes. Add the scallions, stir, and serve.

Nacho Casserole

MICROWAVE ONLY

ENERGY LEVEL:
high, 100%, to cook meat;
medium, 50%, for the casserole

SERVINGS:
4

COMPLETE RECIPE TIME:
about 25 minutes

COOKING TIME:
15 to 17 minutes

MICROWAVE COOKWARE:
2-quart mixing bowl and deep
2-quart glass or plastic casserole
or ring pan

COVERING:
plastic wrap or the dish cover to
contain heat and assure even
cooking

This is not yo' usual nacho chip platter, but it tastes great and makes a nice pot luck dish. It can also be frozen and served later.

1 pound lean ground beef

2 tablespoons chili powder

1 4-ounce can diced green chiles

2 cups prepared salsa or taco sauce

1 16-ounce can chili beans or kidney beans, drained

½ bag nacho chips, about 6 ounces

4 ounces shredded Cheddar cheese

Break up the meat and place in a 2-quart mixing bowl. Microwave on high for 5 minutes. Crumble the meat with a fork and pour off the fat. Mix with the remaining ingredients, except half of the cheese. Place mixture in a deep 2-quart microwavable casserole or ring pan. Top with the rest of the cheese. Cover the casserole with plastic wrap or the dish cover and microwave on medium, 50%, power for 10 to 12 minutes or to an internal temperature of 140 degrees.

Variations: Use leftover chicken or other meat instead of the beef. Or omit meat for a vegetarian casserole.

Pork

Pork is probably the easiest meat to cook by microwave. All you have to be concerned about is cooking it until it is done and tender. Some cuts of beef must be cooked so the inside is rare, but with pork you want all of it to be well done. By that I don't mean cooked to death, but cooked until it is done throughout, with no rare portions. Today's pork is also more lean and marketed with less fat. Because of this, when you cook it in a conventional, hot oven you must be careful not to cook it too long, which causes it to become dry.

In microwave cooking you don't have to worry about that because you are always cooking in a moist environment. I like to cook pork in the microwave to 160 to 170 degrees. Just be sure to cook all cuts of pork at least over 140 degrees to eliminate the possibility of contracting trichinosis, which although extremely rare still does exist. This is another reason to get an instant-read thermometer so you know you have cooked chicken and pork to the proper temperature to avoid any health problems. When I lived in New York City, I had a roommate from the Midwest who always described pork as the sweetest of meat. I think that best describes the satisfaction derived from a good pork recipe.

I hope I don't "boar" you with the following recipes. Here are my general rules for cooking pork:

1. Always cover the dish securely with its cover or plastic wrap or use plastic cooking bags. This retains the steam so that the meat is cooked by microwave and steam and even if you have a microwave that has hot spots the meat will be cooked throughout.

2. Before serving always check and make sure that the meat is at a temperature of 160 to 170. Many years ago the FDA advised that people not cook pork with a microwave oven because of the uneven heating pattern of some ovens. They were warning that portions of the meat might not be completely cooked when you served it. Well folks, I can undercook pork and chicken in my conventional oven, my frying pan, on the charcoal grill and even in a pressure cooker. Machines don't cook, people cook! So before you serve anything, check and make sure it's cooked properly.

3. Cook on high power if you are using some liquid in the recipe. The addition of liquid slows the cooking process.

4. Cook on medium-high or medium when no extra liquid is added to the recipe.

5. Remove all visible fat from the pork cuts. Since you are cooking in a moist environment and the cooking vessels don't get hot you don't need the lubrication provided by fat that is necessary in conventional cooking.

6. Microwave pork sausages about 1 minute each before you fry or barbecue them. This removes a lot of fat and also prevents flare-ups on the barbecue. And you don't have to cook them so long on the grill or in the pan. Cut the sausages open lengthwise and lay flat on a plate. Make cuts across the skin side so sausages will lay flat when you grill or fry them.

7. Allow about 1 minute per slice for refrigerated bacon. Room temperature bacon will take less time. Microwave thick-sliced bacon on medium power so it has time to brown and crisp before it burns. Microwave thin-sliced ba-

con about 45 seconds per slice or it will burn. When making lots of bacon as for BLTs, make layers between paper towels and cook the whole amount, up to ½ pound at a time. Many people will cook only one layer at a time, which is not very efficient.

8. Microwave all pork cuts until done before grilling them outdoors. Then only cook on the charcoal grill to char the surface and enhance the flavor. The meat stays juicy and flare-ups are minimized because you have already cooked off most of the fat. Also because the meat is fully cooked, there is less chance of spoilage.

Leg of Pork

MICROWAVE ONLY

ENERGY LEVEL:
high, 100%

SERVINGS:
6 to 8

COMPLETE RECIPE TIME:
about 1 hour

COOKING TIME:
50 to 60 minutes

MICROWAVE COOKWARE:
9- × 13-inch glass, ceramic, or
plastic baking pan or similar dish
large enough to accommodate the
meat

COVERING:
plastic wrap and aluminum foil for
a very large leg

A leg of pork is a ham that hasn't been cured. It is usually very inexpensive and a wonderful piece of meat to serve for a large group. I can say without fear of argument that microwaving this cut of meat is better than any other way of cooking it. For a large party or gathering, microwave a really big one, around 20 pounds.

1 5- to 6-pound leg of pork   Salt and fresh ground pepper

Trim off all of the skin and surface fat. Season with salt and pepper. Place the leg in a microwave pot that is big enough to accommodate it snugly. (I have a 4-quart oval roasting pan that is perfect.) Cover with plastic wrap and microwave on high for 10 to 12 minutes per pound or to an internal temperature of 160 to 170. Turn over once during the cooking and remove accumulated fat and juices. If you microwave a really big leg of pork, cover the entire top surface with foil after you turn it over, re-cover with plastic wrap. This will prevent it from drying out on the top. Serve with boiled potatoes and/or sauerkraut.

You can also remove the meat from the bone and discard all fat. Shred meat with two forks, blend with a prepared barbecue sauce of choice, and use it for barbecue sandwiches.

Optional: Cover the leg with crushed caraway seeds and insert garlic cloves into 1-inch-deep incisions.

Pork Loin Stuffed with Dried Fruit

I prepared this recipe on one of my television shows and when I sliced it for serving I could almost hear the oohs and aahs from the audience at home. If you want to impress your dinner guests, serve this.

1 4-ounce package pitted mixed dried fruit

1 medium apple, cored and diced

1 3- to 4-pound boneless loin pork roast

½ cup apple juice

½ cup orange marmalade or chutney of choice

MICROWAVE AND CONVENTIONAL OVEN (OPTIONAL)

ENERGY LEVEL:
medium, 50%; conventional oven, 500 degrees (optional)

SERVINGS:
5 or 6

COMPLETE RECIPE TIME:
about 1 hour

COOKING TIME:
30 to 40 minutes

MICROWAVE COOKWARE:
glass loaf pan or 8-inch-square glass baking pan

COVERING:
plastic wrap to contain steam and prevent uneven cooking

Place the dried fruit in 1 cup water and microwave for 5 minutes on high. Let stand until soft. Combine with the apple. Run a thin blade knife through the roast lengthwise and cut a bit to make a pocket. Stuff the mixed fruit into the pocket and close the slits with toothpicks. Place the roast and the apple juice in a glass loaf pan or 8-inch-square glass baking pan. Cover with plastic wrap and microwave on medium, 50%, for about 10 to 12 minutes per pound or to an internal temperature of 160 degrees. Pour off the juices, place the roast on a platter, and spread the marmalade over it. Or, pour off the juices, spread the roast with the marmalade, and place in a preheated 500 degree oven until the glaze bubbles and thickens. Remove the toothpicks and slice into 1-inch rounds. Serve with the pan juices.

Optional: Mix the softened dried fruit with a prepared stuffing mix or cooked wild rice.

Roast Pork Calypso

MICROWAVE AND CONVENTIONAL
OVEN (OPTIONAL)

ENERGY LEVEL:
medium, 50%, conventional oven,
500 degrees

SERVINGS:
4

COMPLETE RECIPE TIME:
about 30 minutes

COOKING TIME:
20 to 25 minutes

MICROWAVE COOKWARE:
8½- × 3½- × 2½-inch glass loaf
pan

COVERING:
plastic wrap to contain steam and
prevent uneven cooking

1 2-pound boneless loin pork roast

½ cup brown sugar, light or dark, your choice

2 tablespoons rum, light or dark, your choice

1 tablespoon minced garlic

1 teaspoon ground ginger

¼ teaspoon ground cloves

1 tablespoon cornstarch or arrowroot dissolved in 3 tablespoons fresh lime juice

Remove any surface fat and score the top of the roast with an X pattern about ¼-inch deep. Mix all ingredients together, except the cornstarch mixture, and rub into the top of the roast. Place in an 8½- × 3½- × 2½-inch glass loaf pan or other similar glass or ceramic pan. Cover with plastic wrap and microwave on medium, 50%, power for 18 to 20 minutes, or 10 minutes per pound, to an internal temperature of 160 to 170. Mix the cornstarch and lime juice with the juices from the roast. Microwave on high, uncovered, about 2 to 3 minutes, or until the sauce thickens. Pour over the roast and serve. Or place in a preheated 500 degree oven for about 5 minutes to brown.

ZAP TIP: Instead of using cornstarch to thicken the pan juices you can pour them off into a frying pan and reduce them over high heat. Sauces reduce much faster on the stove than in the microwave.

Pork Tenderloin Cooked in Milk

Pork tenderloin may seem expensive, but when you consider that there is no waste or surface fat, it's really quite a bargain.

1 pound pork tenderloin

1 tablespoon dried rosemary

1 tablespoon puréed garlic

Salt and fresh ground pepper to taste

½ cup milk

2 tablespoons Worcestershire sauce

Sear the loin in a very hot fry pan and place in a 1-quart microwave dish. Add the remaining ingredients. Cover and microwave on high for 10 to 12 minutes or to an internal temperature of 160 degrees. (Or use a glass skillet for the recipe.) Pour juices into skillet and reduce by about half. Slice into ½-inch rounds and serve with the pan juices.

MICROWAVE AND SKILLET COMBINATION

ENERGY LEVEL:
high, 100%

SERVINGS:
4

COMPLETE RECIPE TIME:
about 20 minutes

COOKING TIME:
15 minutes

MICROWAVE COOKWARE:
shallow 1-quart casserole or glass skillet

COVERING:
plastic wrap or the dish cover

Picnic Ham

Whenever I mention cooking hams in the microwave, people exclaim, "Gee, I never thought of cooking a ham in the microwave!" The next time you cook a ham think about doing it in your microwave oven because it will turn out spectacularly and in about one third of the time it takes in a conventional oven. You can also remove all of the surface fat, thereby reducing the amount retained in the meat.

1 picnic ham, up to 20 pounds

Remove the skin and all of the surface fat from the ham. Place in an appropriate microwave container and add water 1 inch deep to the pan. Cover with plastic wrap and microwave on medium-high, 80%, power for about 8 minutes per pound or to an internal temperature of 160 to 170 degrees. Turn the ham over halfway through the cooking and taste the water. If it is very salty pour it off and add fresh hot water. If you see any portions of the ham drying out and becoming hard you may want to cover these areas with foil to protect them. (I personally like to chew on those hard crusty nubbins of ham.)

For a very large ham, 18 to 22 pounds, after turning it over, cover the entire top surface with foil and re-cover with plastic wrap. Gravity pulls the moisture down away from the top of the meat and when you cook for a long period of time the top will dry out. Once I made a large ham for a party and didn't turn it over or protect it with foil. When it was done the top was like a turtle shell. I pried off a 1-inch-thick petrified piece that I could have used for a salad bowl. Let my experience be your guide and cover the top with foil.

Simple Glaze for Ham

1 15½-ounce can crushed
   pineapple with juice

½ cup brown sugar

2 tablespoons cornstarch

Mix all ingredients and microwave on high, uncovered, for about 5 minutes, or until glaze thickens. Spread over the cooked ham and serve. Or place ham in a hot 500 degree oven for 5 to 10 minutes.

MICROWAVE ONLY

ENERGY LEVEL:
medium-high, 70 to 80%

SERVINGS:
about 25

COMPLETE RECIPE TIME:
about 2 1/2 hours

COOKING TIME:
about 2 1/2 hours

MICROWAVE COOKWARE:
large glass, ceramic, or plastic oval or rectangular baking pan. I have a ceramic oval roaster, 15 inches long, that works perfectly

COVERING:
plastic wrap to contain heat and steam and aluminum foil to protect ham from drying out

Canned Ham

MICROWAVE ONLY

ENERGY LEVEL:
high, 100%

SERVINGS:
allow 6 ounces per serving

COMPLETE RECIPE TIME:
10-pound cooked whole, about 1 hour; sliced on a platter, about 20 minutes

COOKING TIME:
whole ham, 5 minutes per pound; sliced on a platter, about 1 minute per pound

COVERING:
plastic wrap

I don't serve canned ham often because it's so easy to make a picnic ham, which I think has a much better taste. But, if you want to heat a canned ham, do it in your microwave. Since they are completely cooked and ready to eat, all you have to do is to microwave it until it reaches an internal temperature of 140 degrees. Because they are so dense, it still takes about 5 minutes per pound.

Remove the ham from the can and place on a serving platter. Cover with plastic wrap and microwave on high for about 5 minutes per pound or to an internal temperature of 140 degrees. An easier way to do it is to slice the ham and place the slices on a serving platter in an overlapping pattern. Cover with plastic wrap and microwave on medium-high until heated throughout, about 1 minute per pound. People are always asking me how you tell when something is hot enough to serve. Feel it, sweethearts, just feel it. For your information, it has been determined through surveys that the temperature that Americans prefer their food is 140 degrees.

Stroganoff Chops

MICROWAVE ONLY

ENERGY LEVEL:
high, 100%

SERVINGS:
4

COMPLETE RECIPE TIME:
about 15 minutes

COOKING TIME:
10 to 12 minutes

MICROWAVE COOKWARE:
shallow 1-quart glass or
plastic casserole

COVERING:
plastic wrap or the dish cover

When you get home from work and don't want to put much effort into cooking, try this simple recipe.

1 teaspoon dillweed

6 mushrooms, sliced

4 lean thin pork chops, ½ inch thick

½ can cream of mushroom soup mixed with an equal amount of water

Stir the dill and mushrooms into the soup. Place the chops in a 1-quart shallow microwave dish and pour soup over them. Cover the dish with plastic wrap or the dish cover and microwave on high for 10 to 12 minutes, or until the chops are done.

Smoked Pork Butt with Cabbage or Kraut

MICROWAVE ONLY

ENERGY LEVEL:
high, 100%

COMPLETE RECIPE TIME:
about 25 minutes

COOKING TIME:
about 20 minutes, or 10 minutes
per pound of meat

MICROWAVE COOKWARE:
deep 2-quart glass or plastic
casserole

COVERING:
plastic wrap or the dish cover

A smoked butt is boneless pork shoulder packaged in a Cryovac casing and weighs about 2 pounds. If you can find one, microwave it and enjoy a real taste treat.

1 tablespoon caraway seeds, crushed	1 smoked pork butt, about 2 pounds
1 small cabbage, shredded, or 1 pound Bavarian-style (sweet) sauerkraut or regular kraut, not rinsed	

Mix the caraway seeds with the cabbage or kraut in a 2-quart microwave dish and bury the butt in the mixture. Cover with plastic wrap or the dish cover and microwave on high for about 15 minutes. Slice into ½-inch rounds and serve with the cabbage.

Paupiettes of Pork

These long meat rolls can be made as fancy or as simple as you like. Serve them on a bed of microwaved vegetables, with a sauce, or as an hors d'oeuvre. They are also great when charcoal grilled.

4 pork loin medallions, 3 to 4 ounces each

Worcestershire sauce

1 cup cooked rice or prepared stuffing mix

¼ pound seasoned bulk pork sausage

Paprika

MICROWAVE AND SKILLET COMBINATION

ENERGY LEVEL:
high, 100%

SERVINGS:
4

COMPLETE RECIPE TIME:
about 20 minutes

COOKING TIME:
about 12 minutes

MICROWAVE COOKWARE:
shallow 1-quart glass or plastic casserole or a 10-inch glass skillet

ACCESSORY EQUIPMENT:
toothpicks

COVERING:
plastic wrap or the dish cover

Place the medallions between 2 sheets of wax paper and beat with a meat bat or the flat end of a meat tenderizer until very thin, about ⅛ inch. Sprinkle with Worcestershire sauce and spread an equal amount of rice and sausage over the meat. Roll up and secure with toothpicks. Sprinkle with paprika. Place rolls in a shallow microwave dish, cover with plastic wrap or the dish cover, and microwave on high for about 8 minutes. Transfer to a very hot skillet and sear before serving. Or microwave them in a covered glass skillet, then sear in the same dish on stove top.

This is another recipe that can be made ahead of time and frozen until you want to serve it. Just microwave on high without defrosting until the rolls are heated through.

Oriental Pork Rolls: Prepare the meat as directed above but add 2 chopped scallions and 2 tablespoons pickled gingerroot to the filling. Coat with hoisin sauce before microwaving.

Paupiettes Élégantes: Prepare the meat as directed above and stuff with finely chopped mushrooms. Microwave with 4 tablespoons butter and pour sauce over rolls when serving.

Spicy Pork Goulash

MICROWAVE ONLY

ENERGY LEVEL:
medium, 50%; and high, 100%

COMPLETE RECIPE TIME:
about 30 minutes

COOKING TIME:
25 minutes

MICROWAVE COOKWARE:
deep 2-quart glass or plastic
casserole

COVERING:
plastic wrap or the dish cover

The basic recipe for this dish is called Szekeley goulash and I included it in my second cookbook *Microwaves Are for Cooking.* Lots of people commented that it sounded too foreign for them to try. Aside from its name, it is a very simple recipe and so good. The original used sauerkraut and you can still make it that way, but in this version I've substituted *kimchee,* pickled Korean cabbage, for the sauerkraut. It makes the recipe spicy, hot, and different. I love it!

2 pounds pork loin, all fat
    removed and cut into
    1-inch cubes

6 tablespoons paprika

1 jar 12-ounce *kimchee,*
    hotness to taste, available
    in most supermarket
    produce departments

½ pint sour cream or plain
    yogurt

Mix the pork with the paprika and the juice from the *kimchee* in a 2-quart microwave dish, cover with plastic wrap or the dish cover, and microwave on medium, 50%, power for about 15 minutes, or until the pork is no longer pink inside. Add the *kimchee,* re-cover, and microwave on high for 10 minutes. Just before serving, stir in the sour cream or plain yogurt.

Stuffed Pork Chops

MICROWAVE ONLY AND BROILER
(OPTIONAL)

ENERGY LEVEL:
high, 100%

SERVINGS:
4

COMPLETE RECIPE TIME:
about 30 minutes

COOKING TIME:
microwave 15 to 20 minutes;
broiler about 5 minutes (optional)

MICROWAVE COOKWARE:
8-inch-square or 9- × 13-inch
glass baking pan

ACCESSORY EQUIPMENT:
toothpicks

COVERING:
plastic wrap to ensure even
cooking

You can stuff these individual chops with the same dried fruit mixture as in the stuffed pork loin (page 47) or just use a prepared stuffing of choice. A wild rice stuffing is also a nice complement to pork chops.

½ cup dry white wine

1 tablespoon minced fresh sage, or 2 tablespoons dried

4 thick loin pork chops, about ½ pound each

2 cups stuffing mix prepared as directed on package without cooking

Place the wine and sage in an 8-inch-square glass baking pan and microwave on high about 3 minutes. Make a pocket in each chop and fill with the stuffing. Close the opening with toothpicks. Place the chops in the baking pan, cover with plastic wrap, and microwave on high for about 15 to 20 minutes or to an internal temperature of 160 to 170 degrees. Pour the juices into a frying pan and reduce over high heat by about half. Pour over chops when serving. You may want to place the chops under your broiler to brown while you are reducing the juices.

Deli Meat Casserole

MICROWAVE ONLY

ENERGY LEVEL:
high, 100%

SERVINGS:
4

COMPLETE RECIPE TIME:
about 20 minutes

COOKING TIME:
12 to 15 minutes

MICROWAVE COOKWARE:
deep 2-quart glass or plastic casserole or ring pan

COVERING:
plastic wrap or the dish cover

When I was a kid we called deli meats cold cuts. Usually cured and fully cooked, most are ready to eat without further cooking. They are always loaded with flavor and have a high fat content. If you want to reduce the fat in this casserole, microwave the meat for about 5 minutes, then pour off the rendered fat, and continue with the recipe. There is such a variety of deli meats that I'm not going to specify any in this recipe. Just use those that you enjoy most, singularly or combined with others.

1 pound deli meat, such as salami, bologna, mortadella, thüringer, etc., sliced and cut into 1-inch squares

2 medium potatoes, diced

2 medium carrots, sliced

1 medium onion, chopped

1 14½-ounce can stewed tomatoes

Place everything in a 2-quart microwave dish or ring pan. Cover with plastic wrap or the dish cover and microwave on high for 12 to 15 minutes, or until the potatoes are soft.

ZAP TIP: When making a deli meat sandwich, microwave the meat 30 to 40 seconds before adding it to the sandwich. You'll be pleased at how much more flavor you taste.

Sausage and Vegetable Casserole

I make this recipe a lot when I'm demonstrating at food and nutrition shows. It doesn't require much preparation so I just put it together, microwave it, then explain the principles of micro-waving to the audience. They always love it, and when using only toothpicks it's easy to serve lots of people. At home serve it with forks instead of the toothpicks.

1 pound sausage, either raw or cured or cooked, cut into 1-inch pieces (Sometimes I use kielbasa, linguiça, or plain smoked sausage, other times I'll use Italian sausage, bratwurst, or even pork chorizo.)

1 large potato, diced

1 large onion, cut into 1-inch pieces

1 small cabbage, chopped

Place everything into a 2-quart microwave dish or ring pan, cover with plastic wrap or the dish cover, and microwave on high for 12 to 15 minutes, or until the potatoes are soft.

MICROWAVE ONLY

ENERGY LEVEL:
high, 100%

SERVINGS:
4

COMPLETE RECIPE TIME:
about 20 minutes

COOKING TIME:
12 to 15 minutes

MICROWAVE COOKWARE:
deep 2-quart glass or plastic casserole or ring pan

COVERING:
plastic wrap or the dish cover

Bean and Pork Casserole

MICROWAVE ONLY

ENERGY LEVEL:
high, 100%, and medium, 50%

SERVINGS:
8

COMPLETE RECIPE TIME:
about 60 minutes

COOKING TIME:
about 45 minutes

MICROWAVE COOKWARE:
deep 3-quart glass or plastic
casserole or ring pan

COVERING:
plastic wrap or the dish cover

This recipe is something like the classic French dish *cassoulet.* A true *cassoulet* takes days to make, hours to bake, and requires lots of attention to the cooking. Even in a microwave the classic recipe takes 1½ to 2 hours. As this book is more concerned with cooking fast and easy, I've developed the following combination. Serve it with a simple lettuce salad with vinaigrette dressing to cut the richness. A great dish to serve after a day of vigorous activity like skiing or hiking or plowing, even shopping.

2 thick slices bacon	1 medium carrot, chopped
1 pound pork loin, fat removed and cut into 1-inch cubes	4 cloves garlic, minced
	1 8-ounce can tomato sauce
½ pound Polish sausage or other sausage of choice	2 14-ounce cans navy beans with liquid
1 medium onion, chopped	2 cups prepared croutons

Place the bacon between two paper towels and microwave on medium, 50%, power for 4 to 5 minutes until brown and crisp. In a 3-quart microwave casserole or ring pan break the bacon into pieces and add the remaining ingredients, except the tomato sauce, beans, and croutons. Cover with plastic wrap or the dish cover and microwave on high for 10 minutes. Stir in the tomato sauce and beans and top with the croutons. Microwave, uncovered, on medium for 30 minutes. Press the croutons into the casserole before serving.

Sausage and Mashed Potato Pie

4 medium potatoes or 4
    servings instant mashed
    potatoes, prepared as
    directed on the package

1 pound sausage of choice,
    such as bratwurst, Italian,
    Polish, and so on

1 cup grated Cheddar cheese

⅛ teaspoon grated nutmeg

MICROWAVE ONLY

ENERGY LEVEL:
high, 100%

SERVINGS:
4

COMPLETE RECIPE TIME:
if using raw potatoes, about 30
minutes, with instant potatoes,
about 15 minutes

COOKING TIME:
with raw potatoes, 25 minutes;
with instant potatoes, 10 minutes

MICROWAVE COOKWARE:
9-inch glass or ceramic pie plate

If using raw potatoes, microwave them on high 12 to 15 minutes, or until soft and process them with a ricer or peel and mash. Beat in about 4 tablespoons butter or margarine and enough milk to make them smooth.

Remove the skin from the sausages if necessary and cut sausages into 1-inch pieces. Mix with the remaining ingredients and place in a 9-inch glass pie dish. Microwave on high, uncovered, for 10 minutes and serve. You may want to place the pie under your broiler until the surface browns.

Pork and Chorizo Sausage and Chicken Casserole

MICROWAVE ONLY

ENERGY LEVEL:
high, 100%

SERVINGS:
4

COMPLETE RECIPE TIME:
about 30 minutes

COOKING TIME:
about 23 minutes

MICROWAVE COOKWARE:
deep 3-quart glass or plastic
casserole or ring pan

COVERING:
plastic wrap or the dish cover

In this recipe use the soft pork chorizo sausages. They lend great color and flavor. Also, if you are reducing the amount of animal protein in your diet, add only half the suggested amounts in this recipe. Use the meat more as a condiment than as a component with the rice.

1 whole skinned chicken
    breast, cubed

1 pound lean pork loin, cut
    into 1-inch cubes

½ pound pork chorizo sausage,
    skin removed

1 medium bell pepper, seeds
    removed and diced

1 small onion, chopped

1 cup long-grain rice

1¾ cups water

Mix all ingredients in a 3-quart microwave casserole or ring pan, cover with plastic wrap or the dish cover, and microwave on high for 8 minutes and on medium, 50%, for 12 to 15 minutes, or until the rice has absorbed the water and becomes tender.

Sausage and Sauerkraut

You may think that I feature too much sauerkraut in my recipes. If you don't like it, you can substitute cabbage or any other leafy vegetable, but kraut is so good for us that we should all eat more of it. Also, try Bavarian-style kraut, which is slightly sweet, for a little variety.

1 pound sauerkraut, rinsed

1 pound ring bologna or
   knackwurst

1 medium onion, chopped

1 medium hard apple, cored
   and diced

1 tablespoon caraway seeds

Place half of the kraut in a 2-quart microwave casserole or ring pan and add the remaining ingredients. Cover with the remaining kraut, cover with plastic wrap or the dish cover, and microwave on high for 12 to 15 minutes, or until heated through.

MICROWAVE ONLY:

ENERGY LEVEL:
high, 100%

SERVINGS:
4

COMPLETE RECIPE TIME:
about 20 minutes

COOKING TIME:
12–15 minutes

MICROWAVE COOKWARE:
2-quart microwave casserole or ring pan

COVERING:
plastic wrap or the dish cover

Pizza Rice Casserole

MICROWAVE ONLY

ENERGY LEVEL:
high, 100%, medium, 50%

SERVINGS:
4 to 6

COMPLETE RECIPE TIME:
about 25 minutes

COOKING TIME:
about 20 minutes

MICROWAVE COOKWARE:
deep 3-quart glass or plastic
casserole or ring pan

COVERING:
plastic wrap or the dish cover

Here I've just taken the ingredients for a sausage pizza, substituted rice for the crust, and cooked it as a casserole.

1 cup long-grain rice

1¾ cups water

1 cup prepared pizza sauce

½ pound Italian sausage, crumbled

½ pound raw mushrooms, sliced

1 medium bell pepper, cored and diced

2 ounces olives, chopped

2 ounces pepperoni sausage, thinly sliced

½ cup grated Parmesan cheese

1 cup shredded mozzarella cheese

Mix all ingredients, except the cheeses, in a 3-quart microwave casserole or ring pan. Cover with plastic wrap or the dish cover and microwave on high for 8 minutes and on medium, 50%, for 12 to 15 minutes, or until the rice is tender. Stir in the cheeses and let casserole sit for a couple of minutes before serving.

Note: If you want to reduce the fat in this recipe, microwave the sausages for 3 to 4 minutes and pour off the fat before incorporating the sausage in the recipe.

Lamb

Several times I've made presentations on "Cooking Lamb by Microwave" for the American Lamb Council. These have always been a pleasure for me because I really enjoy lamb and love any opportunity to convince people to eat more of it. Most cuts cook beautifully by microwave, especially boned legs and stews. However, I still recommend that chops and steaks be cooked by broiling or grilling because it's so easy and the flavor from charring cannot be duplicated by microwaving.

There is a strange prejudice toward lamb that I can't understand. Lots of people think they don't like it and, therefore, don't cook and serve it. It may be a carry-over from the days when mutton was cooked and served with a lot of fat. Lamb today is very lean and extremely flavorful, so I hope that if you think you don't like it, you'll try these recipes and overcome any bad impressions you may harbor. Lots of times when I serve lamb at food exhibitions, people will sample it without knowing what kind of meat it is and exclaim how wonderful it tastes. When I tell them it's lamb they will screw up their faces and tell me that they don't like it.

I don't want to pull the wool over your heads, nor ram these recipes down your throat, but I think ewe'll love them.

Microwave-Grilled Leg of Lamb

MICROWAVE, CHARCOAL GRILL,
OR BROILER COMBINATION

ENERGY LEVEL:
medium, 50%

SERVINGS:
6 to 8

COMPLETE RECIPE TIME:
about 2 hours, including
marinating

COOKING TIME:
about 30 minutes

MICROWAVE COOKWARE:
9- x 13-inch glass or plastic
baking pan

ACCESSORY EQUIPMENT:
charcoal grill

COVERING:
wax paper or other nonstick paper

I want to start this section with this recipe because it really shows off the delectable flavor and texture of properly cooked lamb. One problem with cooking large pieces of lamb on the grill is that you have to cook them so long to get the interior done that the surface overcooks, dries out, and burns. When you microwave it first, you grill it only long enough to char the surface. The meat is juicier and you still have the flavor from grilling.

1 5-pound leg of lamb, boned, about 3 ½ pounds of meat	2 tablespoons lemon juice
4 tablespoons minced garlic	1 tablespoon dried rosemary
	¼ cup olive oil

Lay the lamb in a 9- x 13- inch baking pan and spread the remaining ingredients over both surfaces. Cover with wax paper and microwave on medium, 50%, power for about 4 minutes per pound or to an internal temperature of about 110 to 120 degrees. Charcoal grill or broil until the surface chars and the internal temperature is 140 degrees for rare and 150 for medium.

Middle East Marinade: Combine 1 cup chopped mint leaves, 1 teaspoon allspice, 4 tablespoons minced garlic, and 1 teaspoon ground cinnamon and spread over the surface of the lamb. Cook as directed above. Use this marinade instead of garlic, lemon, rosemary, and oil.

Chinese-style Barbecued Leg of Lamb: Use 4 tablespoons five spice seasoning, and spread over surface of the lamb. Cook as directed above.

Hot and Spicy Barbecued Leg of Lamb: If you like hot and spicy meats, this is the easiest way to make a really good recipe. Just spread the surfaces with garlic-chili paste or sauce, which is available at Asian specialty stores. Cook as directed above.

Curried Barbecued Leg of Lamb: Mix 4 tablespoons curry powder, 4 tablespoons minced garlic, 4 tablespoons ginger paste, and 4 tablespoons lemon juice and spread over the surface of the lamb. Cook as directed above. You can also buy curry paste at Asian specialty food stores; it works well in this recipe.

Microwaved Boneless Leg of Lamb

4 tablespoons minced garlic

2 tablespoons crushed dried rosemary

2 tablespoons dried or fresh chopped thyme

Salt and fresh ground pepper to taste

1 5- to 6-pound leg of lamb, boned, about 3½ pounds meat

MICROWAVE AND CONVENTIONAL OVEN (OPTIONAL)

ENERGY LEVEL: medium, 50%

SERVINGS: 6 to 8

COMPLETE RECIPE TIME: about 1 hour

COOKING TIME: about 50 minutes

MICROWAVE COOKWARE: shallow 2-quart glass casserole or 8-inch-square glass baking pan

COVERING: wax paper or other nonstick paper to contain the heat but allow moisture to escape

Mix the garlic and herbs and rub all over the meat. Roll and tie the meat and place it in an appropriate glass or ceramic pan. Cover with wax paper and microwave on medium, 50%, power for about 7 to 8 minutes per pound or to an internal temperature of 125 degrees. Turn over once during the cooking and drain off the juices. After microwaving, drain off the juices and place in a preheated hot 500 degree oven for about 10 minutes to brown and crust the surface.

If you don't want to go through the step of finishing the roast in a conventional oven, just microwave it 8 to 10 minutes per pound or to an internal temperature of 130 degrees. Let stand for about 10 minutes before serving.

To make gravy, dissolve 2 tablespoons flour in 2 tablespoons water in a measuring cup and stir in the juices. Microwave for 3 to 4 minutes, or until thickened. You may have to add more water or broth to make enough to serve everyone.

Whole Leg of Lamb

MICROWAVE AND CONVENTIONAL OVEN
(OPTIONAL)

ENERGY LEVEL:
medium, 50%

SERVINGS:
6 to 8

COMPLETE RECIPE TIME:
about 1 hour

COOKING TIME:
40 to 50 minutes

MICROWAVE COOKWARE:
9- x 13-inch glass or ceramic
baking pan or oval roaster of
similar size

COVERING:
wax paper or other nonstick paper

1 5- to 6-pound leg of lamb, short end	2 tablespoons crushed dried rosemary
8 cloves garlic, peeled	Lemon pepper

Make 1-inch incisions evenly spaced on the lamb. Insert the garlic cloves and rub the surface with the rosemary and lemon pepper. Place the roast in an appropriate glass or ceramic pan and cover with wax paper or other nonstick paper. Microwave on medium, 50%, power for about 7 minutes per pound or to an internal temperature of 125 degrees. Turn over once during the cooking and drain off the juices. After microwaving, drain off the juices and place the leg in a preheated 500 degree oven for about 10 minutes to brown and crust the surface. Or simply microwave it 8 to 10 minutes per pound to an internal temperature of 130 degrees. Let stand for about 10 minutes before serving.

To make gravy, see page 67.

Rack of Lamb

Although I recommend that you always broil or grill lamb chops, a rack has enough mass so that it cooks beautifully by microwave. Since you don't have to worry about it burning when cooked by microwave, you can remove all exterior fat and thus enjoy a healthier piece of meat.

1 rack of lamb, about 2 pounds, with 8 ribs	1 tablespoon minced lemon zest
½ cup bread crumbs	2 tablespoons minced garlic
¼ cup minced mint leaves	2 tablespoons mayonnaise

Remove all fat from the meat and cut the rack into 2 equal pieces of 4 ribs each. Place in an 8-inch-square glass pan with the thin ends overlapping. Mix all of the remaining ingredients together and pack down over the meat. Cover with wax paper or other nonstick paper and microwave on medium, 50%, power about 5 minutes per pound or to an internal temperature of 140 degrees.

For a more impressive presentation, have your butcher French the rib bones—that is, remove the meat between them. When you cook the racks intertwine the bones, and leave them uncovered to brown.

MICROWAVE ONLY

ENERGY LEVEL:
medium, 50%

SERVINGS:
4

COMPLETE RECIPE TIME:
about 20 minutes

COOKING TIME:
about 10 minutes

MICROWAVE COOKWARE:
8-inch-square glass baking pan or similar glass or plastic dish

COVERING:
wax paper or other nonstick paper

Crown Roast of Lamb with Dried-Fruit Stuffing

MICROWAVE AND CONVENTIONAL
OVEN (OPTIONAL)

ENERGY LEVEL:
medium, 50%

SERVINGS:
6 to 8

COMPLETE RECIPE TIME:
about 50 minutes

COOKING TIME:
about 30 minutes

MICROWAVE COOKWARE:
10-inch glass or ceramic pie dish
or 9- x 13-inch glass or plastic
baking pan

COVERING:
wax paper or other nonstick paper

A glorious presentation for a small dinner party.

**1 4-ounce package pitted
mixed dried fruit**

**1 6-ounce package prepared
stuffing mix**

**2 racks of lamb tied into a
crown, about 4 pounds
(Ask your butcher to
prepare and tie it for you.)**

Place the fruit in 2 cups water, in a measuring cup and microwave on high for 10 minutes. Let stand until the fruit becomes soft. Press out excess water and mix with the stuffing prepared as directed on the package.

Place the crown in a 10-inch glass pie dish or other appropriate dish and fill the center with the stuffing. Place wax paper or other nonstick paper around and over the roast. Microwave on medium, 50%, power for 7 to 8 minutes per pound or to an internal temperature of 140 degrees. Because the roast cooks for this long a period, it will develop a nice brown color. If you want it darker, place it in a preheated hot 500 degree oven for about 5 minutes.

Lamb Stew with Vegetables

MICROWAVE ONLY

ENERGY LEVEL:
high, 100%

SERVINGS:
4

COMPLETE RECIPE TIME:
40 to 50 minutes

COOKING TIME:
30 to 35 minutes

MICROWAVE COOKWARE:
deep 3-quart glass, ceramic, or plastic casserole dish or ring pan, or plastic cooking bag

COVERING:
plastic wrap or the dish cover

Most people, when making a stew, will brown the meat in a little oil before adding it to the other ingredients. You can do this if you have the time, but I've found that there is little difference in flavor if you just combine the ingredients and cook it until done. Sometime, when you've the time to fool around in the kitchen, make the stew, browning only half the meat. See if you can tell the difference.

This recipe also works very well in a plastic cooking bag.

1 pound lean lamb from the leg, cut into 1-inch cubes

2 tablespoons flour

2 cloves garlic, chopped

1 tablespoon *fines herbes*

2 tablespoons Worcestershire sauce

2 medium potatoes, diced

2 medium carrots, sliced

1 medium onion, cut into large squares

1 14-ounce can crushed tomatoes

1 cup dark beer

1 10-ounce package frozen peas, thawed under running water

Place the lamb and flour in a bag and shake to coat. Place the meat in a 3-quart microwave dish or ring pan with the garlic, *fines herbes,* and Worcestershire sauce, cover with plastic wrap, or use a plastic cooking bag, and microwave on high for 10 minutes. Add the remaining ingredients, re-cover, and microwave on high for 20 to 25 minutes, or until the meat is very tender and the vegetables soft.

Lamb Stew with Parmesan Cheese

MICROWAVE ONLY

ENERGY LEVEL:
high, 100%

SERVINGS:
4

COMPLETE RECIPE TIME:
about 35 minutes

COOKING TIME:
about 28 minutes

MICROWAVE COOKWARE:
deep 2-quart glass or plastic
casserole or ring pan

COVERING:
plastic wrap or the dish cover

1 medium onion, chopped

2 cloves garlic, minced

1 pound lean lamb stew meat

1 large potato, cubed (peel if
  desired)

2 medium carrots, cut into
  1-inch pieces

½ cup dry white wine

½ cup beef broth

½ cup grated Parmesan
  cheese

Fresh ground pepper to taste

Place the onion and garlic in a deep 2-quart glass or plastic casserole and microwave on high for 3 minutes. Add the lamb, cover with plastic wrap or the dish cover, and microwave for 5 minutes. Add the remaining ingredients, except the cheese and pepper, re-cover, and microwave on high for about 20 minutes, or until the lamb is tender. Stir in the cheese and pepper and serve.

Lamb with Rice, Peppers, Olives, and Tomatoes

MICROWAVE ONLY

ENERGY LEVEL:
high, 100%
medium, 50%

SERVINGS:
4

COMPLETE RECIPE TIME:
25 minutes

COOKING TIME:
20 minutes

MICROWAVE COOKWARE:
deep 2-quart glass or plastic
casserole or ring pan

COVERING:
plastic wrap or the dish cover

Another tasty dish that uses very little meat and is easy to prepare, especially when you don't want to spend much time in the kitchen.

½ to ¾ pound lean lamb, cut
  into 1-inch cubes

½ cup long-grain rice

½ cup water

¼ pound mushrooms, sliced

½ medium bell pepper, cored
  and chopped

½ medium onion, chopped

8 canned pitted green olives

1 4-ounce jar or can or
  pimientos, diced

1 tablespoon dried Italian
  herbs

½ can (7 ounces) stewed
  tomatoes

3 tablespoons A-1 brand or
  other steak sauce

Mix all ingredients in a 2-quart microwave casserole dish or ring pan. Cover with plastic wrap or the dish cover and microwave on high for 5 minutes and medium, 50%, power for about 15 minutes, or until the rice is tender.

Lamb with Navy Beans

This recipe can also be made without meat and you will still have a hearty, satisfying dish.

½ to ¾ pound ground lamb

½ medium onion, chopped

1 stalk celery, chopped

½ cup dried tomatoes, chopped (optional)

1 tablespoon dried Italian herbs

½ can (7¼ ounces) Italian-style stewed tomatoes, drained

1 can navy beans with liquid

½ cup grated Parmesan cheese

½ cup chopped parsley

MICROWAVE ONLY

ENERGY LEVEL:
high, 100%

SERVINGS:
4

COMPLETE RECIPE TIME:
15 minutes

COOKING TIME:
10 minutes

MICROWAVE COOKWARE:
deep 2-quart glass or plastic casserole

COVERING:
plastic wrap or the dish cover

Place the lamb, onion, celery, dried tomatoes, and herbs in a 2-quart microwave casserole, cover with plastic wrap or the dish cover, and microwave on high for 5 minutes. Drain off fat and crumble the meat. Add the stewed tomatoes and beans, recover, and microwave on high for 5 minutes. Stir in the cheese and parsley before serving.

Simple Curried Lamb

MICROWAVE ONLY

ENERGY LEVEL:
high, 100%
medium, 50%

SERVINGS:
4

COMPLETE RECIPE TIME:
40 to 50 minutes

COOKING TIME:
30 to 40 minutes

MICROWAVE COOKWARE:
deep 2-quart glass or plastic casserole or ring pan or plastic cooking bag

COVERING:
plastic wrap or the dish cover

By using some of the excellent prepared pastes and sauces available and your microwave, you can make recipes in just minutes that would otherwise take hours of preparation and cooking. This combination is a prime example.

2 pounds lean lamb from the leg, cut into cubes

2 tablespoons curry paste, available at Asian food stores

1 medium onion, chopped

2 cloves garlic, minced

2 tablespoons raw ginger, shredded

1 cup plain yogurt

1 14½-ounce can stewed tomatoes, drained

Mix all the ingredients, except the yogurt and tomatoes, in a 2-quart microwave dish or plastic cooking bag, cover, and microwave on high for 10 minutes. Add the yogurt and tomatoes, re-cover, and microwave on medium, 50%, power for 20 to 30 minutes, or until the lamb is very tender. If you like hot curry add ¼ teaspoon dried red chili flakes to the recipe. Another interesting addition is 2 tablespoons chutney added with the yogurt.

Lamb Curry with Nut Sauce

This is a really elegant recipe that takes a little work but is worth it. Great to serve when you're entertaining friends who like slightly exotic food.

1½ pounds lean leg of lamb, cut into 1-inch cubes

1 medium onion, chopped

4 cloves garlic, minced

2 tablespoons curry powder

½ teaspoon ground cinnamon

½ teaspoon dried red chili flakes

4 tablespoons chopped fresh gingerroot

½ cup raw cashews

½ cup plain yogurt

3 sprigs, stem and leaves, raw coriander, chopped

2 tablespoons lemon juice

Place the lamb, onion, and garlic in a deep 2-quart microwave dish or ring pan. Cover with plastic wrap or the dish cover and microwave on high for 12 to 15 minutes, stirring once during cooking.

Meanwhile place the remaining ingredients, except the coriander and lemon juice, in your processor and blend until smooth. Add the sauce to the lamb, re-cover, and microwave on high for 10 minutes. Stir in the chopped coriander and lemon juice and serve.

MICROWAVE ONLY

ENERGY LEVEL:
high, 100%

SERVINGS:
4

COMPLETE RECIPE TIME:
about 35 minutes

COOKING TIME:
about 25 minutes

MICROWAVE COOKWARE:
deep 2-quart glass or plastic casserole or ring pan

COVERING:
plastic wrap or the dish cover

Turban of Ground Lamb

MICROWAVE ONLY

ENERGY LEVEL:
high, 100%

SERVINGS:
6 to 8

COMPLETE RECIPE TIME:
50 minutes

COOKING TIME:
35–40 minutes

MICROWAVE COOKWARE:
2-quart glass or plastic batter bowl
or charlotte mold

ACCESSORY EQUIPMENT:
large mixing bowl and a serving
platter

COVERING:
plastic wrap or a plate or platter
large enough to cover the top of
the mold

When you want to make something special and are willing to exert a little effort in preparation, make this recipe.

2 pounds ground lamb	½ cup grated Parmesan cheese
4 tablespoons minced garlic	
1 medium onion, chopped	½ cup bread crumbs
3 medium eggplants	½ teaspoon ground allspice
3 tablespoons olive oil	1 cup pitted Greek olives (optional)
2 eggs, beaten	
1 14½-ounce can stewed tomatoes, drained	

Place the lamb, garlic, and onion in a 3-quart microwave dish, cover with plastic wrap or the dish cover, and microwave on high for 10 minutes, stirring once. Drain off fat and set aside. Microwave the eggplants for about 15 minutes, or until soft. In the meanwhile mix all the remaining ingredients with the lamb.

When the eggplants are cool enough to handle without pain, cut them in half and scoop out the pulp all the way to the skin. Be careful not to tear the skin. Chop the pulp and add half of it to the lamb mixture. Line a 2-quart glass batter bowl or charlotte mold with the eggplant skins, overlapping them so there are no gaps between them. Fill the mold with the lamb mixture and fold any exposed eggplant skins over it. Cover with plastic wrap or a plate or platter and microwave on high for 10 to 15 minutes or to an internal temperature of 150 degrees. Remove the cover and place a platter over the mold. Place your hand, protected with a towel or hot pad, under the mold and quickly invert the mold onto the platter. Remove the cooking dish and gaze upon a culinary delight. Serve with a spicy tomato sauce.

Lamb Shanks Italiano

In one of my earlier cookbooks this recipe had eleven ingredients. I've brought it down to three and, believe me, it tastes as good—but it's so much easier.

4 lamb shanks, about 4 pounds   2 tablespoons minced garlic

2 cups prepared Italian
   spaghetti sauce

Place all the ingredients in a plastic cooking bag and close with a rubberband or the tie provided. Or place everything in a 9- x 13-inch glass or plastic baking pan with the thick ends of the shanks toward the edge of the dish. Cover with plastic wrap and microwave on medium, 50%, power for about 40 minutes, or until the shanks are very tender. Serve with the sauce.

Lamb Shanks Mexicano: Substitute picante sauce, as hot as you like, for the spaghetti sauce in the above recipe.

Lamb Shanks in Cranberry Sauce: Use 1 16-ounce can whole berry cranberry sauce to the shanks recipe instead of the tomato-based sauce. This is a little different but oh-so-good.

MICROWAVE ONLY

ENERGY LEVEL:
medium, 50%

SERVINGS:
4

COMPLETE RECIPE TIME:
about 45 minutes

COOKING TIME:
about 40 minutes

MICROWAVE COOKWARE:
plastic cooking bag or 9- x 13-inch glass or plastic baking pan

COVERING:
plastic wrap

Lamb Riblets

MICROWAVE AND BROIL OR CHARCOAL
GRILL COMBINATION

ENERGY LEVEL:
high, 100%

SERVINGS:
4

COMPLETE RECIPE TIME:
about 30 minutes

COOKING TIME:
about 18 minutes

MICROWAVE COOKWARE:
roasting rack or large glass or
plastic bowl or casserole

ACCESSORY EQUIPMENT:
broiling pan or charcoal grill

When I was first married back in 1961 BM (Before Microwave), my wife and I loved to barbecue lamb riblets. I would tend the cooking and she would stand by with a squirt gun extinguishing the flare-ups from the fat dripping into the fire. Well, today when we barbecue riblets, we microwave them first and eliminate most of the fat and the problem of flare-ups. These little bones from the lamb breast have lots of taste and can be eaten when cooked purely by microwave. I like them better, though, when barbecued or broiled after microwaving. They make wonderful finger food when you're having a casual party.

2 pounds lamb riblets

Prepared barbecue sauce

Cut the ribs into individual pieces and place on a microwave roasting rack or in a large microwavable bowl. Microwave on high power for about 7 to 8 minutes, or until cooked and rendered of most of the fat. Baste with sauce and broil or grill them until they develop a crust.

Note: You can also serve these riblets like Buffalo chicken wings—coated with sauce and served with celery sticks and blue cheese dressing.

Stuffed Lamb Breast

There's not much meat on the breast, but with a stuffing you have enough food for a main course.

1 medium onion, chopped

1 stalk celery, chopped

1 medium carrot, chopped

1 6-ounce package prepared stuffing mix

1 3-pound breast of lamb

Kitchen Bouquet or soy sauce or MicroShake browning powder

2 tablespoons dried Italian herbs

Place the onion, celery, and carrot in a mixing bowl, cover with plastic wrap, and microwave on high for 3 to 4 minutes, or until soft. Add stuffing mix and prepare as directed on the package. Make a pocket in the breast by running a boning knife between the bones and the meat. Be careful not to cut all the way through the breast. Or ask your butcher to do it for you. Put stuffing into the pocket just so it's full and not stretching the pocket. (It will expand during cooking.) Place the remaining stuffing in a 9- x 13-inch glass baking pan and top with the breast. Paint the top of the breast with diluted Kitchen Bouquet or soy sauce or microwave browning powder and sprinkle on the herbs. Cover with plastic wrap and microwave on medium-high, 80%, power for about 20 to 25 minutes or to an internal temperature of 160 degrees. If you want a dry, crisp surface on the meat, after microwaving place the breast under the broiler for a few minutes.

MICROWAVE AND BROILER (OPTIONAL)

ENERGY LEVEL:
medium-high, 80%

SERVINGS:
4 to 6

COMPLETE RECIPE TIME:
50 to 60 minutes

COOKING TIME:
about 30 minutes

MICROWAVE COOKWARE:
9- x 13-inch glass or plastic baking pan

ACCESSORY EQUIPMENT:
large glass mixing bowl

COVERING:
plastic wrap

Poultry

There are probably no other entities that cook by microwave as well and as easily as chicken and other poultry. Every conventional recipe except those that call for deep frying can be easily converted to microwave. Most of my recipes use poultry with the skin removed. Skinless poultry does not dry out when cooked by microwave because there's no hot air in the oven. When I microwave a bird with the skin on, I always transfer it to a preheated conventional oven to brown and crisp the skin just for the aesthetic value.

One day when I was a little boy growing up on a farm in northern Wisconsin, I noticed my grandmother chasing all of the chickens out of the barnyard. When I asked her why, she replied, "They were using fowl language!"

I hope you don't foul up any of these recipes.

General rules for microwaving poultry:

1. Estimate 7 to 10 minutes per pound on high power and cook to an internal temperature of 170 degrees.

2. Always cover securely with the dish cover or plastic wrap, except when dry roasting in a combination microwave-convection oven.

3. When microwaving whole birds, turn over half way through the cooking or use a vertical roasting device.

4. Remove the skin to reduce fat and cholesterol.

5. When microwaving chicken breasts, do it in a liquid so the cooking is slowed and the breasts have time to tenderize. Use stock, wine, milk, juice, or whatever you like.

Whole Naked Chicken

MICROWAVE AND CONVENTIONAL OVEN COMBINATION

ENERGY LEVEL:
high, 100%

SERVINGS:
4

COMPLETE RECIPE TIME:
40 to 50 minutes

COOKING TIME:
25 to 40 minutes

MICROWAVE COOKWARE:
deep 3-quart glass or ceramic casserole

ACCESSORY EQUIPMENT:
vertical roasting stand (optional)

COVERING:
plastic wrap or the dish cover

1 3 to 4-pound whole chicken

2 tablespoons salad supreme or salad delight seasoning

These seasonings are made for salads, but the combinations of herbs, salts, and seeds lend them to seasoning chicken superbly. They also usually contain paprika, which gives the chicken a nice color. Remove the skin from the chicken and coat the surface with the seasoning mix. Place in a deep 3-quart casserole, cover with plastic wrap or the dish cover, and microwave on high for 7 to 10 minutes per pound or to an internal temperature of 170 degrees. Turn oven once during the cooking. If you use a vertical roasting stand, place a plastic cooking bag over the bird and you don't have to turn the chicken over. If you don't have an instant-read thermometer to check to see if the chicken is thoroughly cooked, use the techniques used when you cooked conventionally. Wiggle the leg, it should feel loose; or poke the chicken with a knife or skewer—the juices that run out should be clear and not bloody. Incidentally, sometimes you will cook a chicken to perfection and you'll find that the flesh around the bones is reddish in color. Don't worry about it being undercooked because that redness around the bone indicates that the chicken was frozen at one time.

ZAP TIP: To make chicken skin cracklings, remove the skin from a cooked chicken and place it between paper towels. Microwave on high for 3 to 4 minutes. You cook out lots of the fat and the result is simply delicious—a low-fat version of the Jewish snack called griebenes.

Ginger Chicken

This recipe turned out to be one of the favorites in both of my first two cookbooks *More Time for Lovin', Since I Got My Microwave Oven* and *Microwaves Are for Cooking*. I'm going to include it here because it's so good and easy and you may not have purchased those other books. It's even better with a finishing touch in the conventional oven.

1 3- 4-pound whole chicken	2 tablespoons minced garlic
4 tablespoons grated raw ginger	1 teaspoon garlic powder
	½ cup soy sauce
1 teaspoon powdered ginger	1 ounce sweet sherry

Insert the handle of a plastic spatula or a chopstick under the skin of the bird and run it around between the skin and the flesh, making sure you loosen the skin around the legs. Mix the remaining ingredients and pour the mixture under the skin of the bird. Massage it in all over the bird. Place the chicken, breast side down, in a deep 3-quart glass or ceramic container and cover with plastic wrap. Microwave on high for 15 minutes. Turn the bird over, re-cover and microwave on high for 10 to 15 minutes or to an internal temperature of 170 degrees. Remove the plastic wrap, pour off the juices, and place the chicken in a preheated 500 degree oven for about 5 to 10 minutes until the skin becomes crispy and brown. If you use a vertical roasting stand, place a plastic cooking bag over the bird and you don't have to turn the chicken.

ZAP TIP: To make chicken skin cracklings, see above.

MICROWAVE AND CONVENTIONAL OVEN COMBINATION

ENERGY LEVEL:
high, 100%

SERVINGS:
4

COMPLETE RECIPE TIME:
40 to 50 minutes

COOKING TIME:
25 to 40 minutes

MICROWAVE COOKWARE:
deep 3-quart glass or ceramic casserole

ACCESSORY EQUIPMENT:
vertical roasting rack (optional)

COVERING:
plastic wrap or the dish cover or plastic cooking bag

Red Hot Chicken on a Bed of Tomatoes

MICROWAVE ONLY

ENERGY LEVEL:
high, 100%

SERVINGS:
4

COMPLETE RECIPE TIME:
30 to 35 minutes

COOKING TIME:
20 to 25 minutes

MICROWAVE COOKWARE:
large glass or ceramic serving
platter or 9- x 13-inch glass or
plastic baking pan

COVERING:
plastic wrap

This recipe makes a beautiful presentation, but be sure you serve it only to folks who love hot foods. It's so efficient when you cook microwave; you can cook right on the serving platter. No cooking pots to wash!

1 3–4-pound whole chicken

½ cup garlic-chili sauce or paste, available at Asian markets or in the gourmet section of your supermarket, or combine 2 tablespoons pressed garlic, ½ cup tomato paste, and 1 tablespoon dried chili pepper flakes

3 large ripe tomatoes, sliced; or 1 14 ½-ounce can tomato chunks or stewed tomatoes

½ cup chopped coriander (cilantro)

Cut the backbone out of the chicken and press the chicken flat, breaking the breastbone. Remove the skin and tuck the wing tips behind the wings. Make slits in the skin between the lower breast and leg and tuck the ends of the legs into the slits. Paint the garlic-chili sauce over the surface of the chicken. Lay the tomato slices on a large serving platter and place the chicken over the tomatoes. Cover with plastic wrap and microwave on high for 20 to 25 minutes or to an internal temperature of 170 degrees. Remove plastic wrap and sprinkle coriander over the chicken.

Chicken Picante

This combination is a little unusual, but I love it and hope you'll give it a try. If you don't like it, your cats will—and it's probably cheaper than cat food.

1 3–4-pound frying chicken, cut up and skin removed

3 tablespoons anchovy paste

1 3-ounce jar capers, drained

6 gherkins, chopped

½ cup chopped parsley

Place the chicken in a 2-quart casserole or ring pan, cover with plastic wrap or the dish cover, and microwave on high for 20 to 25 minutes or to an internal temperature of 170 degrees. If using a casserole dish, rearrange the pieces halfway through the cooking. This is not necessary if you cook it in a ring pan. Mix the remaining ingredients, except the parsley, and spread over the chicken. Microwave on high for 5 minutes. Sprinkle parsley over top when serving.

MICROWAVE ONLY

ENERGY LEVEL:
high, 100%

SERVINGS:
4

COMPLETE RECIPE TIME:
about 30 minutes

COOKING TIME:
25 to 30 minutes

MICROWAVE COOKWARE:
2-quart glass or plastic casserole or ring pan

COVERING:
plastic wrap or the dish cover

Chicken Parmesan

ENERGY LEVEL:
high, 100%

SERVINGS:
4

COMPLETE RECIPE TIME:
about 40 minutes

COOKING TIME:
20 to 30 minutes

MICROWAVE COOKWARE:
8-inch-square glass baking pan

COVERING:
plastic wrap

1 3–4-pound chicken, cut up and skin removed

2 14½-ounce cans stewed tomatos, drained

1 tablespoon dried Italian herb blend

¼ teaspoon dried crushed red pepper

2 tablespoons cornstarch

¾ cup grated Parmesan cheese

Place chicken in an 8-inch-square glass baking pan. Mix the remaining ingredients, except the cheese, and pour over the chicken. Cover with plastic wrap and microwave on high for 20 to 25 minutes or to an internal temperature of 170 degrees. Sprinkle cheese over the chicken and allow it to melt from the temperature of the chicken. If you like, run the dish under a preheated broiler for a browned appearance.

Chicken Paprika

MICROWAVE ONLY

ENERGY LEVEL:
high, 100%

SERVINGS:
4

COMPLETE RECIPE TIME:
about 30 minutes

COOKING TIME:
about 25 minutes

MICROWAVE COOKWARE:
3-quart glass or plastic casserole

COVERING:
plastic wrap or the dish cover

This recipe is so good and yet so simple that it's almost embarrassing to accept the accolades you will receive when you serve it.

1 3-pound frying chicken, cut up and skin removed

1 medium onion, chopped

2 cloves garlic, chopped

1 to 2 tablespoons sweet or hot Hungarian paprika

2 tablespoons flour

1 cup sour cream or plain yogurt

Place chicken, onion, garlic, and paprika in a 3-quart glass or plastic casserole and stir to coat the chicken with the paprika. Cover with plastic wrap or the dish cover and microwave on high for about 20 minutes or to an internal temperature of 170 degrees. While the chicken is cooking, whisk the flour into the sour cream or yogurt. Add the mixture to the chicken and stir to blend. Re-cover and microwave 5 minutes on high. Transfer the chicken to a platter and serve with the sauce. Best served with rice, fettuccine, or egg noodles.

Variation: To make a really pretty chicken paprika, add ½ each of red and green bell pepper, diced.

Chicken in Salsa

MICROWAVE ONLY

ENERGY LEVEL:
high, 100%

SERVINGS:
4

COMPLETE RECIPE TIME:
30 to 35 minutes

COOKING TIME:
20 to 25 minutes

MICROWAVE COOKWARE:
3-quart glass or plastic casserole or ring pan

COVERING:
plastic wrap or the dish cover

These days some commercially prepared sauces are just wonderful. Find one that you particularly like and use it in this recipe. I'm not going to mention my favorite because there are some available locally in your area that are really superb and not available in other areas.

1 medium yellow onion, chopped

1 green bell pepper, cored and diced

2 cloves garlic, minced

1 3–4-pound frying chicken, cut up and skin removed

1½ cups medium hot picante, salsa, or taco sauce

Place the onion, pepper, and garlic in a 3-quart glass or plastic casserole dish or ring pan, cover with plastic wrap or the dish cover, and microwave on high for 4 minutes, or until the vegetables are soft. Add the chicken and sauce, re-cover, and microwave on high for about 20 to 25 minutes, or until the chicken is cooked, or to an internal temperature of about 170 degrees.

An interesting variation to this recipe is to add 1 4-ounce package dried fruit with the chicken and sauce.

Buttermilk Chicken

MICROWAVE ONLY

ENERGY LEVEL:
high, 100%

SERVINGS:
4

COMPLETE RECIPE TIME:
30 to 35 minutes

COOKING TIME:
20 to 25 minutes

MICROWAVE COOKWARE:
deep 3-quart glass or plastic
casserole or ring pan

COVERING:
plastic wrap or the dish cover

I like to use buttermilk in recipes because it is low in fat and calories and gives recipes an interesting flavor.

1 3–4-pound frying chicken, cut up and skin removed

½ cup flour

1 cup buttermilk

1 tablespoon crushed garlic or 4 cloves, pressed

2 tablespoons horseradish mustard or 1 tablespoon mustard with seeds mixed with 1 tablespoon prepared horseradish

Chopped parsley

Place chicken and flour in a bag and shake to coat. Then place into a 3-quart glass or plastic casserole or ring pan and add the remaining ingredients, except the parsley. Cover with plastic wrap or the dish cover and microwave on high for 20 to 25 minutes or to an internal temperature of 170 degrees. Sprinkle with the parsley when serving.

Chicken in Spaghetti Sauce

MICROWAVE AND BROILER
COMBINATION

ENERGY LEVEL:
high, 100%

SERVINGS:
4

COMPLETE RECIPE TIME:
about 45 minutes

COOKING TIME:
about 35 minutes

COVERING:
plastic wrap

A simple, impressive dinner for four that can be prepared with a minimum of effort.

2 small fryers, 2 ½ pounds each

1 28-ounce jar prepared spaghetti sauce or 1 28-ounce can crushed tomatoes plus 2 tablespoons spaghetti sauce seasoning and 4 tablespoons minced garlic

Salt and fresh ground pepper

Cut the backs from the chickens and cut the chickens in half. Pour the sauce into a 9- x 13-inch glass baking pan or oval roaster and place the chicken halves over it. Do not cover the top surface with sauce. Salt and pepper the poultry and cover with plastic wrap. Microwave on high for about 30 minutes or to an internal temperature of 170 degrees.

In the meantime make a pot of spaghetti and a nice salad. When the chicken is done, remove the plastic wrap and place the dish under your broiler for about 5 minutes, or until the chicken browns and crisps. Serve the chicken on a bed of the pasta and top with the sauce.

Microwave Chicken for Grilling

Before grilling on charcoal or under the broiler, I like to microwave my chickens in a marinade. This serves two purposes: The flavors of the marinade permeate the chicken meat and, secondly, you cook off much of the fat, especially when the skin is removed, so you virtually eliminate any flare-ups when grilling.

1 4-pound fryer, skin removed and cut into 8 pieces (cut the breasts in half)

MARINADE

¼ cup triple sec or other similar liqueur of choice

¼ cup soy sauce

¼ cup fresh lime juice

1 tablespoon bitters (optional)

MICROWAVE AND CHARCOAL GRILL COMBINATION

ENERGY LEVEL:
high, 100%

SERVINGS:
4

COMPLETE RECIPE TIME:
about 1½ hours, including marinating

COOKING TIME:
about 30 minutes

MICROWAVE COOKWARE:
plastic cooking bag

ACCESSORY EQUIPMENT:
charcoal grill

Mix the ingredients for the marinade.

Place the chicken and ¾ of the marinade in a roasting bag. Allow to marinate for at least 1 hour or overnight.

Close the bag with the ties provided or a rubberband and make sure the opening is about the size of your thumb. Place the bag of chicken and marinade in a microwavable dish and microwave on high for about 20 minutes or to an internal temperature of 160 degrees. Charcoal grill when ready and baste with the remaining marinade. You can use the juices from the cooking bag as a sauce.

ZAP TIP: Precooking chicken is an especially good idea if you are going to grill it for a picnic. The chances of it spoiling are greatly reduced when it is precooked.

Flattened Cornish Hens

MICROWAVE AND SKILLET COMBINATION

ENERGY LEVEL:
high, 100%

SERVINGS:
4

COMPLETE RECIPE TIME:
about 1 hour

COOKING TIME:
about 40 to 45 minutes

MICROWAVE COOKWARE:
9- x 13-inch glass or plastic baking pan

ACCESSORY EQUIPMENT:
large skillet and large cooking pot, like a pasta pot

COVERING:
plastic wrap

This is a recipe that I've adapted from one of my many Russian cookbooks. By microwaving the hens before you cook them in a hot pan, you preserve the juices and still get a wonderful crispy exterior. Serve it right after cooking or cold, for a picnic.

4 Cornish hens, about 1 to
   1 ¼ pounds each

Salt and fresh ground pepper
   to taste

4 tablespoons margarine

4 tablespoons sour cream

Cut the backbones out of the hens and lay the hens, cut side down, on a cutting board. Press firmly on the breastbones to flatten. Tuck the wing tips behind the wings. Make a small incision in the skin between the lower breast and thigh on both sides and tuck the ends of the legs through it. Season with salt and pepper. Place in a 9- x 13-inch glass or plastic baking pan, cover with plastic wrap, and microwave on high for about 5 minutes per pound or to an internal temperature of 160 degrees.

In a large skillet or frying pan melt 2 tablespoons each of the margarine and sour cream and place 2 hens in the pan. Fill a large cooking pot, the same diameter as the skillet, halfway with water and place on top of the hens. Fry until very crisp on both sides, about 5 minutes per side. Place the cooked hens in a 200 degree oven while you fry the remaining hens.

Venice-Style Chicken

This dish has more ingredients than I like to include in my recipes, but it's a good one. Give it a try.

2 tablespoons olive oil

1 medium onion, chopped

1 large carrot, chopped

1 stalk celery, chopped

1 pound mushrooms, sliced

2 whole cloves

¼ teaspoon ground cinnamon

1 3-4-pound fryer, skin removed and cut up

½ cup dry white wine

1 14½-ounce can tomato wedges or whole tomatoes, drained, quartered

Place oil, vegetables, and spices in a 3-quart glass or plastic casserole or ring pan. Cover with plastic wrap or the dish cover and microwave on high for 10 minutes. Add the chicken, wine, and tomatoes and microwave on high, covered with wax paper or other nonstick paper, for 20 to 25 minutes, or until the chicken reaches an internal temperature of 170 degrees. Microwaving covered with wax paper allows the moisture to escape and the sauce to thicken.

MICROWAVE ONLY

ENERGY LEVEL:
high, 100%

SERVINGS:
4

COMPLETE RECIPE TIME:
about 50 minutes

COOKING TIME:
30 to 35 minutes

MICROWAVE COOKWARE:
deep 3-quart glass or plastic casserole or ring pan

COVERING:
plastic wrap or the dish cover and wax or nonstick cooking paper

Chicken on Stuffing

MICROWAVE AND BROILER COMBINATION (OPTIONAL)

ENERGY LEVEL:
high, 100%

SERVINGS:
4

COMPLETE RECIPE TIME:
about 50 minutes

COOKING TIME:
20 to 25 minutes

MICROWAVE COOKWARE:
9- x 13-inch glass or plastic baking pan

COVERING:
plastic wrap

I make a lot of presentations on the Nashville Network and one of the sponsors is a prepared stuffing mix. For a busy person these stuffings are very convenient to use and very tasty. Instead of going through the bother of putting the stuffing inside the chicken, just make a bed of stuffing and place the bird on top.

1 package 6-ounce stuffing mix prepared as directed on the package, but without any oil, butter, or margarine

2 2½-pound fryers, skin removed and cut in half

Salt and fresh ground pepper

In a 9- x 13-inch glass or plastic baking pan make 4 equal mounds of stuffing and place the chicken halves on top of each mound. Salt and pepper the chicken and cover with plastic wrap. Microwave on high for 20 to 25 minutes, or until the chicken reaches an internal temperature of 170 degrees. You may prefer to leave the skin on and after microwaving run the dish under your broiler to crisp the outside.

Chicken and Rice

A simple, no-fail, one-dish meal.

1 cup long-grain rice

1 3-pound frying chicken, cut up and skin removed

½ pound mushrooms, sliced

1 green bell pepper, cored and diced

2 tablespoons dried Italian herbs

1 cup water

Salt and fresh ground pepper to taste

Place rice on the bottom of a 3-quart microwave dish or ring pan and add the remaining ingredients. Cover securely with plastic wrap or the dish cover and microwave on high for 25 to 30 minutes, or until the chicken reaches an internal temperature of 170 degrees and the rice is tender.

Variation: Use 1 14-ounce can stewed tomatoes in place of the water.

MICROWAVE ONLY

ENERGY LEVEL:
high, 100%

SERVINGS:
4

COMPLETE RECIPE TIME:
about 35 minutes

COOKING TIME:
about 30 minutes

MICROWAVE COOKWARE:
3-quart glass or plastic casserole dish or ring pan

COVERING:
plastic wrap or the dish cover

Chicken and Pork Stew

MICROWAVE ONLY

ENERGY LEVEL:
high, 100%, and medium, 50%

SERVINGS:
4

COMPLETE RECIPE TIME:
50 to 60 minutes

COOKING TIME:
40 minutes

MICROWAVE COOKWARE:
deep 3-quart glass or plastic
casserole or ring pan

COVERING:
plastic wrap or the dish cover

Most recipes for stew advise that you sear the meat before completing the recipe. There is a flavor enhancement from browning meat, but many times it is lost in the complexity of this stew. So you don't have to do it; and the stew tastes great; and you've saved the time and bother of frying and the cleaning of the pan.

¾ pound boned chicken thighs	1 teaspoon dried red chili flakes
¾ pound pork shoulder, trimmed of fat and cut into cubes	1 stick cinnamon
	2 whole cloves
1 8-ounce smoked ham hock	¼ teaspoon ground thyme
¾ cup dry white wine	1 tablespoon malt vinegar
2 tablespoons brown sugar	1 tablespoon paprika

Mix all ingredients in a deep 3-quart casserole or ring pan. Cover with plastic wrap or the dish cover and microwave on high for 10 minutes. Stir, re-cover, and microwave on medium, 50%, power for 30 minutes, or until the pork is very tender.

Chicken Vindaloo

MICROWAVE AND CHARCOAL GRILL OR
BROILER COMBINATION

ENERGY LEVEL:
high, 100%

SERVINGS:
4

COMPLETE RECIPE TIME:
about 50 minutes

COOKING TIME:
about 40 minutes

MICROWAVE COOKWARE:
plastic cooking bag or deep
3-quart glass or plastic casserole
or ring pan

ACCESSORY EQUIPMENT:
charcoal grill, small mixing bowl,
and basting brush

COVERING:
plastic wrap or the dish cover

You can find vindaloo paste at Asian markets. It keeps forever and can also be used in vegetarian dishes to make them more interesting. If you can't find vindaloo paste, make another recipe; it has too many ingredients to make from scratch.

2 2½-pound fryers, skin
    removed and cut in half

MARINADE

2 tablespoons vindaloo paste   2 tablespoons vegetable oil

¼ cup lemon juice   ¼ cup water

2 tablespoons minced garlic

Mix the marinade and spread three-quarters of it over the chicken pieces. Place in a plastic cooking bag or large glass or plastic casserole and microwave on high for about 20 to 25 minutes, or until the chicken reaches an internal temperature of 160 degrees. Grill the chicken over charcoal coals or under a preheated broiler, basting with the remaining marinade.

Chorizo and Chicken Casserole

MICROWAVE ONLY

ENERGY LEVEL:
high, 100%

SERVINGS:
4

COMPLETE RECIPE TIME:
about 25 minutes

COOKING TIME:
12 to 15 minutes

MICROWAVE COOKWARE:
deep 2-quart glass or plastic
casserole

COVERING:
plastic wrap or the dish cover

This recipe is similar to the potato chip chicken recipe that follows but has a Mexican flair.

2 beef chorizo sausages, skin removed and chopped

2 chicken breasts, skin removed and diced or 2 cups chopped cooked chicken or turkey

1 4-ounce can diced green chili peppers

1 10-ounce can tomatoes or Mexican-style stewed tomatoes

½ pint cottage cheese

4 ounces shredded Cheddar cheese

3 corn tortillas

Mix all the ingredients, except the Cheddar and tortillas. In a glass or ceramic container about the diameter of the tortillas make a layer of the mixture and top with a tortilla. Continue to make layers and finish with the Cheddar cheese. Cover with plastic wrap and microwave on high for 12 to 15 minutes, or until the temperature in the center of the casserole is 170 degrees. Cut into quarters and serve.

Potato Chip Chicken Casserole

A recipe similar to this one won a major recipe contest sponsored by a soup company. I've changed it a bit and converted it to microwave so it's easier to make. This is also a great recipe for leftover meat, especially ham.

2 cups chopped cooked chicken or turkey

1 14½-ounce can stewed tomatos, drained and chopped

1 10-ounce can cream of chicken or mushroom soup

1 4-ounce can diced chiles

5 to 6 ounces low-salt potato chips

4 ounces shredded Cheddar cheese

In a deep 2-quart glass or plastic casserole mix all of the ingredients. Cover with the dish cover or plastic wrap and microwave on high, 100%, power for 10 to 12 minutes or to an internal temperature of 140 degrees in the center of the casserole.

MICROWAVE AND BROILER (OPTIONAL)

ENERGY LEVEL:
high, 100%

SERVINGS:
4

COMPLETE RECIPE TIME:
about 20 minutes

COOKING TIME:
10 to 12 minutes

MICROWAVE COOKWARE:
deep 2-quart glass or plastic casserole

COVERING:
plastic wrap or the dish cover

Chili Chicken

MICROWAVE ONLY

ENERGY LEVEL:
high, 100%

SERVINGS:
4

COMPLETE RECIPE TIME:
about 30 minutes

COOKING TIME:
25 minutes

MICROWAVE COOKWARE:
deep 2-quart glass or plastic casserole

COVERING:
plastic wrap or the dish cover

I was never very fond of canned chili, but when used in this recipe it lends a wonderful flavor and texture to a simple chicken dish.

2½ pounds chicken legs and thighs, skin removed

1 15-ounce can vegetarian chili

Place the chicken and chili in a deep 3-quart plastic casserole, cover with plastic wrap or the dish cover, and microwave on high for about 25 minutes, or until the chicken reaches an internal temperature of 170 degrees. Stir once during cooking.

Chili Chicken with Cornbread Topping

MICROWAVE ONLY

ENERGY LEVEL:
high, 100%

SERVINGS:
4

COMPLETE RECIPE TIME:
about 35 minutes

COOKING TIME:
20 to 25 minutes

MICROWAVE COOKWARE:
deep 2-quart glass or plastic casserole

ACCESSORY EQUIPMENT:
medium mixing bowl

This recipe makes an impressive and unique presentation.

2½ pounds chicken legs and thighs, or whole chicken, cut up and skin removed

1 15-ounce can vegetarian chili

1 8½-ounce package corn muffin mix mixed as directed on package

Place the chicken and chili in a deep 2-quart glass or plastic casserole and top with the muffin mix. Microwave on high for 20 to 25 minutes or to an internal temperature of 170 degrees.

Tarragon Chicken

Here are two versions of a simple but uniquely different tasting recipe.

1 3–4-pound fryer, skin removed and cut up

4 tablespoons margarine or butter

2 tablespoons dried tarragon

Salt and fresh ground pepper to taste

2 tablespoons flour

1 cup evaporated milk or light cream

Place chicken in a shallow glass or ceramic casserole. Melt the margarine and pour over the chicken. Sprinkle with the tarragon and salt and pepper. Cover with the dish cover or plastic wrap and microwave on high for 25 to 30 minutes, or until the chicken reaches an internal temperature of 170 degrees.

In a 1-quart measuring bowl or mixing bowl make a paste of the flour and 4 tablespoons of the milk. Pour the juices from the chicken and the remaining milk into the flour paste. Stir and microwave the sauce for about 3 or 4 minutes, or until thickened. Serve with the chicken.

Tarragon Chicken #2: Soak the tarragon in ½ cup dry white wine and pour over the chicken. Cook as directed above and thicken the juices using 1 tablespoon cornstarch dissolved in 2 tablespoons water.

MICROWAVE ONLY

ENERGY LEVEL:
high, 100%

SERVINGS:
4

COMPLETE RECIPE TIME:
about 45 minutes

COOKING TIME:
30 to 35 minutes

MICROWAVE COOKWARE:
shallow glass or ceramic casserole

ACCESSORY EQUIPMENT:
medium mixing bowl

Tandoori Chicken

MICROWAVE AND BROIL OR CHARCOAL
GRILL COMBINATION

ENERGY LEVEL:
high, 100%

SERVINGS:
4

COMPLETE RECIPE TIME:
about 5 hours, including the
marinating

COOKING TIME:
about 40 minutes

MICROWAVE COOKWARE:
plastic cooking bag

ACCESSORY EQUIPMENT:
shallow dish to hold the cooking
bag, basting brush, charcoal grill

This recipe is usually cooked in a tandoor—an East Indian, vertical clay oven, heated to a very high temperature. Chicken and other meats are cooked suspended in the oven and the high temperature gives the meat quite a dry texture. By using your microwave combined with your conventional oven or charcoal grill, you can achieve almost the same result as with a tandoor but more moist, which I prefer.

4 tablespoons chopped garlic

4 tablespoons grated raw ginger

1 10-ounce can tomatoes or Cajun-style stewed tomatoes, drained

3 tablespoons curry powder

1 cup plain yogurt

1 tablespoon fresh ground black pepper

½ teaspoon cayenne pepper (optional)

2 2½-pound chickens, skin removed and cut in half

1 tablespoon red food color mixed with ½ cup water

Lime wedges (optional)

Place all the ingredients, except the chicken, food coloring, and lime wedges in a large plastic cooking bag and squeeze to mix. Add the chicken and marinate for about 4 hours or overnight in the refrigerator. Place the bag in a shallow microwave container and microwave on high for 20 to 25 minutes, or until the chicken reaches an internal temperature of 160 degrees.

Remove the chicken from the bag and place in a Pyrex or metal pan and brush with the food coloring. Broil in a preheated broiler for about 10 to 15 minutes or grill over charcoal very close to the coals until slightly burned. Serve with the marinade and the juices from the cooking bag. Squeeze limes over the chicken if you wish.

Optional: Baste with Ghee (recipe follows) during the broiling or grilling.

Ghee (Indian Clarified Butter)

MICROWAVE ONLY

ENERGY LEVEL:
high, 100%

YIELD:
about ½ cup

COMPLETE RECIPE TIME:
about 10 minutes

COOKING TIME:
7 to 9 minutes

MICROWAVE COOKWARE:
2-quart Pyrex mixing bowl or other similar bowl

COVERING:
paper towel, wax paper, or other nonstick paper to allow the moisture to escape and prevent spattering

G*hee* is made by separating the milk solids from butter and then continuing the cooking until all of the moisture is eliminated. The remaining oil has a unique nutty flavor and can be stored for a long time without spoiling. When making *ghee* on your stove top, you must watch it carefully to avoid burning. When you make it in your microwave that problem is virtually eliminated. But still be careful because you can overcook and burn it toward the end of the cooking time.

½ pound butter

Place the butter in a large Pyrex bowl or batter bowl, cover with a paper towel or wax paper or other nonstick paper, and microwave on high about 7 to 9 minutes, until all of the moisture has been cooked from the butter. Let stand for a couple of minutes, then pour the butter through a coffee filter or paper towel into a small jar. Store in the refrigerator.

Fast Food Fried Chicken

You may have noticed that the chicken in my recipes is usually devoid of skin to help reduce fat and cholesterol consumption. However, now and then, there's nothing as tasty and satisfying as fried chicken. When you make it at home, it's a real job and a real mess. Since there are so many excellent fried chicken take-out restaurants, I advocate stocking up on your favorite and freezing it in servings of one or two, then reheating it when the urge for fried chicken strikes you.

Here's the best way: Microwave in a cooking bag or closed container on high until the chicken is heated through. In the meantime, preheat your conventional oven to 500 degrees. Transfer the chicken to the oven and heat until the skin and/or breading becomes very crispy. You'll have to watch it and time it yourself to get it perfect.

Chicken Breasts Cordon Bleu

This is an elegant dish that requires a bit of preparation but is very easy to cook by microwave. It can also be made up ahead of time and cooked at a moment's notice or frozen to be used at a later date. If you slice it into rounds and skewer it with toothpicks, it makes a nice appetizer.

2 large chicken breasts, boned and skinned and cut in half

Dijon mustard

4 thin slices Swiss cheese

4 thin slices boiled ham

½ cup chopped fresh parsley

Place the chicken breast halves on a sheet of plastic wrap and cover with another sheet of plastic wrap. Pound thin with a mallet or meat bat. Cover with a slather of mustard, a slice of cheese, and a slice of ham. Roll up in the sheet of wax paper or nonstick cooking paper and tuck in the ends. Repeat with each chicken breast half. Place in a dish or on a plate and microwave on high for about 2 to 3 minutes per roll or to an internal temperature of 160 degrees. Remove paper from each roll and serve plain or with Mornay Sauce (page 287). Sprinkle with parsley.

MICROWAVE ONLY

ENERGY LEVEL:
high, 100%

SERVINGS:
4

COMPLETE RECIPE TIME:
about 25 minutes

COOKING TIME:
about 12 minutes

MICROWAVE COOKWARE:
shallow 1-quart casserole or dinner plate

ACCESSORY EQUIPMENT:
Plastic wrap, wax paper, or nonstick cooking paper, meat bat or mallet

COVERING:
none

Chicken Breasts Florentine

MICROWAVE ONLY

ENERGY LEVEL:
high, 100%

SERVINGS:
4

COMPLETE RECIPE TIME:
about 35 minutes

COOKING TIME:
About 12 minutes

MICROWAVE COOKWARE:
shallow 1-quart glass or plastic
casserole

ACCESSORY EQUIPMENT:
meat bat or mallet, food
processor, toothpicks

COVERING:
Plastic wrap or the dish cover

This recipe is made exactly like the Cordon Bleu recipe that precedes it, but uses a spinach/cheese mixture. It also makes a nice appetizer when sliced into rounds that are secured with toothpicks. Try it topped with a Mexican salsa, which is absolutely delicious.

1 10-ounce package frozen spinach	2 large chicken breasts, boned and skinned and cut in half
3 ounces cream cheese	Dijon mustard
	4 thin slices boiled ham

Microwave the spinach in the box set in a bowl on high for 7 minutes. Allow to cool and squeeze out as much water as possible. Place in your food processor with the cream cheese and blend.

While the spinach is cooking, place each chicken breast half on a sheet of plastic wrap and cover with another sheet of plastic wrap. Pound thin with a mallet or meat bat. Spread with mustard and a thin layer of the spinach mixture. Top with a slice of ham and roll up and tuck in the ends and secure with a toothpick. Repeat with each chicken breast half. Place the rolls in a shallow 1-quart casserole and spread the remaining spinach mixture over each chicken roll. Cover the dish with its cover or plastic wrap and microwave on high for 2 to 3 minutes per roll or to an internal temperature of 160 degrees. Serve with Mornay sauce or for more festive occasions Hollandaise sauce, or with a prepared salsa.

Chicken Breasts aux Duxelles Follow the same procedure as for Chicken Breasts Florentine but substitute *duxelles* for the spinach mixture. See page 291 for the recipe. You'll be surprised at how easy it is to make *duxelles* by microwave and it can be frozen if you make a large batch.

Roll of Chicken

You can serve this chicken roll as a first course or an appetizer or for a small luncheon buffet.

1 chicken breast, both halves (called a supreme), about 8 ounces

½ cup coarsely chopped boiled or baked ham

1 tablespoon Dijon mustard or prepared *pesto*

4 tablespoons duxelles (page 291) or chopped raw mushrooms

1 cup chopped raw spinach

½ cup bread crumbs or 1 tablespoon cornstarch

½ cup blue cheese dressing

MICROWAVE ONLY

ENERGY LEVEL:
high, 100%

SERVINGS:
4 as appetizer; or 2 as entrée

COMPLETE RECIPE TIME:
12 to 15 minutes, plus cooling time

COOKING TIME:
about 5 minutes

MICROWAVE COOKWARE:
plastic cooking bag or nonstick cooking paper

Pound the chicken breast until it is very thin. Mix the remaining ingredients, except the cheese dressing, and spread over the chicken. Roll up the chicken and filling while tucking in the edges. Roll tightly in a plastic cooking bag or nonstick cooking paper. Microwave on high for 4 to 5 minutes or to an internal temperature of 160 to 170 degrees. Allow to cool and cut into ½-inch slices. Spread the cheese dressing in a plate and set the chicken slices on top of it.

Turkey

The biggest challenge to cooking a turkey conventionally is to prevent it from drying out. If you microwave it, you virtually eliminate the problem. However, some other concerns arise when microwaving turkeys. First, a turkey should be turned over once during the cooking and if you're cooking a very large one it's difficult to do. Second, the wings and legs tend to overcook before the entire bird is done. Before microwaving any large whole bird, make an incision at the joints of the legs and wings where they join the body and cut the tendons that secure the joint together. Then, as it cooks, the legs and wings won't flex away from the body. You also have to tie or skewer these parts to the body. You DO NOT have to remove the metal leg retainer from the turkey. I stress this because so many microwave "experts" tell you to be sure to discard it. That small amount of metal will have no effect on the cooking process.

Small to Medium (6- to 16-pound) Turkeys

MICROWAVE AND CONVENTIONAL OVEN COMBINATION

ENERGY LEVEL:
medium-high, 70 to 80%, power

SERVINGS:
for small turkeys, 6 to 10 pounds, estimate ¾ to 1 pound per person; for larger birds, estimate ½ to ¾ pounds per person

COMPLETE RECIPE TIME:
microwave estimate about 5 to 7 minutes per pound plus about 15 minutes preparation time, plus about 1 hour conventional oven cooking

COOKING TIME:
microwave 5 to 7 minutes per pound plus about 1 hour conventional oven cooking

MICROWAVE COOKWARE:
9- x 13-inch glass or ceramic lasagne pan or 13- to 16-inch oval glass or ceramic roasting pan

ACCESSORY EQUIPMENT:
basting bulb, 1-quart glass measuring cup, or mixing bowl

COVERING:
plastic wrap

Make a small incision at the joints where the legs and wings join the body and cut the tendons that secure the joints. Tie or skewer the legs and wings to the body of the bird. Season inside and out with salt, pepper, and poultry seasoning. Place the bird, breast side down, in a 9- x 13-inch glass or ceramic lasagne pan or other appropriate dish. Cover with plastic wrap. Estimate the cooking time at 7 minutes per pound (a 10-pound bird should cook about 70 minutes). Microwave on medium-high, 70 to 80%, power for one half the cooking time.

Turn the bird over and remove the accumulated juices with a basting bulb, saving them in a 1-quart glass measuring cup or mixing bowl. Re-cover the turkey with the plastic wrap and finish the microwave cooking. The turkey should have an internal temperature of about 160 degrees after microwaving. Remove the plastic wrap and draw off the juices. Transfer the turkey to a preheated 400 degree oven and roast for about 10 minutes, or until thoroughly browned.

Note: If you notice any part of the bird overcooking and drying out, place aluminum foil over these areas during the microwave part of the cooking.

Small Turkey with Fruit Stuffing

This recipe makes a nice Sunday dinner for the family. It doesn't take long to cook so you don't have to spend much time in the hot kitchen and you'll have some leftovers for another meal or sandwiches. You can stuff the dressing into the turkey, but with so many cases of food poisoning from improperly cooked dressing, I prefer to cook it outside the bird.

1 6-ounce package stuffing mix prepared as directed but without any butter or oil added

1 4-ounce package mixed dried fruit, reconstituted (covered with water and microwave on high for 10 minutes)

2 stalks celery, chopped

1 small onion, chopped

½ cup chopped nuts of choice

1 10- to 12-pound turkey

MICROWAVE AND CONVENTIONAL OVEN COMBINATION

ENERGY LEVEL:
medium-high, 70-80%

SERVINGS:
estimate ¾ to 1 pound per person

COMPLETE RECIPE TIME:
about 2 hours

COOKING TIME:
about 1¾ hours

MICROWAVE COOKWARE:
glass or ceramic 9- x 13-inch lasagne pan or other similar dish

COVERING:
plastic wrap

Mix the stuffing with the remaining stuffing ingredients and spread it in a 9- x 13-inch glass baking pan or oval roaster. Cut the backbone out of the turkey; spread the turkey open, and press on the breastbone to flatten the bird. Place the turkey over the dressing and cover with plastic wrap. Microwave on medium-high, 70 to 80%, power for about 1½ hours or to an internal temperature of 160 degrees. Remove the plastic wrap. Transfer the turkey to a preheated 450 degree oven for about 15 minutes or to an internal temperature of 170 degrees.

Turkey Breast

Nothing could be easier than cooking a turkey breast by microwave. Allow about 7 minutes per pound and always cover the dish securely with its lid or plastic wrap.

Turkey Breast for Sandwiches

MICROWAVE ONLY

ENERGY LEVEL:
high, 100%

SERVINGS:
¼ to ½ pound per person

COMPLETE RECIPE TIME:
7 minutes per pound plus 5
minutes preparation time

COOKING TIME:
7 minutes per pound

MICROWAVE COOKWARE:
shallow glass or plastic dish about
the area of the breast

COVERING:
plastic wrap or the dish cover

Make your own instead of buying the pressed kind that always tastes a little manufactured. It's also a little cheaper when you cook it yourself.

Use turkey breast with the bone or boneless. If you use one with the bone, make stock or soup with it.

2 to 5 pounds turkey breast   **Salt and seasonings to taste**
1 cup water

If using a breast with the bone, place it, bone side up, in a 3- to 4-quart microwave dish. Add water to pan and season the turkey. Cover with plastic wrap or the dish cover and microwave on high for about 7 minutes per pound or to an internal temperature of 165 to 170 degrees. Slice to the thickness desired.

Note: Since you're cooking by weight, it makes no difference whether the bone is in or not.

Large (18- to 20-Pound) Turkeys

If you must cook a large turkey, place it breast side up in a large glass or ceramic dish. (I have a large oval clay dish that is perfect.) Microwave the bird, covered with plastic wrap, on medium-high, 70 to 80%, power for about 5 minutes per pound or to an internal temperature of about 120 degrees. Remove the plastic wrap and draw off the juices with a basting bulb, reserving them. Transfer the turkey to a preheated 350 degree conventional oven for about 1 hour or to an internal temperature of 170 degrees. The turkey will be very moist and browned to perfection and the cooking time will be cut about in half.

Turkey Gravy: My wife always makes turkey gravy with the fat and the juices, whereas I like to separate the fat and make the gravy with just the juices. There is no difference in the actual making of the gravy but hers is a lot richer.

In a 1-quart measuring cup or mixing bowl make a paste of ¼ cup flour and ¼ cup of the cooking juices. Add the remaining juices slowly, stirring with a whisk. Microwave, uncovered, for 3 to 4 minutes, or until it is as thick as you like. Stir once or twice during the cooking

Browned Flour Gravy: Browned flour gives a richer taste to gravy but is really a task to make conventionally. By microwave it is very easy and fast. Just place ¼ cup flour in a 1-quart Pyrex measuring cup and microwave, uncovered, on high for 2 to 3 minutes, until it browns. Be cautious, it can burn. Use as directed above in Turkey Gravy.

Turkey Breast with Stuffing

1 package stuffing mix prepared as directed on package but without any butter or margarine

1 2- to 3-pound boneless turkey breast, skin removed

Place the stuffing in an appropriate microwave dish, arrange the turkey breast over it, and cover with plastic wrap. Microwave on high for 8 to 10 minutes per pound or to an internal temperature of 165 to 170 degrees. Slice and serve with the stuffing.

MICROWAVE ONLY

ENERGY LEVELS:
high, 100%

SERVINGS:
¼ to ½ pound per person

COMPLETE RECIPE TIME:
8 to 10 minutes per pound plus about 10 minutes preparation time

COOKING TIME:
8 to 10 minutes per pound

MICROWAVE COOKWARE:
shallow glass or plastic dish about the area of the breast

COVERING:
plastic wrap or the dish cover

Turkey Breast with Spaghetti Sauce

MICROWAVE ONLY

ENERGY LEVEL:
high, 100%

SERVINGS:
4

COMPLETE RECIPE TIME:
about 15 minutes

COOKING TIME:
8 to 10 minutes

MICROWAVE COOKWARE:
1-quart glass or plastic casserole

COVERING:
plastic wrap or the dish cover

1 pound boneless and skinless turkey breast, cubed	1 cup spaghetti sauce

Pour sauce over turkey breast in a 1-quart microwave dish, cover with plastic wrap or the dish cover, and microwave on high for 8 to 10 minutes, stirring once, or until the turkey is cooked.

Creamed Turkey Breast

MICROWAVE ONLY

ENERGY LEVEL:
high, 100%

SERVINGS:
4

COMPLETE RECIPE TIME:
about 20 minutes

COOKING TIME:
about 15 minutes

MICROWAVE COOKWARE:
1-quart glass or plastic casserole dish

COVERING:
plastic wrap or the dish cover

1 small onion, chopped	2 tablespoons flour
1 small bell pepper, chopped	1 pound boneless or skinless turkey breast, cubed
2 tablespoons butter or margarine	1 cup milk

Place the onion, pepper, butter, and flour in a 2-quart batter bowl or mixing bowl. Cover with plastic wrap or the dish cover and microwave on high for 3 to 4 minutes, or until the vegetables are soft. Add the turkey and microwave on high, covered, for about 7 minutes. Stir and add the milk and microwave on high for about 5 minutes, or until thickened.

Variation: Use ½ can condensed soup of choice and an equal amount of milk instead of only milk in the recipe.

Galantine of Turkey Breast

This elegant dish may seem to be a lot of work but when you want to make something for a party that will impress the guests try this.

2 pounds boneless turkey breast, skin removed

4 tablespoons Dijon mustard

1 pound ground turkey

1 tablespoon dried tarragon

1 teaspoon ground nutmeg

1 ounce sherry

½ cup heavy cream

½ pound baked ham, diced

8 whole medium mushrooms

Salt and fresh ground pepper

1 envelope plain gelatin

4 tablespoons mayonnaise

Fresh herb sprigs, sliced mushrooms, or bell pepper rings for garnish

MICROWAVE ONLY

ENERGY LEVEL:
medium, 50%

SERVINGS:
8 to 16

COMPLETE RECIPE TIME:
about 40 minutes plus 2 hours chilling time

COOKING TIME:
20 to 25 minutes

MICROWAVE COOKWARE:
glass or plastic bread loaf pan or plastic cooking bag

ACCESSORY EQUIPMENT:
heavy object to place on the roll while cooling

COVERING:
plastic wrap

Butterfly the breast and pound it to ⅜-inch thickness. Spread the mustard over it. Mix the ground turkey, tarragon, nutmeg, sherry, and cream and spread over the breast. Lay the ham over the filling and make a row of mushrooms alternating upright and upside down on one end of the breast. Roll up the breast from the end with the mushrooms. Place the roll in a glass bread loaf pan, season with salt and pepper, and cover with plastic wrap. Or place the roll in a plastic cooking bag and roll up tightly. Microwave on medium, 50%, power for 20 to 25 minutes or to an internal temperature of 160 degrees. Drain off the juices, reserving them in a cup, and place a weight—a full bottle of wine on its side works nicely—on top, and chill for a couple of hours.

Dissolve the gelatin in the reserved juices and add enough water to make 1 cup liquid. Stir in the mayonnaise. When the breast roll has cooled, unmold it onto a serving platter. Microwave the gelatin mixture until it softens and spread it over the roll. Decorate with herb sprigs, sliced mushrooms, or bell pepper rings. Slice and serve.

Fish and Seafood

You just can't miss when you microwave fish.
Cook it whole, in steaks or in fillets,
it's easy to cook in so many ways.
Whether you cook it plain or in a broth
with herbs or spices, or in a sauce.
Cook it in a dish, bowl, or even on your plate,
anyway you do it, it'll turn out great.
Just make sure you cover it securely
or it'll dry out most assuredly.
And most important of all, you'll only go wrong
if you microwave your fish a little too long.

Most everyone who owns a microwave oven agrees that you can cook fish in it beautifully. The only way you can't make it in the microwave is fried or deep fried. But we all should cut down on our consumption of fried foods anyway, so cook your fish by microwave and you'll have a healthier diet.

It takes 4 to 5 minutes per pound to cook fish properly. However, if the fish is very cold it will take a little longer. As with anything else, do not overcook it. Always cover fish securely with plastic wrap or the dish cover.

Cooked Seviche

MICROWAVE ONLY

ENERGY LEVEL:
high, 100%

SERVINGS:
8 as a side dish

COMPLETE RECIPE TIME:
15 minutes plus 1 hour for
marinating

COOKING TIME:
8 to 10 minutes

MICROWAVE COOKWARE:
2-quart glass or plastic casserole

COVERING:
plastic wrap or the dish cover

Seviche is raw fish that is marinated and cured in an acidic brine. I think it is delicious and have served it often. However, lately I've found that some folks are getting squeamish about eating uncooked fish. One of my guests once complained about this, so, being an accommodating host, I offered to cook it for him. With a microwave oven, it was no problem at all. He really enjoyed it as did everyone else who tried it. See for yourself and compare it with the traditional uncooked version.

1 pound, very fresh firm-bodied fish, snapper, cod, and so on, without skin or bones, cut into 1-inch cubes

1 pound bay scallops

Juice of 8 limes

1 jalapeño chili pepper, seeded and minced

1 medium yellow onion, minced

1 large ripe tomato, diced, or canned tomato wedges, drained and chopped

½ cup chopped coriander leaves (cilantro)

Place all ingredients in a 2-quart glass bowl and allow to marinate for at least 1 hour. Cover with plastic wrap or the dish cover and microwave on high for 8 to 10 minutes, or until the fish becomes opaque or reaches an internal temperature of 150 degrees.

Note: If you microwave the limes about 30 seconds each before squeezing them, you will get a lot more juice.

Fish Steaks with Mayonnaise

MICROWAVE ONLY

ENERGY LEVEL:
high, 100%

SERVINGS:
4

COMPLETE RECIPE TIME:
about 10 minutes

COOKING TIME:
6 to 8 minutes

MICROWAVE COOKWARE:
8-inch-square glass baking pan or
other similar glass or plastic dish

COVERING:
plastic wrap or the dish cover

When I first tried this recipe, I thought that all kinds of funny things would happen to the mayonnaise when it was cooked. However, nothing weird occurred, and the dish turned out to be very delicious. And there are now low-calorie and cholesterol-free mayonnaises available if you're cutting back a bit.

4 fish steaks, such as salmon, halibut, shark, and so on, about 1½ pounds total

4 tablespoons mayonnaise

Dillweed (optional)

Place the fish, with the thinner edges toward the center, in an 8-inch-square glass baking dish or other similar microwave dish and spread the mayonnaise over the top of each steak. Sprinkle with the dill if desired. Cover securely with plastic wrap or the dish cover and microwave on high for about 6 to 8 minutes or to an internal temperature of 150 degrees.

Halibut with Ginger Butter

MICROWAVE ONLY

ENERGY LEVEL:
high, 100%

SERVINGS:
4

COMPLETE RECIPE TIME:
about 15 minutes

COOKING TIME:
6 to 8 minutes

MICROWAVE COOKWARE:
8-inch-square glass baking pan or other similar dish

COVERING:
plastic wrap

You can find ginger paste in tubes or jars at Asian food stores, or just shred raw ginger with the finest grater you have and blend it with the butter.

4 tablespoons butter or margarine, softened

2 tablespoons ginger paste or finely grated raw ginger

4 halibut steaks or other fish of choice, about 1½ pounds total

2 tablespoons chopped coriander leaves (cilantro; optional)

Mix the butter and ginger. Place the fish in an 8-inch-square glass baking pan or other similar dish and spread with the ginger butter. Cover securely with plastic wrap and microwave on high for about 6 to 8 minutes, or until the fish is done. Sprinkle with the coriander if desired.

Sea Bass with Horseradish Sauce

MICROWAVE ONLY

ENERGY LEVEL:
high, 100%

SERVINGS:
4

COMPLETE RECIPE TIME:
about 12 minutes

COOKING TIME:
6 to 8 minutes

MICROWAVE COOKWARE:
shallow 1-quart glass or plastic casserole

COVERING:
plastic wrap or the dish cover

I like to use the Japanese horseradish, called *wasabi*, for this recipe, but you can use plain grated horseradish or even creamed horseradish. *Wasabi* comes in tubes or powdered in cans, which you reconstitute with water. If you eat it plain, you can really clear your sinuses.

4 sea bass or other heavy flesh fish fillets, about 1½ pounds

½ cup dry white wine, fish stock, or clam juice

3 tablespoons *wasabi* paste

3 tablespoons soy sauce

¾ cup plain yogurt

Place the fish and wine in a shallow 1-quart microwave dish, cover securely with plastic wrap or the dish cover, and microwave on high for about 6 to 8 minutes, or until the fish is done. Mix the remaining ingredients and serve over the fish.

Cod with Red Bell Pepper Sauce

MICROWAVE ONLY

ENERGY LEVEL:
high, 100%

SERVINGS:
4

COMPLETE RECIPE TIME:
about 25 minutes

COOKING TIME:
15 minutes

MICROWAVE COOKWARE:
8-inch-square glass baking pan or
other similar dish

COVERING:
plastic wrap or the dish cover

In another of my cookbooks I featured a recipe called fish on a bed of peppers. It was a truly beautiful concoction with the white flesh of the fish on a bed of red, green, and yellow bell peppers. This recipe is virtually the same except you make a sauce of the peppers after cooking them.

1 medium red bell pepper, core and seeds removed, sliced

1 medium yellow bell pepper, core and seeds removed, sliced

½ red onion, sliced thinly

2 cloves garlic, minced

2 tablespoons olive oil

1 teaspoon bottled hot sauce (optional)

4 cod fillets, about 1½ pounds

Place all the ingredients, except the fish, in an 8-inch-square glass baking dish. Cover securely with plastic wrap or the dish cover, and microwave on high for about 10 minutes, or until the peppers are very soft. Place the fish on top of the peppers, re-cover, and microwave on high for about 5 minutes, or until the fish is just done. (You are cooking the fish for a shorter period of time because the peppers are already hot.) Remove the fish to a serving platter, place the other ingredients in your food processor, and blend until smooth. Serve the sauce over the fish.

Tuna in Salsa

Here again the simplicity of this recipe makes it ideal for busy folks who don't want to expend the time it usually takes in the kitchen to make something really good.

1½ cups prepared salsa or picante sauce

4 pieces raw tuna, about 1 pound

Lemon slices

Place half the salsa in a shallow 1-quart glass or plastic casserole or similar microwave dish. Top with the fish and cover with the remaining salsa. Cover securely with plastic wrap or the dish cover and microwave on high about 6 to 8 minutes. With tuna, you can leave the center a little rare and it tastes wonderful. Serve garnished with lemon slices.

Another simple way to make this recipe is to heat the salsa in your microwave and sear the tuna in a really hot skillet just so the surfaces are charred and the center is still raw. Delicious served with the salsa.

Variation: Add 2 ounces canned crushed pineapple, drained, to the salsa for a unique taste treat.

MICROWAVE OR SKILLET AND MICROWAVE

ENERGY LEVEL:
high, 100%

SERVINGS:
4

COMPLETE RECIPE TIME:
about 10 to 12 minutes

COOKING TIME:
6 to 8 minutes

MICROWAVE COOKWARE:
shallow 1-quart glass or plastic casserole

ACCESSORY EQUIPMENT:
skillet (optional)

COVERING:
plastic wrap or the dish cover

Yucatán-Style Fish

MICROWAVE OR CHARCOAL GRILL

ENERGY LEVEL:
high, 100%

SERVINGS:
4

COMPLETE RECIPE TIME:
microwave, 13 to 15 minutes;
charcoal grill, 1 hour and 10
minutes

COOKING TIME:
microwave, 6 to 8 minutes;
charcoal grill, 6 to 8 minutes

MICROWAVE COOKWARE:
shallow 1-quart glass or plastic
casserole

ACCESSORY EQUIPMENT:
food processor and charcoal grill

COVERING:
plastic wrap or the dish cover

Microwave the fish in this recipe or let it marinate for a couple of hours in the sauce below, then throw it on your charcoal grill.

4 red snapper fillets, about 1½ pounds

3 ounces frozen orange juice concentrate

3 tablespoons lemon juice

4 scallions, white part only

4 sprigs coriander (cilantro)

1 small pickled jalapeño pepper

Place the fish in a shallow microwave dish. In a food processor or blender process or blend together the remaining ingredients and pour over the fish. Cover securely with plastic wrap or the dish cover and microwave on high for 6 to 8 minutes, or until the fish is done. Or, let the fish marinate, charcoal grill it, and serve it with the marinade.

Catfish in Cocktail Sauce

I like to use catfish nuggets for this recipe. They are thick bone-·less pieces of catfish about 2 to 3 inches in length and are usually quite inexpensive. You can also use small whole catfish, allowing one per serving.

1½ pounds catfish nuggets   Lemon slices

1 12-ounce jar cocktail sauce

Place the fish and sauce in a 2-quart glass or plastic casserole. Cover securely with plastic wrap or the dish cover and microwave on high for about 8 to 10 minutes, or until the fish is done. Stir once during the cooking. Serve garnished with the lemon slices.

MICROWAVE ONLY

ENERGY LEVEL:
high, 100%

SERVINGS:
4

COMPLETE RECIPE TIME:
10 to 12 minutes

COOKING TIME:
8 to 10 minutes

MICROWAVE COOKWARE:
2-quart glass or plastic casserole

COVERING:
plastic wrap or the dish cover

Fish with Lime and Herbs

This is a recipe that I have done many times on the charcoal grill. Just marinate the fish in the other ingredients and toss it on the coals when ready. An easier and quicker way—just microwave it.

Juice from 2 limes   ½ teaspoon thyme leaves

½ yellow onion, chopped   1 pound fish fillets, 4 pieces,
                                   no skin or bones
½ teaspoon dried chili flakes
                                   4 whole sprigs parsley
1 tablespoon minced garlic

2 bay leaves

Place all ingredients, except the fish and parsley, in a measuring cup and microwave for 1 minute on high. Pour a little of the mixture on the bottom of a shallow 1-quart glass or plastic

MICROWAVE ONLY

ENERGY LEVEL:
high, 100%

SERVINGS:
4

COMPLETE RECIPE TIME:
about 12 minutes

COOKING TIME:
6 to 8 minutes

MICROWAVE COOKWARE:
shallow 1-quart glass or plastic casserole

COVERING:
plastic wrap or the dish cover

dish, lay the fish over it, and pour the rest of the liquid over the fish. Cover with plastic wrap or the dish cover and microwave on high for 6 to 8 minutes, until the fish flakes easily or to an internal temperature of 150 degrees.

Fish Fillets in Lemon Rings

MICROWAVE ONLY

ENERGY LEVEL:
high, 100%

SERVINGS:
4

COMPLETE RECIPE TIME:
about 20 minutes

COOKING TIME:
6 to 8 minutes

MICROWAVE COOKWARE:
shallow 1-quart glass or plastic casserole

COVERING:
plastic wrap or the dish cover

While attending college I also tended bar, and I remember that we would make lemon slices for garnishing drinks by cutting the ends off of the lemons, running a tablespoon between the lemon peel and the flesh, then popping out the flesh, and cutting the peel into rings or strips for garnish. It occurred to me that using these lemon rings to hold fish fillets, like a napkin ring, would make a nice, simple presentation. Also, holding the fish together, instead of laying it flat, increases the mass of the fillet, which is helpful when microwaving fish.

4 thin fish fillets, such as sole, flounder, etc.

4 scallions, cut the length of each fish fillet

2 lemons prepared as described above and cut into 4 rings

½ cup fish stock or clam juice

¼ cup minced parsley

Roll each fillet lengthwise around each scallion and slip a lemon ring over the roll. Place the rolls in a shallow 1-quart casserole. Squeeze the lemon flesh of 1 lemon into the fish stock or clam juice and pour over the fish. Cover with plastic wrap or the dish cover and microwave 6 to 8 minutes or to a temperature of 150 degrees. Pour pan juices over fish when serving and garnish with the parsley.

Fish Medley for Pasta

The colors of this recipe make it beautiful to present. If you want to make it even prettier, serve it with green (spinach) or red (tomato) pasta.

4 servings cooked pasta of choice

¼ pound salmon steak, skin and bones removed

¼ pound halibut steak, skin and bones removed

4 large shrimp, peeled, deveined, and cut in half

½ pint heavy cream

4 tablespoons butter or margarine

6 fresh basil leaves, chopped

¾ cup imitation crab, optional

MICROWAVE, SKILLET, AND POT TO COOK PASTA

ENERGY LEVEL:
high, 100%

SERVINGS: 4

COMPLETE RECIPE TIME:
about 20 minutes

COOKING TIME:
about 15 minutes

MICROWAVE COOKWARE:
shallow 1-quart glass or plastic casserole

ACCESSORY EQUIPMENT:
large skillet and pot to cook pasta

COVERING:
plastic wrap or the dish cover

Cook the pasta according to package directions. In the meantime cut the fish into 1-inch cubes and place it and the shrimp in a 1-quart casserole, cover with plastic wrap or the dish cover, and microwave on high for about 4 minutes, or until the fish is just done and the shrimp becomes pink.

Place the cream, butter, and basil in a large skillet and reduce by about half. When the fish is cooked, drain the juices into the cream mixture and continue reducing until thick enough to coat a spoon. Add the sauce to the fish and shrimp and spoon over the pasta, making sure each serving has an equal amount of fish and shrimp.

ZAP TIP: Make large batches of pasta in advance and freeze it in plastic cooking bags. When needed, microwave on high until hot, about 2 minutes per serving.

Whole Poached Salmon

MICROWAVE ONLY

ENERGY LEVEL:
high, 100%

SERVINGS:
about 8

COMPLETE RECIPE TIME:
about 30 minutes

COOKING TIME:
about 25 minutes

MICROWAVE COOKWARE:
large or turkey-size plastic cooking
bag or a glass or plastic dish big
enough to hold the fish

ACCESSORY EQUIPMENT:
1-quart measuring cup

COVERING:
plastic wrap

Poaching whole fish by microwave is so much easier and faster than doing it conventionally. The only problem is finding a glass or plastic dish with the right dimensions to hold a modest-size fish. I have a long narrow glass dish shaped like a five-pound salmon that works perfectly. I also use a glass oval roaster and it works quite well. If you have neither, use a large size or turkey-size plastic cooking bag.

2 cups water or dry white wine	2 bay leaves
1 stalk celery, chopped	4 peppercorns
1 carrot, shredded	1 whole salmon, about 3
1 onion, chopped	pounds, cleaned and head
½ cup chopped parsley	removed

Place all ingredients, except the salmon, in a 1-quart measuring cup and microwave on high for about 8 minutes, or until the water has boiled for a couple of minutes. Strain the poaching liquid. If using a cooking bag, place the fish in the bag, pour in the poaching liquid, and close the cooking bag with a rubberband or the plastic ties provided, leaving a gap about the size of your thumb. Microwave on high for about 4 to 5 minutes per pound or to an internal temperature or 150 degrees at the thickest part of the fish. Halfway through the cooking, turn the fish over. This is very easy when you're using a cooking bag. If using a container for cooking, pour half of the poaching liquid into the container, put the fish in, and pour the remaining liquid over it. Cover with plastic wrap and microwave on high for 4 to 5 minutes per pound or to an internal temperature of 150 degrees at the thickest part of the fish.

Spicy Poached Salmon: Add ¼ cup bottled hot sauce, but not Tabasco, to the poaching liquid and cook as directed above.

Poached Salmon Steaks or Fillets

4 1-inch-thick salmon steaks or
   fillets, about 1 to 1½
   pound total

1½ cups water, dry white wine,
   or clam juice

½ stalk celery, chopped

½ carrot, shredded

½ yellow onion, chopped

¼ cup chopped parsley

1 small bay leaf

2 peppercorns

1 lemon, quartered

MICROWAVE ONLY

ENERGY LEVEL:
high, 100%

SERVINGS:
4

COMPLETE RECIPE TIME:
about 15 minutes

COOKING TIME:
about 12 minutes

MICROWAVE COOKWARE:
8-inch-square glass baking pan or
similar dish

COVERING:
plastic wrap

Place all ingredients, except the fish, in a 1-quart measuring cup and microwave on high for about 6 minutes, or until the water has boiled for a couple of minutes. Strain the liquid and pour half of it into an 8-inch-square glass baking pan. Add the fish and pour the remaining liquid over it. Cover with plastic wrap and microwave on high for about 4 to 6 minutes. Remove the fish from the liquid and serve with the lemon.

Salmon with Jalapeño Jelly

MICROWAVE ONLY

ENERGY LEVEL:
high, 100%

SERVINGS:
4

COMPLETE RECIPE TIME:
about 10 minutes

COOKING TIME:
7 to 9 minutes

MICROWAVE COOKWARE:
8-inch-square glass baking pan or
similar dish

COVERING:
plastic wrap

I first saw this dish at a restaurant in New York City. My curiosity was piqued, so I had to try it. It was served broiled and was delicious; it turns out just as good microwaved. Try it both ways.

½ cup dry white wine

½ cup jalapeño jelly

4 salmon fillets, about 1½
    pounds

½ cup chopped fresh coriander
    leaves (cilantro)

Place the wine in an 8-inch-square glass baking pan or similar dish, cover with plastic wrap, and microwave on high for 2 minutes. Spread the jelly over each fillet and place the fish in the poaching liquid. Re-cover and microwave on high for about 5 to 7 minutes, or until done. Remove from poaching liquid and sprinkle with coriander before serving.

Salmon in Salad Dressing

MICROWAVE ONLY

ENERGY LEVEL:
high, 100%

SERVINGS:
4

COMPLETE RECIPE TIME:
about 10 minutes

COOKING TIME:
6 to 8 minutes

MICROWAVE COOKWARE:
shallow 1-quart glass or plastic
casserole dish or 10-inch pie pan

COVERING:
plastic wrap or the dish cover

There are many flavorful high-quality salad dressings on the market today. Experiment cooking fish in one that you like. This recipe uses Italian-style dressing and it makes a wonderful fish dish. Remember, cooking easy makes life easier.

t½ cup Italian salad dressing   **4 salmon steaks or fillets, about 1½ pounds**

Spread a little of the salad dressing on the bottom of a shallow 1-quart microwave dish and top with the fish. Pour the remaining dressing over the fish and cover securely with plastic wrap or the dish cover, and microwave on high for about 6 to 8 minutes, or until the fish is done. Serve with the juices from the cooking.

Ginger Salmon

MICROWAVE ONLY

ENERGY LEVEL:
high, 100%

SERVINGS:
4

COMPLETE RECIPE TIME:
about 13 minutes

COOKING TIME:
6 to 8 minutes

MICROWAVE COOKWARE:
shallow 1-quart microwave dish or
10-inch glass pie pan

COVERING:
plastic wrap or the dish cover

There is a recipe in this book for ginger chicken (page 83), which everyone really likes, so I thought why not try it with fish? It works just as well and is just as easy.

4 salmon steaks or fillets, about 1½ pounds total

4 cloves garlic, minced, or 2 tablespoons garlic paste

4 tablespoons shredded raw ginger or 2 tablespoons ginger paste

½ cup soy sauce

4 scallions, 4 inches long and smashed, done by placing the flat side of a French knife or cleaver on the scallions and whacking them

Place the salmon in a shallow 1-quart microwave dish. Combine the garlic, ginger, and soy sauce and pour over the fish. Cover with plastic wrap or the dish cover and microwave on high for about 6 to 8 minutes, or until the fish is done. Serve with one scallion over each piece of fish.

Salmon in Tomato Cups

MICROWAVE ONLY

ENERGY LEVEL:
medium, 50%

SERVINGS:
4

COMPLETE RECIPE TIME:
about 12 minutes

COOKING TIME:
6 to 8 minutes

MICROWAVE COOKWARE:
glass custard cups or a plastic
muffin pan

COVERING:
wax paper or nonstick cooking
paper

This is a nice presentation for a small, informal garden party.

**4 tomatoes, each the size of a
    tennis ball**

**8- to 10-ounces cooked
    salmon, all bones removed**

**4 tablespoons tartar sauce or
    lemon dill sauce**

Cut the tops off the tomatoes and scoop out the insides with a spoon. Fill each tomato with an equal amount of salmon and top with the sauce. Place the tomatoes in custard cups or the cups of a plastic muffin pan. Cover with wax paper and microwave on medium, 50%, power for about 6 to 8 minutes, or until warmed through—to an internal temperature of 140 degrees.

Shrimp by Microwave

Cooking shrimp in your microwave is another way to get to love the machine. Like chicken, it's almost impossible to ruin shrimp. Just make sure you don't cook them too long and be sure to cover the dish securely. Try the following recipe as a confidence builder and serve the shrimp hot or chilled.

Curried Shrimp

MICROWAVE ONLY

ENERGY LEVEL:
high, 100%

SERVINGS:
4

COMPLETE RECIPE TIME:
about 20 minutes if you have to clean the shrimp yourself

COOKING TIME:
4 to 6 minutes

MICROWAVE COOKWARE:
shallow 1-quart glass or plastic casserole dish

COVERING:
plastic wrap or the dish cover

Shrimp cooked this way make a wonderful entrée when served with rice or can be served as a spicy first course.

1 pound peeled and deveined large shrimp

1 tablespoon curry paste, available at Asian food stores, or 2 tablespoons curry powder

4 cloves garlic, minced

2 tablespoons shredded raw ginger

2 tablespoons tomato paste

2 tablespoons lemon juice

Mix all ingredients together and place in a shallow 1-quart glass or plastic container. Cover securely with plastic wrap or the dish cover and microwave on high for about 4 to 6 minutes, or until the shrimp are done. Stir once during the cooking.

Shrimp with Garlic and Oil

1 pound (16 to 21) peeled and deveined large shrimp

4 tablespoons minced garlic

½ cup olive oil

1 tablespoon butter

½ cup chopped fresh parsley

Place all ingredients, except the parsley, in a 1-quart microwave dish, cover with plastic wrap or the dish cover, and microwave on high for 4 to 6 minutes, stirring once, until the shrimp are done and turn pink. Remove the cover, stir, and let sit for a couple of minutes. Sprinkle the parsley over the shrimp and serve with crusty French bread to swab up the juices.

MICROWAVE ONLY

ENERGY LEVEL:
high, 100%

SERVINGS:
4

COMPLETE RECIPE TIME:
about 12 minutes

COOKING TIME:
4 to 6 minutes

MICROWAVE COOKWARE:
shallow 1-quart glass or plastic casserole

COVERING:
plastic wrap or the dish cover

Shrimp in Bisque Soup Sauce

Again, a simple recipe, which makes a simple yet elegant dish.

1 pound peeled and deveined large shrimp

1 10-ounce can shrimp bisque soup

2 tablespoons lemon juice

¼ cup chopped parsley

Mix the shrimp and soup in a 2-quart casserole dish, cover with plastic wrap or the dish cover, and microwave on high for about 6 to 8 minutes, or until the shrimp are pink and just done. Stir once. The juices from the shrimp will dilute the soup perfectly. Add the lemon juice and serve over cooked pasta or rice. Garnish with the parsley.

MICROWAVE ONLY

ENERGY LEVEL:
high, 100%

SERVINGS:
4

COMPLETE RECIPE TIME:
18 to 20 minutes if you have to clean the shrimp yourself

COOKING TIME:
6 to 8 minutes

MICROWAVE COOKWARE:
2-quart glass or plastic casserole

COVERING:
plastic wrap or the dish cover

Shrimp in Coconut Mint Sauce

MICROWAVE ONLY

ENERGY LEVEL:
high, 100%

SERVINGS:
4

COMPLETE RECIPE TIME:
about 20 minutes if you have to
clean the shrimp yourself

COOKING TIME:
about 6 minutes

MICROWAVE COOKWARE:
shallow 1-quart glass or plastic
casserole

COVERING:
plastic wrap or the dish cover

When you feel like something a little exotic try this recipe.

1 pound (16 to 21) peeled and
   deveined large shrimp

2 tablespoons minced shallots

½ cup shredded raw coconut

1 tablespoon bottled hot sauce

½ cup heavy cream or plain
   yogurt

½ cup fresh mint leaves,
   chopped

Mix all ingredients except the mint, and place in a 1-quart microwave dish, cover securely with plastic wrap or the dish cover, and microwave on high for about 6 minutes, or until the shrimp are done. Sprinkle with mint before serving.

Shrimp and Baby Artichokes in Cream Sauce

MICROWAVE ONLY

ENERGY LEVEL:
high, 100%

SERVINGS:
4

COMPLETE RECIPE TIME:
about 20 minutes

COOKING TIME:
about 15 minutes

MICROWAVE COOKWARE:
2-quart glass or plastic casserole

COVERING:
plastic wrap or the dish cover

This recipe requires a little more work, but when you want to serve something that will garner raves from guests, this will.

1 pound baby artichokes,
   halved top to bottom and
   washed

4 tablespoons olive oil

2 tablespoons butter

4 ounces prepared *pesto* sauce

1 pound (16 to 21) peeled and
   deveined large shrimp

3 ounces heavy cream

Sliced lemons

3 slices prosciutto or thinly
   sliced baked ham,
   shredded (optional)

Place the artichokes, oil, butter, and *pesto* in a 2-quart microwave dish, cover securely with plastic wrap or the dish cover,

and microwave on high for 7 to 10 minutes, or until the artichokes are tender. Add the shrimp, re-cover, and microwave
on high for 4 to 5 minutes, stirring once, until the shrimp are
done. Drain the juices and add to the cream in a hot skillet and
reduce by about half. Pour the sauce over the shrimp and artichokes and serve with the lemon slices.

Variation: Add the shredded prosciutto or ham when you add
the shrimp.

Dairyland Shrimp

MICROWAVE AND SKILLET

ENERGY LEVEL:
high, 100%

SERVINGS:
4

COMPLETE RECIPE TIME:
about 20 minutes if you clean
the shrimp yourself

COOKING TIME:
about 10 minutes

MICROWAVE COOKWARE:
shallow 1-quart glass or plastic
casserole

ACCESSORY EQUIPMENT:
large frying pan

COVERING:
plastic wrap or the dish cover

I once received a critical letter from a woman in Wisconsin who
watched one of my television shows where I made a derogatory
remark about her state. At that time I also discarded some fat
from a recipe. She didn't like the remark about Wisconsin and
believed that all food should be used—nothing should be wasted.
Well, I love Wisconsin, but I also like to tease a bit; as far as her
concern about wasting fat, I try to convey that we should cut
down on our fat consumption but now and then eat and enjoy!
My philosophy is eat conservatively most of the time and eat for
pure joy some of the time without thinking about fat and calories.
Here is a recipe dedicated to her and Wisconsin.

1 pound (16 to 21) peeled and
    deveined large shrimp

1 cup heavy cream from
    Wisconsin

4 tablespoons butter from
    Wisconsin

¼ cup grated Parmesan
    cheese from Wisconsin

¼ cup chopped parsley from
    Wisconsin

Place the shrimp in a 1-quart casserole dish, cover with plastic wrap or the dish cover, and microwave on high for 5 to 6
minutes, or until the shrimp turn pink, stirring once. In the meantime in a frying pan on your stove reduce the cream with the
butter. When the shrimp are done add the juices to the reduc-

tion and continue reducing it until it is thick enough to coat a spoon. Add the cheese, stir, and pour over the shrimp. Sprinkle the parsley over the top. Mop up the sauce with crusty French bread.

Butter Beans and Tuna with Tomatoes

MICROWAVE ONLY

ENERGY LEVEL:
high, 100%

SERVINGS:
4

COMPLETE RECIPE TIME:
8 to 10 minutes

COOKING TIME:
5 minutes

MICROWAVE COOKWARE:
1-quart glass or plastic serving bowl

COVERING:
plastic wrap

Everything in this recipe is precooked, so all you are doing with your microwave is heating the combination up to serving temperature. By mixing the ingredients in a nice serving bowl you won't have to wash a cooking container.

1 14½-ounce can butter beans, drained

1 7-ounce can albacore tuna packed in oil or water, your choice

1 7-ounce can Italian-style canned tomatoes

2 fresh basil leaves, minced, or 1 teaspoon dried basil leaves

Mix all ingredients in an appropriately sized serving bowl, cover with plastic wrap, and microwave on high for about 5 minutes, or until hot. Stir after cooking.

Microwave Steamed Lobsters

1 cup dry white wine or water

2 1¼ to 1½-pound live Maine lobsters

¼ pound butter or margarine, melted

MICROWAVE ONLY

ENERGY LEVEL:
high, 100%

SERVINGS:
2

COMPLETE RECIPE TIME:
about 15 minutes

COOKING TIME:
about 12 minutes

MICROWAVE COOKWARE:
9- × 13-inch glass lasagne pan or other shallow glass or plastic container, or a large plastic cooking bag

COVERING:
plastic wrap

Place the liquid in a 9- × 13-inch glass pan, lasagne pan, or other large shallow plastic pan. Cover with plastic wrap and microwave on high for 4 to 5 minutes. With a paring knife, cut the spinal cord of the lobsters at the first joint behind the head. Place the lobsters, head to head, in the cooking container and cover with the plastic wrap. Microwave on high for about 10 to 12 minutes, or until they turn pink. Note: Sometimes the large claws don't turn pink. Don't worry. When the body is pink the whole lobster is cooked. Lift a corner of the plastic wrap and pour off the liquid. Remove the plastic wrap and serve with the melted butter.

Variation: Microwave the liquid in a measuring cup for 3 to 4 minutes. Sever the spinal cord of the lobsters as directed above and place them in a large plastic cooking bag. Pour in the hot liquid and secure the bag as close to the lobsters as possible with the ties provided or with a rubberband. Microwave on high for about 10 to 12 minutes, or until the lobsters turn pink. Serve with the melted butter.

Lobsters in Picante Sauce

MICROWAVE ONLY

ENERGY LEVEL:
high, 100%

SERVINGS:
2

COMPLETE RECIPE TIME:
about 20 minutes

COOKING TIME:
about 14 to 16 minutes

MICROWAVE COOKWARE:
9- × 13-inch glass lasagne pan or
other large shallow glass or plastic
dish, or a large plastic cooking
bag

COVERING:
plastic wrap

This is a perfect recipe when you want to enjoy an evening with someone but don't want to spend time in the kitchen away from that someone. The sauce cuts the richness of the lobster. Serve with a nice salad and some garlic bread.

2 cups prepared picante sauce or salsa	**2 small (1- to 1¼-pound) live lobsters**

Place the sauce in a 9- × 13-inch glass pan, lasagne pan, or other large, preferably oval, shallow casserole dish, cover with plastic wrap, and microwave on high for about 8 minutes, or until very hot. Add the lobsters, re-cover, and microwave on high for another 8 minutes, or until the lobsters turn bright pink.

Note: You can put the lobsters in the sauce and cook them right from the start, but for humane reasons before microwaving cut the spinal cord behind the head.

Variation: Microwave the sauce in a 2-cup measuring container for 4 to 5 minutes. Place the lobsters in a large plastic cooking bag, pour the sauce over, and close the bag as close to the lobsters as possible with the ties provided. Microwave on high for 10 to 12 minutes, or until the lobsters turn pink.

In one of my cooking classes, I mentioned that opening live oysters can be quite dangerous. One of the students asked, very seriously "Do they bite?" I, of course, was referring to the fact that if the knife slips, you can give yourself a nasty wound.

Do not use this technique if you are going to serve the oysters raw.

To open oysters easily using your microwave, place 6 oysters, convex side down, on a platter in glass custard cups; or in a plastic muffin pan, which works perfectly because each cup holds an oyster in place. Microwave on high for about 3 minutes, or until each oyster opens its lips slightly. Be careful not to microwave too long because the oysters will shrivel up. Slip a short, thin-blade knife between the lips and cut the muscle from the top shell. Discard the top shell and add filling or flavoring. Microwave about 20 to 30 seconds for each oyster and serve. Save and wash the shells for future recipes using raw oysters sold by the jar. In fact, unless you have an ample supply of raw oysters off your shore or must serve authentic, just-opened oysters, I recommend that you use the raw, fresh-packed ones in a jar. They're available at almost every fish store in the country and are always fresh, plump, and delicious.

Oysters Microwaved Many Ways

MICROWAVE ONLY

ENERGY LEVEL:
high, 100%

SERVINGS:
6 oysters

COMPLETE RECIPE TIME:
5 to 10 minutes

COOKING TIME:
2 to 6 minutes

MICROWAVE COOKWARE:
glass custard cups or plastic muffin pan

ACCESSORY EQUIPMENT:
2-cup glass or plastic measuring cup

COVERING:
wax paper or other nonstick cooking paper

Oysters Casino

6 oysters

Salt

½ cup each chopped celery,
    bell pepper, onion, bacon
    bits, real or imitation

Worcestershire sauce

Bottled hot sauce

Place 6 oysters, on the half shell, on a platter that has been spread with ¼ inch of salt to hold the oysters upright or place the oysters in the cups of a plastic muffin pan. Or use raw shucked oysters placed in small cups or on plastic scallop shells or previously cooked real shells. Place the vegetables in a bowl and microwave on high for 3 minutes, or until cooked but still crunchy. Place an equal amount of the vegetables on the oysters and give each a dash of Worcestershire and hot sauce. Cover with wax paper or other nonstick cooking paper and microwave on high for about 2 to 3 minutes, or until cooked.

Oysters with Blue Cheese: Place 1 tablespoon crumbled blue or Roquefort cheese or 1 tablespoon prepared blue cheese dressing over each oyster and cook as directed above.

Oysters in Cream and Parmesan Cheese: Pour 1 tablespoon heavy cream over each oyster, sprinkle grated Parmesan cheese, and cook as directed in the Oysters Casino recipe.

Oysters Rockefeller: Mix 5 ounces frozen or canned spinach, squeezed dry, with ¼ cup grated Parmesan cheese, 2 tablespoons minced garlic, 1 tablespoon anchovy paste, and ½ cup bread crumbs. Place an equal amount on each oyster and add a dash of Worcestershire sauce. Cook as directed in the Oysters Casino recipe.

Oysters with Salsa: Place 1 heaping tablespoon of salsa on top of each oyster and cook as directed in the Oysters Casino recipe.

Oysters Pesto: Place 1 tablespoon of prepared *pesto* sauce on each oyster and cook as directed in the Oysters Casino recipe.

Oysters in Lemon Cups: Cut 3 lemons in half and run a tablespoon between the rind and the flesh and remove the flesh. Cut off just enough of the other ends, so the cups will sit upright, but not through to the cavity. Slip 1 or 2 raw oysters into each lemon cup and top with a dash of bottled hot sauce. Place the lemons with oysters in the cups of a plastic muffin pan or set in a circle on a large platter. Cover with wax paper or other non-stick cooking paper and microwave on high for about 2 to 3 minutes or 20 to 30 seconds per cup until the oysters are cooked.

Scallops

You can substitute scallops for all of the shrimp recipes in this book. Scallops are so easy to cook; no cleaning is required.

Scallop Sauté

1 pound scallops

4 tablespoons butter or margarine

½ teaspoon paprika

2 cloves garlic, minced

Salt and fresh ground pepper to taste

3 tablespoons lemon juice

Chopped parsley

Place all ingredients, except the lemon juice and parsley, in a 1-quart microwave dish, cover with plastic wrap or the dish cover, and microwave 4 to 6 minutes, or until the scallops are just done, stirring once during the cooking. They become opaque in appearance. Stir in the lemon juice and parsley and serve.

MICROWAVE ONLY

ENERGY LEVEL:
high, 100%

SERVINGS:
4

COMPLETE RECIPE TIME:
about 8 minutes

COOKING TIME:
4 to 6 minutes

MICROWAVE COOKWARE:
shallow 1-quart glass or plastic casserole

COVERING:
plastic wrap or the dish cover

Scallops Mayonnaise

MICROWAVE ONLY

ENERGY LEVEL:
high, 100%

SERVINGS:
4

COMPLETE RECIPE TIME:
about 10 minutes

COOKING TIME:
4 to 6 minutes

MICROWAVE COOKWARE:
shallow 1-quart glass or plastic
casserole

COVERING:
plastic wrap or the dish cover

1 pound scallops

6 tablespoons mayonnaise

3 tablespoons chopped chives

Pinch of cayenne pepper

Place scallops and mayonnaise in a 1-quart microwave dish, cover with plastic wrap or the dish cover, and microwave 4 to 6 minutes, or until the scallops are cooked. Add the chives and pepper and serve.

Scallops au Gratin

MICROWAVE AND BROILER
COMBINATION

ENERGY LEVEL:
high, 100%

SERVINGS:
4

COMPLETE RECIPE TIME:
about 20 minutes

COOKING TIME:
about 15 minutes

MICROWAVE COOKWARE:
4 glass or ceramic soup bowls

COVERING:
plastic wrap

4 tablespoons minced onions

2 tablespoons minced garlic

4 tablespoons capers

1 pound scallops

1 cup Mornay Sauce (page 287), made with Parmesan cheese

Microwave the onions, garlic, and capers in a measuring cup for 2 to 3 minutes, or until the onions are soft. Place an equal amount of the mixture in 4 small soup bowls or similar glass or ceramic bowls. Add an equal amount of scallops to each bowl and place on a glass or ceramic serving platter. Cover with plastic wrap and microwave on high for 4 to 6 minutes, or until the scallops are cooked. Remove the plastic wrap and top each bowl with mornay sauce. Place under a preheated broiler for a couple of minutes until the tops are browned.

One of my most enjoyable elements of my brief, but pleasurable, tour in the army was my introduction to the joy of eating clams. I was stationed near Virginia Beach, Virginia, where beachside restaurants served a variety of raw and cooked clams. Many hours of a weekend pass were spent consuming platters of raw cherrystones on the half shell or huge bowls of steamers with broth and, of course, copious amounts of adult beverages.

When I started cooking by microwave, I found that clams and, for that matter, all shellfish cook beautifully in a microwave oven. Just make sure you cover the cooking container tightly so you use the steam created from the juices to cook along with the microwave energy. Use a 4-quart glass, ceramic, or plastic container or a large plastic cooking bag for microwaving these shellfish.

Always scrub the shells and rinse the clams several times to rid them of sand before cooking. If you are using soft-shell or long-neck clams it may be wise to soak them in a brine of 1 gallon of water and ⅓ cup of salt for a few hours before cooking.

Use only tightly closed clams and discard any that don't open after cooking.

Clams

Steamed Clams

ENERGY LEVEL:
high, 100%

SERVINGS:
2 to 4

COMPLETE RECIPE TIME:
about 30 minutes

COOKING TIME:
about 14 minutes

MICROWAVE COOKWARE:
4-quart glass or plastic container
or large plastic cooking bag

COVERING:
plastic wrap or the dish cover

24 soft-shell or long-neck clams or small littlenecks	4 tablespoons butter or margarine, melted

Scrub the shells and rinse the clams several times in cold water to rid them of sand. Place them in a 4-quart glass or plastic container or large plastic cooking bag. Cover the container with its cover or plastic wrap or close the bag with the ties provided and leave an opening about the size of your thumb. Microwave on high, 100%, power for 8 to 12 minutes, or until most of the clams have opened.

Note: The colder the clams, the longer it will take to cook them. Stir halfway through the cooking or if using a plastic cooking bag jostle the clams around halfway through the cooking. Transfer the opened clams to a serving dish and continue cooking the unopened ones for 2 to 4 minutes. If they don't open after that time discard them. Strain the juices through cheesecloth and mix with the butter or margarine and serve alongside the clams.

Clams in Salsa

24 small littleneck or
cherrystone clams

1 cup prepared salsa, hotness
to taste

Scrub the shells and rinse the clams several times in fresh water. Place the clams and salsa in a 4-quart glass or plastic container or a large plastic cooking bag. Cover the container with plastic wrap or its cover, or if using a plastic cooking bag, close the opening with the ties provided, leaving an opening about the size of your thumb.

Microwave on high, 100% power, for 8 to 12 minutes, or until most of the clams have opened. Stir the clams in the container or shake the bag halfway through the cooking. Transfer the opened clams to a serving dish and microwave the unopened ones for 2 to 4 minutes or until they are open. Discard any that haven't opened after this. Pour the salsa and juices over the cooked clams and serve.

ENERGY LEVEL:
high, 100%

SERVINGS:
2 to 4

COMPLETE RECIPE TIME:
about 30 minutes

COOKING TIME:
about 14 minutes

MICROWAVE COOKWARE:
4-quart glass or plastic container
or large plastic cooking bag

COVERING:
plastic wrap or the dish cover

Clams with Sausage and Tomatoes

MICROWAVE ONLY

ENERGY LEVEL:
high, 100%

SERVINGS:
2 to 4

COMPLETE RECIPE TIME:
about 30 minutes

COOKING TIME:
about 20 minutes

MICROWAVE COOKWARE:
4-quart glass or plastic container
or large plastic cooking bag

COVERING:
plastic wrap or the dish cover

I discovered this recipe at a Portuguese food festival outside Honolulu. The atmosphere isn't quite the same as when cooked over an open fire, but the recipe tastes just as good when cooked in your microwave oven.

½ pound linguica or other smoked sausage, casing removed and thinly sliced

1 medium onion, thinly sliced

2 cloves of garlic, minced

¼ teaspoon dried crushed red pepper

1 14½-ounce can stewed tomatoes, drained

24 littleneck or cherrystone clams

Place everything except the clams in a 4-quart glass or plastic container or large plastic cooking bag and cover with plastic wrap or the dish cover, or close the bag with the ties provided, leaving an opening the size of your thumb. Microwave on high, 100%, power for 5 minutes. In the meantime, scrub the clams and rinse several times in fresh water. Add the clams to the other ingredients, re-cover, and microwave 8 to 10 minutes or until most of the clams have opened. Stir the clams in the container or tumble the bag halfway through the cooking. Transfer the opened clams to a serving container and continue cooking the unopened ones for 2 to 4 minutes. Discard any unopened ones after this. Pour the sausage mixture and juices over the clams and serve.

The thing I like most about mussels, besides their great taste, is the fact that you get three times more meat per pound than clams, so they are much cheaper to buy.

To prepare them for cooking, all you have to do is wash them and pull or cut off the beards. As with clams, be sure you cover the cooking container securely to retain the steam created from heating the juices.

Mussels

Steamed Mussels

2 pounds (about 40) mussels, washed and beards removed

4 cloves garlic, minced

½ cup dry white wine

4 tablespoons butter or margarine or vegetable oil

½ cup chopped parsley

Place everything except the parsley in a 4-quart glass or plastic container or plastic cooking bag. Cover with plastic wrap or the dish cover, or close the cooking bag with the ties provided, leaving an opening the size of your thumb. Microwave on high, 100%, power for 12 to 14 minutes. Stir the mussels in the container or tumble the bag halfway through the cooking. Transfer the opened mussels to a serving dish and cook the unopened mussels for 2 to 4 minutes. Discard any that haven't opened after that. Pour the juices over the mussels and stir in the parsley.

MICROWAVE ONLY

ENERGY LEVEL:
high, 100%

SERVINGS:
2 to 4

COMPLETE RECIPE TIME:
about 25 minutes

COOKING TIME:
about 16 minutes

MICROWAVE COOKWARE:
4-quart glass or plastic container or large plastic cooking bag

COVERING:
plastic wrap or the dish cover

Mussels à l'Escargot

MICROWAVE ONLY

ENERGY LEVEL:
high, 100%

SERVINGS:
2 to 4

COMPLETE RECIPE TIME:
about 25 minutes

COOKING TIME:
about 15 minutes

MICROWAVE COOKWARE:
4-quart glass or plastic container
or large plastic cooking bag

COVERING:
plastic wrap or the dish cover

If you like escargot, you've got to try this recipe. Mussels are much cheaper than using snails but just as good and much easier to prepare.

2 pounds (about 40) mussels, washed and beards removed

¼ pound butter or margarine

½ cup chopped parsley

4 cloves garlic, minced, or 2 tablespoons garlic puree

Place everything in a 4-quart glass or plastic container or large plastic cooking bag. Cover with plastic wrap or the dish cover, or close the bag with the ties provided, leaving an opening the size of your thumb. Microwave on high, 100%, power for 10 to 12 minutes, or until most of the mussels have opened. Stir the mussels in the container or tumble the bag halfway through the cooking. Transfer the opened mussels to a serving dish and continue cooking the unopened mussels for 2 to 4 minutes or until they open. Discard any unopened ones. Pour the juices over the mussels or serve alongside.

Paella

This Spanish dish is named for the shallow round metal pan in which it is cooked. With a microwave, it is counter-productive to cook in a metal pan, but paella is such a good and easy recipe to make by microwave that I must include it here. No matter what you cook it in it's a great one-dish meal. Classically paella calls for saffron for color and flavor, but I've found that the saffron flavor is lost in the complexity of ingredients included in the recipe. And because saffron is so expensive, I've substituted paprika.

Paella is not a spicy dish, so if you like hot recipes, add Tabasco, other bottled hot sauce, or cayenne pepper. Be creative!

MICROWAVE ONLY

ENERGY LEVEL:
high, 100%

SERVINGS:
4

COMPLETE RECIPE TIME:
about 40 minutes

COOKING TIME:
25 to 30 minutes

MICROWAVE COOKWARE:
large shallow glass, plastic, or ceramic casserole

COVERING:
plastic wrap or the dish cover

1 cup long-grain converted rice

1 14½-ounce can stewed tomatoes

1 small yellow onion, chopped

1 small green bell pepper, seeded, cored, and diced

2 cloves garlic, chopped

1 whole chicken breast, quartered

¼ pound chorizo sausage, sliced

1 10-ounce package frozen peas

1 teaspoon dried fines herbes

4 jumbo shrimp (16 to 21), peeled and deveined

4 cherrystone clams, washed and scrubbed

8 mussels, cleaned and scrubbed

In a large shallow glass, plastic, or ceramic pan place all ingredients, except the seafood. Stir, cover with plastic wrap or the dish cover, and microwave on high for about 20 minutes. Stir halfway through the cooking. Check the rice after 20 minutes; it should be al dente. if not, re-cover and microwave 5 minutes more. Add the seafood, re-cover, and microwave on high for 5 to 8 minutes, or until the clams are open. (They take longest to cook.)

Note: Because you're cooking by microwave, evaporation is less than in conventional cooking so you may end up with a moist recipe. Serve it this way or drain off the excess liquid. I assure you the recipe will be great either way.

Soups and a Few Stews

Small-quantity soups are easy to make by microwave. However, when making a large amount of soup remember that the microwave oven becomes very inefficient with large amounts of water. It may be wiser to make a large amount of soup on your stove top. Or cook the components by microwave and the stock or broth on top of your stove. Then incorporate the two for the final result.

There are so many recipes for soup that it's almost impossible for anyone to include them all in a cookbook. But once you try the ones I've collected here, I'm sure you'll develop the knowledge and skill to make any soup you want in your microwave.

For health reasons, it's best to remove most of the animal fat from the foods we eat. Fat always floats to the top of any liquid and it's relatively easy to lift off if you have time to allow it to cool and solidify. However, if you are in a hurry and would like to separate fat from your soups and stocks here's the best way:

ZAP TIP: Insert a bulb baster in the liquid below the fat and draw the clear broth into the tube. Squeeze the broth into another container and repeat until you have drawn out most of the broth and all that remains in the cooking container is the fat. There are also fat separators available with a tube or valve attached to the bottom, which allow you to pour off the broth from the bottom as the fat remains in the separator.

Chicken Stock

MICROWAVE ONLY

ENERGY LEVEL:
high, 100%

YIELD:
about 2 cups

COMPLETE RECIPE TIME:
about 35 minutes

COOKING TIME:
about 30 minutes

MICROWAVE COOKWARE:
3-quart glass or plastic container or ring pan

Most of the chicken recipes in this book have the skin removed to reduce the fat and cholesterol. Save and freeze chicken skin and wing tips, backs and necks, and hearts and gizzards and when you have enough make stock. Then chill the stock, skim off the fat, and freeze the stock in one- and two-cup quantities in plastic bags until needed.

1 pound chicken parts	1 carrot, chopped
1 quart water	2 bay leaves
1 stalk celery, chopped	4 sprigs parsley

Place all ingredients in a 3-quart microwave dish and microwave, uncovered, on high for about 30 minutes. Strain the stock and chill for a couple of hours, or until the fat solidifies on the top. Or use my ZAP TIP and remove the stock with a bulb baster.

Beef Stock

I think James Beard's method of making beef stock is the best recipe for it because you get a meal out of the effort of making the stock. He makes a *pot au feu*, drains off the liquid, then serves the ingredients for a meal. Later he reduces the liquid to make a nice rich stock. You can do the same with your microwave oven but for a smaller recipe.

2 pounds beef shank, cut into 2-inch rounds

2 carrots, cut into 1-inch pieces

2 stalks celery, cut into 1-inch pieces

1 large onion, diced

2 bay leaves

1 tablespoon dried thyme

3 sprigs parsley

6 cups water

Place the shanks under your broiler and brown almost to burning. Transfer to a 4-quart microwave dish or ring pan and add the remaining ingredients. Cover with a paper towel or wax paper and microwave on high for 15 minutes and 45 minutes on medium, 50%, power. Strain the liquid into a pan and transfer the solid ingredients to a serving platter for a meal for 2 persons. Separate the fat from the liquid and reduce the liquid on your stove top to the point where the broth coats a spoon. Use as the base for brown sauces or freeze until needed.

MICROWAVE AND BROILER

ENERGY LEVEL:
high, 100%, and medium, 50%

YIELD:
about 3 cups

COMPLETE RECIPE TIME:
about 1½ hours

COOKING TIME:
about 1 hour and 15 minutes

MICROWAVE COOKWARE:
4-quart glass or plastic container or ring pan

ACCESSORY EQUIPMENT:
broiler pan

COVERING:
paper towel or wax paper

Vegetable Stock

Whenever you cook vegetables in your microwave oven, save the water left over from the cooking. Since you use so little extra water in microwaving, the juices left after cooking are very rich in vegetable nutrients. I keep a one-quart plastic container with a lid in my freezer to accumulate these juices. Just add new juice from each cooking to the frozen contents until you have enough to make a good soup or stew.

Fish Stock

MICROWAVE ONLY

ENERGY LEVEL:
high, 100%

YIELD:
about 3 cups

COMPLETE RECIPE TIME:
about 25 minutes

COOKING TIME:
about 20 minutes

MICROWAVE COOKWARE:
3-quart glass or plastic container or ring pan

Most of the fish that I cook is in the form of steaks or fillets. The times that I do cook a whole fish are rare, but I do freeze the head, bones, and fins along with shrimp shells until I have enough for stock. I also use bottled clam juice and *dashi* (dried bonito) available at Asian food stores.

1 pound fish bones, fins, heads, tails and/or shrimp shells	1 stalk celery, chopped
	1 small onion, chopped
1 quart water or 2 cups water and 2 cups dry white wine	1 tablespoon anchovy paste

Place all ingredients in a 3-quart microwave dish and microwave, uncovered, on high for 20 minutes. Remove any scum and strain to remove solid ingredients. Freeze in 1- and 2-cup quantities.

Very Easy Vegetable Soup

This is such a good recipe if you're trying to lose a few pounds. Little fat, lots of vitamins and fiber, and so filling and satisfying. Serve with a heavy multigrain bread.

2 stalks celery, sliced across the grain ½ inch thick

2 carrots, sliced

1 medium onion, chopped

1 large Russet potato, diced (peeled optional)

2 tablespoons dried *fines herbes* or Italian herb blend

4 cups Vegetable Stock (page 152) or Chicken Stock (page 150)

2 tablespoons Vegemite or other concentrated vegetable flavor enhancer

Place all ingredients, except the stock and Vegemite, in a 3-quart microwave dish, cover securely with plastic wrap or the dish cover, and microwave on high for about 15 minutes, or until the vegetables are soft. Add the stock and Vegemite and microwave on high for 8 to 10 minutes, or until very hot. To save time, heat the stock and Vegemite on the stove top, then add to the vegetables when they are cooked.

MICROWAVE ONLY; STOVE TOP, OPTIONAL

ENERGY LEVEL:
high, 100%

SERVINGS:
4

COMPLETE RECIPE TIME:
about 25 to 35 minutes

COOKING TIME:
about 15 to 25 minutes

MICROWAVE COOKWARE:
3-quart glass or plastic container or ring pan

ACCESSORY EQUIPMENT:
1½-quart metal pot if heating stock on stove top

COVERING:
plastic wrap or the dish cover

Puréed Raw Vegetable Soup

MICROWAVE ONLY

ENERGY LEVEL:
high, 100%

SERVINGS:
4

COMPLETE RECIPE TIME:
about 25 to 30 minutes

COOKING TIME:
about 10 to 15 minutes

MICROWAVE COOKWARE:
2-quart glass or plastic container
or batter bowl

ACCESSORY EQUIPMENT:
food processor

COVERING:
plastic wrap or the dish cover

Any raw vegetable can be used in this recipe. The cooking times will vary because of the density and freshness of the vegetable, but you can estimate the time and test the softness of the item and cook it longer if necessary. You want the vegetables to be very soft so when they are puréed they will be very smooth.

1 pound fresh raw asparagus or cauliflower or broccoli or cabbage or carrots or onions, etc.

4 cups stock, Vegetable (page 152) or Chicken (page 150)

Cut the vegetables into small pieces and place in a 2-quart microwave bowl or glass batter bowl with 1 cup of the stock. Cover with plastic wrap or the dish cover and microwave on high for 10 to 15 minutes, or until the vegetables are very soft. Place vegetables and stock in food processor and process until smooth. Gradually add the remaining stock. Pour back into the cooking vessel and microwave on high for 3 to 4 minutes, or until hot.

Variation: Add 1 teaspoon frozen limeade concentrate per serving for a unique taste treat.

Cream of Puréed Vegetable Soup

MICROWAVE ONLY

ENERGY LEVEL:
high, 100%

SERVINGS:
4

COMPLETE RECIPE TIME:
about 35 minutes

COOKING TIME:
about 25 minutes

MICROWAVE COOKWARE:
2-quart glass or plastic container
batter bowl

ACCESSORY EQUIPMENT:
food processor

Follow the directions for Puréed Raw Vegetable Soup, but use 2 cups stock and 2 cups milk. When the soup is in the processor, place 2 tablespoons flour and 2 tablespoons butter in the cooking bowl and microwave on high, uncovered, for 2 minutes, stirring once. Add the soup and microwave on high, uncovered, 5 to 10 minutes, or until thickened.

Variation: Add ½ cup grated Parmesan cheese after cooking.

Manhattan-Style Clam Chowder

MICROWAVE ONLY

ENERGY LEVEL:
high, 100%

SERVINGS:
4

COMPLETE RECIPE TIME:
about 30 minutes

COOKING TIME:
about 25 minutes

MICROWAVE COOKWARE:
3-quart glass or plastic container
or ring pan

COVERING:
plastic wrap or the dish cover

You're a lucky person if you have live littlenecks available. Most of us must do with canned clams for this recipe.

1 large Russet potato, diced (peeled optional)

1 medium onion, diced

1 green bell pepper, cored and diced

3 tablespoons flour

3 tablespoons butter

1 14-ounce can stewed tomatoes

1 cup clam juice

1 cup water

2 6-ounce cans minced clams or 20 raw littlenecks, soaked and scrubbed

Place the potato, onion, pepper, flour, and butter in a 3-quart microwave dish or ring pan and stir to coat the vegetables with the flour and butter. Cover with plastic wrap or the dish cover and microwave on high for 10 to 12 minutes, or until the potato is tender. Add the remaining ingredients, re-cover, and microwave on high for 10 to 12 minutes, or until the soup has thickened and all of the raw clams, if used, have opened.

Variation: Add cooked crumbled bacon to the chowder after it is cooked.

New England–Style Clam Chowder: Omit the pepper and tomatoes from Manhattan-style Clam Chowder and substitute milk for the water.

Corn Chowder

MICROWAVE ONLY

ENERGY LEVEL:
high, 100%

SERVINGS:
4

COMPLETE RECIPE TIME:
about 25 minutes

COOKING TIME:
about 20 minutes

MICROWAVE COOKWARE:
2-quart glass container

COVERING:
plastic wrap or the dish cover

If you have fresh corn from your garden or market, shave off the kernels and use them in this recipe. Otherwise use frozen or canned, whichever you like best.

4 slices bacon, chopped

1 medium onion, chopped

2 tablespoons flour

1 medium red bell pepper, cored and diced (optional)

1½ cups raw corn kernels or 1 10-ounce package frozen corn, defrosted, or 1 11-ounce can corn kernels, drained

3 cups milk

4 tablespoons bottled hot sauce or 1 teaspoon Tabasco (optional)

Place the bacon in a 2-quart glass microwave dish and microwave on high for about 4 minutes, or until it becomes brown and crisp. Add the onion, flour, and bell pepper and stir to coat with the bacon grease and flour. Cover with plastic wrap and microwave 4 to 5 minutes, or until the onion and pepper are soft. Add the remaining ingredients and microwave, uncovered, for about 10 minutes, or until the soup has thickened.

Cuban Black Bean Soup

1 small onion, chopped

2 cloves garlic, minced

4 ounces baked ham, chopped

2 tablespoons annato oil or 2 tablespoons oil and 1 tablespoon paprika

1 14-ounce can black beans with juice

1 14-ounce can stewed tomatoes

2 cups Chicken Stock (page 150)

2 tablespoons malt vinegar (optional)

4 dollops of sour cream or plain yogurt (optional)

MICROWAVE ONLY

ENERGY LEVEL:
high, 100%

SERVINGS:
4 to 6

COMPLETE RECIPE TIME:
about 30 minutes

COOKING TIME:
About 20 minutes

MICROWAVE COOKWARE:
3-quart glass or plastic container or ring pan

ACCESSORY EQUIPMENT:
food processor (optional)

COVERING:
plastic wrap or the dish cover

Place the onion, garlic, ham, and oil in a 3-quart microwave dish or ring pan , cover with plastic wrap or the dish cover, and microwave on high for about 5 minutes, or until the onion is soft. Add the remaining ingredients, except the vinegar and sour cream, re-cover, and microwave on high for about 15 minutes, or until heated through. Stir in the vinegar. Top each serving with a dollop of sour cream. To make a thicker soup, process the beans with a little of the stock and return to the soup.

Vegetarian Black Bean Soup: Substitute 1 can drained corn kernels for the ham and use Vegetable Stock (page 152) instead of chicken stock.

Navy Bean Soup

MICROWAVE ONLY

ENERGY LEVEL:
high, 100%

SERVINGS:
4

COMPLETE RECIPE TIME:
about 20 minutes

COOKING TIME:
about 13 minutes

MICROWAVE COOKWARE:
3-quart glass or plastic container
or ring pan

ACCESSORY EQUIPMENT:
food processor

COVERING:
plastic wrap or the dish cover

1 small onion, chopped

2 cloves garlic, minced

2 14-ounce can navy beans

1 14-ounce can tomato wedges or 4 ripe plum tomatoes, chopped

2 cups Chicken Stock (page 150)

2 tablespoons minced fresh thyme

½ cup cream or evaporated milk

1 cup unseasoned croutons

Salt and fresh ground pepper to taste

Place the onion and garlic in a 3-quart microwave dish or ring pan, cover with plastic wrap or the dish cover, and microwave on high for about 3 minutes, or until the onion is soft. Purée the beans. Add the puréed beans, tomatoes, stock, and thyme to the onion mixture. Re-cover and microwave on high for about 10 minutes, or until heated through. Stir in the cream. Top each serving with croutons and season with salt and pepper.

ZAP TIP: To make croutons in your microwave, dice French or other bread and sprinkle with oil and seasonings. Microwave, uncovered, about 1 minute per cup of bread cubes. Stir and let sit for a couple of minutes until hardened.

Split Pea Soup Picante

This recipe takes a relatively long time to cook, but you can set it and forget it and when you return home, you'll have a nice hearty soup awaiting you.

½ carrot

1 stalk celery

1 small onion

½ cup parsley

2 ham hocks or 1 pound lean
    baked ham, diced, or 1
    ham bone with lots of meat
    still on it

2½ cups water

1 cup stewed tomatoes

½ cup hot picante sauce

1 cup dried split green peas

Finely chop or in a food processor process the carrot, celery, onion, and parsley and place in a 3-quart microwave dish or ring pan, cover with plastic wrap or the dish cover, and micro-wave on high for 3 or 4 minutes, or until the vegetables are soft. Add the remaining ingredients, re-cover and microwave on high for 10 minutes and medium, 50%, power for 25 to 30 minutes, or until the peas are soft. Remove the meat from the bones and return to the soup. To make a thicker soup, purée 1 cup of the soup and stir purée back into dish.

Variation: Garnish each serving with chopped Bavarian-style sauerkraut.

MICROWAVE ONLY

ENERGY LEVEL:
high, 100%, medium, 50%

SERVINGS:
4

COMPLETE RECIPE TIME:
about 50 minutes

COOKING TIME:
about 45 minutes

MICROWAVE COOKWARE:
3-quart glass or plastic container
or ring pan

ACCESSORY EQUIPMENT:
food processor

COVERING:
plastic wrap or the dish cover

East Indian Cream of Peanut Soup

MICROWAVE ONLY

ENERGY LEVEL:
high, 100%

SERVINGS:
4

COMPLETE RECIPE TIME:
about 16 minutes

COOKING TIME:
about 11 minutes

MICROWAVE COOKWARE:
3-quart glass or plastic container
or ring pan

COVERING:
plastic wrap or the dish cover

Here's a dandy recipe if you're looking for something a little different. I guarantee that anyone who likes peanut butter will love this soup.

1 medium onion, chopped

2 cloves garlic, minced

1 tablespoon freshly grated
   raw ginger

3 tablespoons sesame seeds,
   toasted and mashed

1 tablespoon curry powder

½ cup chunky peanut butter

4 cups Chicken Stock (page
   150)

2 tablespoons cornstarch

1 tablespoon lemon or lime
   juice

½ cup plain yogurt

Chopped roasted peanuts

Fresh coriander (cilantro)
   leaves, minced

Place the onion, garlic, ginger, curry powder, and sesame seeds in a 3-quart microwave dish or ring pan, cover with plastic wrap or the dish cover, and microwave on high for 3 to 4 minutes, or until the onion is soft. Add the peanut butter, stock, and cornstarch. Stir to blend and microwave uncovered on high for 5 to 7 minutes, or until the soup thickens. Stir in the lemon or lime juice and yogurt. Garnish each serving with the nuts and coriander leaves.

ZAP TIP: To toast sesame seeds, place 3 tablespoons of the seeds in a measuring cup and microwave on high for 4 to 5 minutes, or until they start to brown. Stir every minute.

Leek, Potato, and Ham Soup

If you want to make this or any of these soups really fast, heat the stock on your stove while you cook the other ingredients in your microwave. Stir the two together and you've got soup in half the time.

2 tablespoons butter or
   margarine

3 leeks, white part only, thinly
   sliced and washed

2 large Russet potatoes, diced

½ pound baked ham, diced

4 cups Chicken Stock (page
   150)

Fresh ground pepper

2 scallions, thinly sliced

Place the butter, leeks, potatoes, and ham in a 3-quart microwave dish or ring pan, cover with plastic wrap or the dish cover, and microwave on high for about 15 minutes, or until the potatoes are tender. Add the stock, re-cover, and microwave for 5 minutes, or until heated through. Season each serving with the pepper and garnish with the scallions. To make a creamy soup, purée half of the potatoes and leeks after they have been cooked and stir them back into the soup.

MICROWAVE ONLY

ENERGY LEVEL:
high, 100%

SERVINGS:
4

COMPLETE RECIPE TIME:
about 25 minutes

COOKING TIME:
about 20 minutes

MICROWAVE COOKWARE:
3-quart glass or plastic container
or ring pan

ACCESSORY EQUIPMENT:
food processor

COVERING:
plastic wrap or the dish cover

Salad Soups

MICROWAVE ONLY

ENERGY LEVEL:
high, 100%

SERVINGS:
4

COMPLETE RECIPE TIME:
about 17 minutes

COOKING TIME:
about 12 minutes

MICROWAVE COOKWARE:
2-quart glass or plastic container
or ring pan

COVERING:
plastic wrap or the dish cover

If you have a tendency to make too much salad, use what is leftover to make this soup.

3 cups leftover salad, chopped	1 cup salsa
2 cups Chicken Stock (page 150)	½ cup tomato juice
1 14-½-ounce can tomatoes	Salt and fresh ground pepper to taste

Place the salad and ½ cup of the stock in a 2-quart microwave dish or ring pan, cover with plastic wrap or the dish cover, and microwave on high for 5 to 7 minutes, or until the salad vegetables are soft. Add the remaining ingredients, re-cover, and microwave on high for 5 minutes, or until heated through.

Optional: Process the vegetables after cooking for a pureed soup.

BLT Soup: Microwave 4 strips of bacon until crisp, drain, and crumble over each serving of Salad Soup.

French Onion Soup

Whenever you use a conventional recipe for this soup you are always admonished not to burn the onions when sautéing them. With a microwave, you don't have to worry about that because the cooking container never gets hot enough to scorch the onions.

4 medium yellow onions, cut in half and thinly sliced

½ cup butter or margarine

1 tablespoon brown sugar

3 tablespoons flour

3 cups canned beef broth

1 ounce cognac (optional)

4 2½-inch rounds of toast, hardened

1 to 2 cups shredded Swiss cheese

Place the onions, butter, and sugar in a 3-quart microwave dish, cover with plastic wrap or the dish cover, and microwave on high for 12 to 15 minutes, or until the onions are soft. Stir in the flour, add the broth and the cognac if using. Microwave, uncovered, for about 10 minutes. Place 1 toast round each in 4 soup bowls and pour equal amounts of the soup into each bowl. Serve with the cheese.

Optional: Divide the soup among 4 soup bowls and place a toast round on top of each. Top the rounds with cheese. Place the bowls on a cookie sheet and run under a preheated broiler for a few minutes until the cheese melts and browns.

ZAP TIP: Cut out bread rounds and toast them in the microwave, uncovered, on high for 3 minutes.

Oyster Stew

MICROWAVE ONLY

ENERGY LEVEL:
high, 100%

SERVINGS:
4

COMPLETE RECIPE TIME:
about 13 minutes

COOKING TIME:
about 10 minutes

MICROWAVE COOKWARE:
1-quart glass or plastic container
or ring pan

If live oysters in the shell are available and cheap in your area, use them in this recipe. Otherwise, the raw shelled ones available at fish markets are superb for making stew.

ZAP TIP: It's really a chore, even if you're experienced, to open live oysters. See page 137 to open them by microwave. Use this technique only if you are going to cook the oysters, not eat them raw.

2 tablespoons butter	1 pint shucked oysters
2 tablespoons flour	Salt and fresh ground pepper
3 cups light cream or milk	4 tablespoons chopped chives

Place the flour and butter in a 4-cup glass measuring cup and microwave, uncovered, on high for 2 minutes. Add the cream and microwave on high for about 5 minutes, or until thickened. Add the oysters and microwave, uncovered, on high for about 3 minutes, or until the oysters are just cooked. Season and serve garnished with the chives.

Variation: Add bottled hot sauce to taste after the stew is cooked.

Creamy Mussel Soup

MICROWAVE ONLY

ENERGY LEVEL:
high, 100%

SERVINGS:
4

COMPLETE RECIPE TIME:
about 22 minutes

COOKING TIME:
about 15 minutes

MICROWAVE COOKWARE:
4-quart glass or plastic container
or ring pan

COVERING:
plastic wrap or the dish cover

Eastern mussels are available almost everywhere. If they aren't featured at your local fish market, ask the clerk to order some for you because they are delicious and a much better buy than clams or oysters in the shell. The ratio of meat to shell is much greater.

2 shallots, minced

2 scallions, thinly sliced

1 cup dry white wine

1 tablespoon minced parsley

2 tablespoons bottled hot
    sauce or ¼ teaspoon
    Tabasco

1 teaspoon fresh thyme

2 pounds mussels

2 cups heavy cream

4 thin slices of lemon

Place all ingredients, except the mussels, cream, and lemon in a 4-quart microwave dish. Cover securely with plastic wrap or the dish cover, and microwave on high for 4 minutes.

Scrub the mussels and remove the beards. Discard any mussels that do not close when tapped. Add the mussels to the dish, re-cover, and microwave on high for 5 to 8 minutes, or until all the mussels have opened, stirring once. Remove the mussels from their shells and return to the soup. Add the cream and microwave, uncovered, for 3 minutes. Garnish each serving with a lemon slice.

Bouillabaisse

MICROWAVE ONLY

ENERGY LEVEL:
high, 100%

SERVINGS:
4

COMPLETE RECIPE TIME:
about 30 minutes

COOKING TIME:
about 25 minutes

MICROWAVE COOKWARE:
4-quart glass or plastic container
or ring pan

COVERING:
plastic wrap or the dish cover

I probably should call this recipe a fish and shellfish stew because someone always insists that a true *bouillabaisse* can only be made with *fruits de mer,* found in Marseilles, France. Call this imitation *bouillabaisse* and enjoy!

½ stalk celery, chopped

1 medium onion, chopped

2 cloves garlic, minced

¼ cup olive oil

1 tablespoon dried *fines herbes*

½ teaspoon fennel seeds, crushed

1 14-ounce can Cajun-style or traditional stewed tomatoes

1 cup bottled clam juice

1 cup dry red wine

Pinch of saffron (optional)

Bottled hot sauce to taste (optional)

8 large shrimp

sea scallops

cherrystone clams

½ pound fish, such as snapper, cod, and so on, cut into large cubes

Place the celery, onion, garlic, and oil in a 4-quart microwave dish or ring pan and microwave on high for 3 or 4 minutes, or until soft. Add the remaining ingredients, except the fish and shellfish, cover, and microwave on high for 10 minutes. Add the clams, re-cover, and microwave for 5 minutes. Add the fish, shrimp, and scallops, re-cover, and microwave on high for about 5 minutes, or until the fish is cooked.Ladle into 4 bowls, dividing the fish and shellfish equally.

Borscht

There are as many recipes for borscht as there are cooks. Use your imagination and the vegetables and meats that are plentiful when you make this soup. The one ingredient that is essential is beets. Prepare them from scratch as directed on page 181 or opt for canned ones, which are just about as good and easier to use.

½ pound pork loin, cut into
  ½-inch cubes

½ pound kielbasa or other
  cooked sausage, cut into
  ½-inch slices

1 medium onion, chopped

1 stalk celery, chopped

1 cup chopped cabbage

1 15-ounce can beets, chopped

3 cups beef broth, canned or
  homemade (page 151)

4 dollops of sour cream or
  plain yogurt

MICROWAVE ONLY

ENERGY LEVEL:
high, 100%

SERVINGS:
4

COMPLETE RECIPE TIME:
about 30 minutes

COOKING TIME:
about 20 minutes

MICROWAVE COOKWARE:
4-quart glass or plastic container
or ring pan

COVERING:
plastic wrap or the dish cover

Place all ingredients, except the broth, in a 4-quart microwave dish or ring pan, cover with plastic wrap or the dish cover, and microwave on high for 12 to 15 minutes, or until the pork is cooked and the vegetables are soft. Add the broth and microwave 5 minutes, or until heated through. Garnish each serving with sour cream or yogurt.

Corned Beef Borscht: Substitute a 1-pound can corned beef for the pork and sausage in the above recipe and cook only 10 minutes before adding the broth. If cutting back on fat, first microwave the corned beef for 3 minutes and press out the fat with a paper towel.

Meatless Borscht

MICROWAVE ONLY

ENERGY LEVEL:
high, 100%

SERVINGS:
4

COMPLETE RECIPE TIME:
about 27 minutes

COOKING TIME:
about 22 minutes

MICROWAVE COOKWARE:
3-quart glass or plastic container
or ring pan

COVERING:
plastic wrap or the dish cover

2 cups shredded cabbage

1 large Russet potato, diced

1 15-ounce can beets, shredded

1 16-ounce can kidney beans, drained

1 14-ounce can stewed tomatoes with juice

3 cups beef broth, canned or homemade

Salt and fresh ground pepper to taste

4 dollops sour cream or plain yogurt

Place the cabbage and potato in a 3-quart microwave dish or ring pan, cover with plastic wrap or the dish cover, and microwave on high for 8 to 10 minutes, or until the potato is tender. Add the remaining ingredients, except the sour cream, and microwave 10 to 12 minutes, or until heated through. Season and serve with the sour cream.

Chicken Stew

MICROWAVE ONLY

ENERGY LEVEL:
high, 100%

SERVINGS:
4

COMPLETE RECIPE TIME:
about 35 to 45 minutes

COOKING TIME:
about 25 to 35 minutes

MICROWAVE COOKWARE:
4-quart glass or plastic container
or ring pan

COVERING:
plastic wrap or the dish cover

1 small onion, chopped

1 stalk celery, chopped

1 carrot, chopped

2 tablespoons butter or margarine

1 ear of raw corn, husked and cut into 1-inch pieces

1 3-pound frying chicken, skinned and cut into 8 pieces

1 tablespoon poultry seasoning

4 cups Chicken Stock (page 150)

Place the onion, celery, carrot, and butter in a 4-quart microwave dish or ring pan, cover with plastic wrap or the dish cover, and microwave 3 to 4 minutes, or until the vegetables are soft. Add the remaining ingredients, except the stock, re-cover, and microwave on high for 20 minutes, or until the chicken is cooked or it reaches an internal temperature of 170 degrees. Add the stock and microwave for 10 minutes. Or heat the stock on your stove top and add to the chicken. Serve.

Creamed Chicken Stew: Combine 4 tablespoons flour with the onion, celery, carrot, and butter in the above recipe. Use 2 cups milk and 2 cups chicken stock as the liquid.

Tomato and Red Bell Pepper Soup

If fresh pimientos are in season use them in this recipe instead of the red peppers.

2 red bell peppers, cored and diced

1 medium yellow onion, chopped

1 stalk celery, chopped

4 tablespoons olive oil

1 14-ounce can Italian-style stewed tomatoes

2 tablespoons paprika

2 cups Chicken Stock (page 150)

Place the peppers, onion, celery, and oil in a 3-quart microwave dish or ring pan, cover with plastic wrap or the dish cover, and microwave on high for 10 minutes, or until the vegetables are soft. Add the remaining ingredients and microwave 10 minutes. For a thicker soup, you may want to process all or half of the soup before serving.

MICROWAVE ONLY

ENERGY LEVEL:
high, 100%

SERVINGS:
4

COMPLETE RECIPE TIME:
about 25 minutes

COOKING TIME:
about 20 minutes

MICROWAVE COOKWARE:
3-quart glass or plastic container or ring pan

ACCESSORY EQUIPMENT:
food processor (optional)

COVERING:
plastic wrap or the dish cover

Cheesy Potato and Popcorn Soup

MICROWAVE ONLY

ENERGY LEVEL:
high, 100%

SERVINGS:
4

COMPLETE RECIPE TIME:
about 20 minutes

COOKING TIME:
about 13 minutes

MICROWAVE COOKWARE:
3-quart glass or plastic container
or ring pan

COVERING:
plastic wrap or the dish cover

Here's an interesting soup recipe I picked up while traveling in Minnesota.

1 large Russet Potato, washed and diced (peeled optional)	1 14-ounce can cheese soup
1 14-ounce can chicken broth	4 cups popped popcorn

Place the potato and ½ cup of the broth in a 2-quart microwave dish or ring pan. Cover with plastic wrap or the dish cover and microwave on high for about 8 minutes, or until the potato is tender. Add the remaining broth and the cheese soup and stir until smooth. Microwave on high 5 minutes and pour into 4 bowls. Use the popcorn as you would croutons.

Three Pea Soup

MICROWAVE ONLY

ENERGY LEVEL:
high, 100%

SERVINGS:
4

COMPLETE RECIPE TIME:
about 20 minutes

COOKING TIME:
about 15 minutes

MICROWAVE COOKWARE:
2-quart glass or plastic container
or ring pan

COVERING:
plastic wrap or the dish cover

1 14-ounce can pea soup	1 cup raw shelled peas, when available
1 10-ounce package frozen peas	
1 cup canned chicken broth	4 dollops of sour cream or plain yogurt
1 tablespoon curry powder or ½ teaspoon Tabasco (optional)	

Mix all ingredients, except the raw peas and sour cream, in a 2-quart microwave dish. Cover with plastic wrap or the dish cover, and microwave on high about 15 minutes, or until the frozen peas are hot. Pour equal amounts into 4 bowls and garnish with the raw peas and sour cream.

Scotch Broth

Here is a hearty soup best served during cold weather after outdoor activity. You'll probably want to take a nap after eating it. Because the soup takes a while to cook you can make it as a one-dish, one-step meal. You can brown the meat on the stove top before adding it to the soup but the difference in taste is almost negligible.

½ cup pearl barley

1 pound lamb stew meat, trimmed of fat

2 carrots, cut into 1-inch pieces

1 medium onion, chopped

1 stalk celery, chopped

4 cups beef broth, canned or homemade

1 ounce Scotch whisky (optional)

Salt and fresh ground pepper

Place all ingredients in a 3-quart microwave dish or ring pan, cover with plastic wrap or the dish cover, and microwave on high for 10 minutes and medium, 50%, for 20 to 25 minutes, or until the barley is soft.

MICROWAVE ONLY

ENERGY LEVEL:
high, 100%, medium, 50%

SERVINGS:
4

COMPLETE RECIPE TIME:
about 40 minutes

COOKING TIME:
about 35 minutes

MICROWAVE COOKWARE:
3-quart glass or plastic container or ring pan

COVERING:
plastic wrap or the dish cover

Dumplings for Soup

MICROWAVE ONLY

ENERGY LEVEL:
high, 100%, medium-high, 80%

YIELD:
16 cubes

COMPLETE RECIPE TIME:
about 40 minutes

COOKING TIME:
about 28 minutes, including the
preparation of the mashed
potatoes

MICROWAVE COOKWARE:
large mixing bowl and a glass or
plastic bread loaf pan

ACCESSORY EQUIPMENT:
potato masher or ricer

COVERING:
plastic wrap

You need rapidly boiling water to cook dumplings and since water doesn't boil well in a microwave oven I don't advise making dumplings by microwave. However, you can make a dumpling loaf in your microwave, then cut the loaf into cubes. This is a nice addition to any soup.

POTATO DUMPLING LOAF

3 cups mashed potatoes made from 4 medium potatoes, microwaved about 15 to 20 minutes and forced through a ricer; or use instant mashed potatoes

1 cup bread crumbs

2 tablespoons butter or margarine

½ cup flour

4 eggs or egg substitute equivalent

1 cup sauerkraut, rinsed and chopped (optional)

1 tablespoon fennel seeds, crushed

4 tablespoons chopped chives

Salt and fresh ground pepper

Mix all ingredients and place in a 8 ½- × 3 ½- × 2 ½-inch glass loaf pan. Microwave, covered with plastic wrap, on medium-high, 80% power, for 6 to 8 minutes, or until the loaf has set. Cool and slice into 4 equal pieces. Cut the pieces into quarters. Add to soup or stew near the end of its cooking time so the pieces heat through but don't break up.

Combination Soups

I'm including these soups in this chapter because we all should eat more vegetables and they are so easy to cook by microwave I like to suggest using them whenever convenient. These soups are just an embellishment of canned, concentrated ones, which are generally quite good. The combinations are simple to make in a hurry and result in a soup that is a step above the canned variety.

I suggest a few here and hope that you will create your own using your imagination and taste.

Asparagus-Asparagus Soup

1 pound raw asparagus, tough ends removed and spears cut into 1-inch pieces

1 10-ounce can cream of asparagus soup

1½ soup cans milk or water

Place the asparagus in a 2-quart microwave dish, cover with plastic wrap or the dish cover, and microwave on high for 5 minutes. Add the soup and milk or water, stir to blend, and microwave on high for 3 to 5 minutes, or until heated through.

Asparagus-Rice Soup: Add 1 cup cooked rice—white, brown, or wild—to the above recipe with the canned soup.

Celery-Celery Soup

3 stalks celery, cut into ½-inch pieces

1 10-ounce can cream of celery soup

1½ soup cans water or milk

¼ teaspoon Tabasco (optional)

Place the celery in a 2-quart microwave dish, cover with plastic wrap or the dish cover, and microwave on high for 5 minutes, or until the celery is soft. Add the soup, water or milk, and Tabasco if using; stir to blend, and microwave 3 to 5 minutes, or until heated through.

Mushroom-Mushroom Soup

½ pound raw mushrooms, sliced

3 tablespoons butter or margarine

1 10-ounce can cream of mushroom soup

1½ soup cans water or milk

Place the mushrooms and butter in a 2-quart microwave dish and microwave, uncovered, for 5 minutes. Add the soup and water and stir to blend. Cover and microwave on high for 5 minutes.

Tomato-Tomato Soup

1 14-ounce can tomato wedges

1 10-ounce can tomato soup

1 soup can water

1 tablespoon dried dillweed or 1 tablespoon curry powder or 1 tablespoon bottled hot sauce, not Tabasco

Place all ingredients in a 2-quart microwave dish, cover with plastic wrap or the dish cover, and microwave on high for 6 to 8 minutes, or until heated through.

Vegetables

Vegetables cooked by microwave are bright in color, tasty, and nutritious. They can be cooked al dente or soft and mushy—any way you like them. There are many advantages to cooking them by microwave. You don't need much water; you can cook and serve them in the same container; vegetables cook in a fraction of the time needed for conventional cooking; you don't have to watch and tend them as you do when steaming or boiling; and you use less energy than with conventional cooking. Generally, just wash the vegetables and cook them with the residual water left on for about 5 to 7 minutes per pound for an al dente texture. Always cover them securely with the dish cover or plastic wrap or they can dry out and become tough.

Try my recipes or convert your favorite conventional ones. Learn to cook with your microwave using vegetables, which are usually inexpensive, so you won't have to worry about blowing a lot of money if the result doesn't turn out right. The best container for cooking vegetables is the ring pan. However, you can cook them in serving dishes and top them with Béchamel or Mornay sauce (page 287); place under the broiler for a couple of minutes until the top browns and you have a beautiful vegetable au gratin.

ZAP TIP: Freeze the water that remains from cooking vegetables in a tall plastic container. Continue adding to it until you have enough to make Vegetable Stock (page 152). It'll be loaded with vitamins and minerals.

Artichokes

Can you imagine how hungry the first person to eat an artichoke must have been? To pick them you have to avoid the spikes on the leaves and if you eat them raw they are so bitter you're left with a permanent pucker. Then if you succeed in cooking them, there is a thistle inside that could choke you to death. Anyway, they're delicious and fun to eat, which can be a challenge if you're not familiar with the technique. The edible portions are located in the stem and the heart and the base of the leaves where they are attached to the heart. To eat them, break off a leaf, place the stem end between your teeth, and pull it through your clenched teeth to strip off the little bit of meat on the bottom. Usually you dip the end into melted butter or mayonnaise before eating it. The inner leaves can be eaten totally. When all of the leaves have been removed from the heart, remove the choke and cut the heart into pieces for everyone to enjoy.

The advantages of cooking artichokes by microwave is that you don't waste all the time and energy bringing a big pot of water to a boil and the chokes don't end up soggy.

4 medium artichokes	**4 tablespoons olive oil or Italian-style salad dressing**

Cut off the stem and 1 inch of the top. Snip off the remaining spikes with a scissors. Spread the leaves and hold them under the faucet for a few seconds to wash out any dirt or insects within. Leave the water from washing in the artichoke and quickly invert them into a large ring pan or other large cooking container so the stem end is up. This way the thick meaty end is exposed to more microwave energy and the leaves are in the water at the bottom of the pot. Otherwise the leaves tend to dry and shrivel up. Pour oil over each choke and cover securely with the dish cover or plastic wrap. Microwave on high for about 5 to 7 minutes per artichoke. Poke the ends with a knife or toothpick to determine if they're done. Serve with mayonnaise, melted butter, Hollandaise sauce, blue cheese dressing, or other salad dressing.

**1 pound whole trimmed
    artichokes**

Leave the stem on and just cut off the tip. Cut away all of the tough part of the leaves revealing the choke. Cut off the choke and place the trimmed artichokes in a 2-quart glass or plastic casserole. Add ½ cup water, cover with plastic wrap or the dish cover, and microwave on high for about 7 to 10 minutes.

**1 pound whole trimmed baby
    artichokes**

When you find these little artichokes at the market, buy them. They are easier to fix than the big ones and just as good. Just pull off any dried outer leaves and put them in a 2-quart glass or plastic casserole with ½ cup water or Italian-style salad dressing. Cover with plastic wrap or the dish cover and micro-wave on high about 7 minutes per pound or until tender.

Asparagus

1 pound asparagus spears

Break off the tough end and wash. Turn half of the spears around so the tougher bases are mixed with the tender tips. Place in a 1-quart cooking container and cover securely with the dish cover or plastic wrap. Microwave on high for 5 to 7 minutes.

1 pound asparagus spears

Cut the spears into 1-inch pieces and cook as above. Serve with melted butter and lemon juice or top with a dollop of hollandaise or tartar sauce or Asian sauce.

Asian Sauce

2 scallions, chopped

2 tablespoons olive oil

1 teaspoon sesame oil with chili

1 tablespoon sesame seeds

1 tablespoon lemon juice

Mix all ingredients and serve over vegetables.

Beans

This category includes green beans, yellow wax, Italian wide beans, haricots verts, and Chinese long beans.

1 pound trimmed beans

The best way to cook beans by microwave is to place trimmed beans in a plastic cooking bag with ½ cup water. Close the bag as close to the beans as possible and microwave on high for about 7 minutes. Or place the beans in a pot and add water to cover. Cover with plastic wrap and microwave on high for about 10 to 12 minutes, or until the beans are tender.

Twice-Cooked Beans

After the beans are cooked, heat 2 tablespoons olive oil and 2 cloves garlic, smashed, in a frying pan until the garlic starts to brown. Discard the garlic, add the beans, and fry them for 1 to 2 minutes.

Beans in Stewed Tomatoes

1 pound green beans, trimmed

1 14½-ounce can stewed
    tomatoes

½ cup imitation bacon bits

Place the beans and tomatoes with their juice in a 1-quart glass or plastic casserole, cover with plastic wrap or the dish cover, and microwave on high for 10 to 12 minutes, or until the beans are tender. Drain off the excess juice and top with the bacon bits.

Green Beans Orientale

1 pound green beans, trimmed
    and cut into 2-inch pieces

8 small mushrooms, sliced

2 scallions, sliced

1 tablespoon soy sauce

1 tablespoon peanut oil

1 tablespoon cornstarch

¼ cup peanuts

3 tablespoons fresh chopped
    coriander (cilantro)

Place the beans, mushrooms, and scallions in a 1-quart microwave dish, cover with plastic wrap or the dish cover, and microwave on high for 8 to 10 minutes. Mix the soy sauce, oil, and cornstarch. Add to the cooked beans, stir in the peanuts, and microwave on high 40 to 60 seconds, or until the sauce is thickened. Garnish with the coriander to serve.

Raw Shelled Beans

These beans also have a tendency to dry out when cooked by microwave, so you must cover them with water and cook as long as you would cook them conventionally. The advantage of cooking by microwave is that the oven turns off automatically and you don't have to be concerned aobut removing the pot from the burner.

1 pound beans

Place the beans in a microwave pot, cover with water, and cover the pot. Microwave on high for 15 to 25 minutes, or until tender. Check often after 15 minutes to determine when the beans are done.

Beets

1 pound beets

Beets cook very well by microwave. Cut off leaves, wash, and place the beets in a plastic ring pan or other microwave pot and add ½ cup water. Cover the dish and microwave on high for about 3 to 5 minutes per beet, depending upon the size. Poke the beets with a knife to determine when done. Let cool and slip off the outer skin and slice or dice for serving.

Tarragon Beets

4 raw beets, the size of a
    tennis ball

½ cup water

3 tablespoons tarragon vinegar

1 tablespoon fresh tarragon
    leaves

2 small sweet gherkins,
    chopped

3 tablespoons margarine,
    melted

Trim the beets and place in a 2-quart microwave dish with ½ cup water. Cover with plastic wrap or the dish cover and microwave on high for 15 to 20 minutes, or until tender. Drain off the water, slip off the skins, and dice. Stir in remaining ingredients and microwave 1 more minute.

Beets in Yogurt Sauce

4 raw beets, each the size of a
    tennis ball

1 tablespoon crushed garlic

1 cup plain yogurt

1 tablespoon lemon juice

1 tablespoon mint jelly

Trim the beets and place in a 2-quart microwave dish. Cover with plastic wrap or the dish cover and microwave on high for 15 to 20 minutes, or until tender. Slip off skins and shred or chop. Stir in remaining ingredients and microwave for 1 minute.

Harvard Beets

1 tablespoon cornstarch

½ cup white vinegar

½ cup sugar

½ teaspoon ground allspice

1 pound cooked beets, sliced

Make a paste with the cornstarch and a little of the vinegar and mix with the sugar, allspice, and remaining vinegar. Place the beets in a medium mixing bowl and stir in the vinegar mixture. Microwave on high for 3 to 5 minutes, stirring a couple times during the cooking, until the sauce thickens and coats the beets.

Bok Choy

This is a wonderful vegetable that I hope you cook often. Serve it with Asian Sauce (page 178).

1 pound bok choy

Pull apart, wash, and cut the leaves from the stem. Chop leaves into 1-inch squares. Cut the stem into 1-inch pieces. Place stem and leaves in a 1-quart glass or plastic dish and cover with plastic wrap or the dish cover. Microwave on high for about 7 minutes, or until tender.

Broccoli

1 pound broccoli

Cut off flowerets with 2 inches of stem and break flowerets apart. Peel the remaining stalk and cut into ½-inch slices. Wash and place in a 2-quart microwave pot. Cover with plastic wrap or the dish cover and microwave on high for 5 to 7 minutes.

Broccoli-Cauliflower Mold

This is an impressive way to serve both these vegetables, particularly for a formal dinner party. Pour Hollandaise Sauce (page 289) or cheese sauce over the mold before serving.

1 large head cauliflower   **2 large bunches broccoli**

Wash and cut the flowerets of both vegetables from their stems, retaining about 2 inches of stem. Leave about a 3-inch diameter of the crown of the cauliflower. Place the crown piece in the bottom of a 2-quart glass batter bowl and surround it with broccoli flowerets with the stem ends toward the center. Top the broccoli with a ring of cauliflower and continue making layers until all the vegetables are used. Cover with plastic wrap and microwave on high for about 12 minutes, or until the vegetables are tender. (Insert a thin blade knife into the centermost vegetables to determine doneness.) Remove plastic wrap and place a saucer over the vegetables. Press down to form the mold. Hold the saucer firmly on the vegetables and pour off the water. Remove the saucer and place a serving platter over the mold. Invert the molded vegetables onto the platter. Remove the batter bowl. Isn't it beautiful?

Note: If you don't have a batter bowl for the mold you can use a large clean clay flowerpot or similar shaped glass or ceramic bowl.

Broccoli-Cauliflower Wreath

This is a timely and very nice dish to serve around the Christmas holidays because of its shape and colors. To serve with Hollandaise Sauce, see page 289.

1 large head cauliflower

2 large bunches broccoli

1 large red bell pepper, cored and cut into star shapes

Wash and cut the flowerets from the cauliflower and broccoli, leaving about 2 inches of stem. In a 2-quart microwave ring pan make a ring of cauliflowerets around the bottom of the pan. Place broccoli flowerets on each side of the cauliflower with the stems overlapping the cauliflower. Make a ring of cauliflower over the broccoli with the stems toward the center. Continue making alternate rings until all of the vegetables are used. Cover with plastic wrap and microwave on high for about 12 minutes, or until the vegetables are tender. Insert a thin blade knife in the centermost vegetables to determine doneness. With the plastic wrap in place, press down on the vegetables with a folded dish towel to form the mold. Hold the vegetables in place and pour off the water. Remove the plastic wrap and place a serving platter over the ring pan. Invert the mold onto the platter and remove the ring pan. Pour hollandaise or a cheese sauce over the top and space the pepper stars on it.

Brussels Sprouts

1 pound brussels sprouts

Cut off the stem nub and pull off the outer leaves on each sprout. Wash and place in a 1-quart microwave casserole. Cover with plastic wrap or the dish cover and microwave on high for about 7 minutes, or until tender.

Burning Brussels Sprouts

Prepare the sprouts as directed above and place them in a 1-quart Mason jar or other tall narrow container. Add ¾ cup white vinegar and ¼ cup bottled hot sauce and water to cover. Cover with plastic wrap and microwave on high for 7 minutes. Let cool and store in the jar. Serve as appetizers or add to Martinis.

Southern-Style Brussels Sprouts

Prepare the sprouts as directed above and add to them ½ medium onion, chopped, 1 7-ounce can stewed tomatoes, 1 slice bacon. Place in a 2-quart casserole, cover with plastic wrap or the dish cover, and microwave on high for about 10 minutes, or until the sprouts are tender.

Cabbage

1 pound cabbage

Remove the outer leaves and cut the head into quarters. Remove and discard the core. Quarter or shred cabbage. Wash and place in a 2-quart microwave pot, cover with plastic wrap or the dish cover, and microwave on high for 8 to 10 minutes, or until tender. Cabbage stays crunchy when cooked this way. If you like it soft, add 1 cup water before microwaving.

Colcannon (Cabbage and Potatoes)

Once I was scheduled for a radio interview in San Francisco that happened to fall on St. Patrick's Day. The hostess asked me to offer some Irish recipes to commemorate the day. I didn't want to do the standard corned beef and cabbage, which incidentally is a purely American dish, because it doesn't cook all that well by microwave. I delved into my files for some traditional Irish dishes and found colcannon. There are many variations on it and all are as delightful as the Irish spirit. You'll like this one or me name is not Donovan. I've doubled the recipe because it's so good the next day.

2 large Russet potatoes
  (peeled optional)

1 medium cabbage, chopped

½ cup water

Milk

¼ pound margarine

8 scallions, thinly sliced

Fresh ground pepper

Place the potatoes, cabbage, and water in a 3-quart microwave dish, cover with plastic wrap or the dish cover, and microwave on high for 15 to 20 minutes, or until the potatoes are tender. Mash the potatoes with the water from cooking and add as much milk and margarine as is needed to render the mixture smooth but not thick. Stir back into the cabbage with the rest of the margarine and the scallions. Add pepper to taste and serve.

Variations: Use kale instead of cabbage. Add a couple of parsnips or a small rutabaga. Dice the potatoes instead of mashing them. Use your imagination. After all, it's an Irish dish.

Carrots

1 pound carrots

Carrots, like edible pod beans, don't cook by microwave any better than they do on the top of the stove. They tend to shrivel and dry out unless you cover them with water and whenever you have a lot of water the microwave loses its efficiency. The only advantage when you cook by microwave is that you don't have to watch the pot and remove it from the heat when the cooking is done.

Peel the carrots and slice into 1-inch pieces or cut into julienne strips. Place in a 1-quart microwave pot, barely cover with water, cover with plastic wrap or the dish cover, and microwave on high 8 to 10 minutes, or until tender.

Carrots in Sherbet

1 pound carrots, peeled and
cut into ½-inch slices

½ pint orange or lemon
sherbet (yes, frozen
sherbet)

Place the carrots and sherbet in a 1-quart casserole, cover with plastic wrap or the dish cover, and microwave on high for about 10 minutes, stirring once or twice, or until the carrots are tender.

Glazed Carrots

After microwaving carrots, heat a frying pan and add 2 tablespoons butter or margarine and 2 tablespoons brown sugar. Heat until the mixture starts to bubble, add the carrots, and heat until they are coated with the glaze, about 2 minutes.

Variations: Chutney Carrots: Use prepared chutney instead of sugar—very interesting and good.

Parsleyed Carrots: Add butter and chopped parsley to cooked carrots.

Cauliflower

**1 whole medium head
cauliflower**

Trim off the outer leaves and cut out the core. Wash and place whole head in a 2-quart casserole or other appropriate dish, cover with plastic wrap or the dish cover, and microwave on high for about 7 minutes, or until tender.

Or break head into flowerets. Wash and place in a microwave ring pan or other microwave pot, cover with plastic wrap or the dish cover, and microwave on high for 5 to 7 minutes, or until tender.

Cauliflower with Cheddar Cheese Sauce

**1 whole cauliflower cooked as
directed above**

**1 cup shredded Cheddar
cheese**

¼ cup minced onion

¼ cup Dijon mustard

¼ cup mayonnaise

Mix together the sauce ingredients and spread over the top of the cooked whole cauliflower as soon as you remove it from the microwave. The heat of the cauliflower will usually melt the sauce. If not, return it to the oven for 1 to 2 minutes.

Curried Cauliflower

1 cauliflower, broken into
    flowerets and cooked as
    directed on page 190

1 medium onion, chopped

2 tablespoons curry powder

¼ teaspoon cloves

1 7-ounce can stewed
    tomatoes

1 cup plain yogurt

Place the onion and spices in a large measuring cup and microwave on high for 3 minutes. Sir in the remaining ingredients and add to the cooked cauliflower. Stir to coat with the sauce and microwave 1 minute on high to heat through.

Cauliflower Mold

1 whole cauliflower, cooked as
    directed on page 190

Mornay Sauce (page 287) made
    with ½ cup grated
    Parmesan cheese

Place the cauliflower in a shallow 1-quart ceramic or glass casserole dish and cover with the sauce. Run under the broiler for about 1 minute, or until the sauce starts to brown.

Celery

1 pound celery

I prefer celery raw rather than cooked but if you want to cook it do so.

Cut celery into 1-inch slices, wash and place in a 1-quart microwave pot, cover with plastic wrap or the dish cover, and microwave on high for about 7 minutes, or until tender.

Celery Root

1 pound celery root

Cut off the top and peel away the tough outer skin. Dice or cut into ¼-inch slices. Wash and place in 1-quart microwave dish with ½ cup water. Cover with plastic wrap or the dish cover and microwave on high for about 7 minutes, or until tender. Serve with butter or margarine.

Chayote (Mirliton)

1 pound chayote

Use the whole squash, including the seed. Wash and cut in half and slice or dice into ½-inch cubes. Place in a 1-quart casserole and add ½ cup water. Cover with plastic wrap or the dish cover and microwave on high for about 7 minutes, or until tender. Drain off the water and add salt and pepper and butter or margarine.

Stuffed Chayotes

2 chayotes, cut in half

1 pound bulk pork sausage

½ package (3-ounce) prepared stuffing mix

Place the chayotes in a 1-quart microwave dish, cover with plastic wrap or the dish cover, and microwave on high for 7 minutes, or until tender. Prepare the stuffing as directed on the package but without any butter or oil. Mix with the sausage and pack over the chayotes. Re-cover and microwave on high for 12 minutes, or to an internal temperature of 160 degrees.

Corn on the Cob

4 ears corn

The easiest way to microwave corn on the cob is to place the ears, still in the husks, in the microwave and cook on high for 2 to 3 minutes per ear. Peel away the husks and eat. Or, remove the husks, wash the ears, and wrap them in wax paper or other nonstick cooking paper (you can butter and salt and pepper them before you wrap them) and microwave on high 2 to 3 minutes per ear. Don't use plastic wrap because it sticks together and is difficult to remove, especially from a hot cob. Or, remove the husks, wash the ears and place in a microwave ring pan or other microwave pot, add ½ cup water, cover with plastic wrap or the dish cover, and microwave on high for 2 to 3 minutes per ear. Or use a plastic roasting bag and after cooking drain off the water. Add butter to the corn in the bag. Massage the butter over the corn and serve.

ZAP TIP: Stick the little metal pronged holders into the ends of the cobs before microwaving. This is much easier to do than when the cobs are hot from cooking.

Cheesy Corn on the Cob: After microwaving the cobs, lay a slice of your favorite cheese over the cob and let it melt. You may have to pop the corn back into your microwave for 1 minute or so if the cheese doesn't melt thoroughly.

Cucumbers

1 pound cucumbers

This is another vegetable I prefer raw, but they do take on brilliant color when microwaved. Cut off the ends and slice or dice the cucumbers. Wash and place in a 1-quart microwave pot, cover with plastic wrap or the dish cover, and microwave on high for just 4 minutes.

Cucumbers with Soy Sauce and Sesame Oil: Stir 2 tablespoons soy sauce and 1 teaspoon sesame oil into the cucumbers before cooking as directed above.

Eggplant

1 pound eggplant

Cut off the stem end and cut into slices or cubes. Place in a 2-quart microwave pot, cover with plastic wrap or the dish cover, and microwave on high about 7 minutes, or until soft.

Eggplant with Artichokes

1 medium unpeeled eggplant,
  cut into cubes

1 1-ounce jar marinated
  artichokes, including oil

1 medium onion, chopped

Place everything in a 2-quart microwave dish, cover with plastic wrap or the dish cover, and microwave on high for about 7 minutes, or until the eggplant is soft. Stir and serve with salt and pepper.

Eggplant with Okra and Tomatoes

½ pound raw okra, trimmed
  and sliced into ½-inch
  pieces

½ medium unpeeled eggplant,
  cut into cubes

1 14½-ounce can stewed
  tomatoes, drained

3 tablespoons olive oil

Place okra in a 2-quart microwave dish, cover with plastic wrap or the dish cover, and microwave on high for 5 minutes. Add the remaining ingredients, re-cover, and microwave on high for 10 minutes. Stir and serve.

Eggplant with Butter and Onions

Using butter instead of oil gives this recipe a really nice flavor.

1 medium unpeeled eggplant,
   cubed

1 medium onion, cut into
   1-inch pieces

4 tablespoons butter or
   margarine

Place all ingredients in a 2-quart microwave dish, cover with plastic wrap or the dish cover, and microwave on high for about 10 minutes.

Eggplant with Sun-Dried Tomatoes and Cheese

1 medium unpeeled eggplant,
   cubed

8 dried tomato slices in oil

½ cup grated Romano cheese

Place the eggplant and tomatoes in a 2-quart microwave dish, cover with plastic wrap or the dish cover, and microwave on high for about 7 minutes, or until the eggplant is soft. Stir in the cheese and serve.

Endive

1 pound endive

Cut off the stem end and remove the outer leaves. Cook whole, or separate the leaves. Wash and place in a 1-quart microwave pot, cover with plastic wrap or the dish cover, and microwave on high for 5 to 7 minutes, or until tender. Add melted butter and lemon juice when serving.

Endive in Cheese Sauce with Walnuts

Microwave 3 ounces cream cheese and ½ cup milk for 1 to 2 minutes on high and stir to blend. Pour over cooked endive and sprinkle chopped walnuts over the top to serve.

Endive with Baked Ham

This is an excellent side dish that uses leftover baked ham. Add 1 cup diced baked ham to raw endive and cook as directed above. Serve with the juices from cooking.

Endive with Dried Tomatoes

Chop 8 dried tomato halves or use 1 cup dried tomato pieces in oil and add to chopped raw endive. Cover with plastic wrap or the dish cover and microwave on high 5 to 7 minutes.

Fennel

This is another vegetable I wish people would serve more often. It's a little unusual and provides a nice change from the more common popular vegetables. Try it raw in salads and as an addition to relish trays.

1 pound fennel	**2 tablespoons butter or olive oil**

Cut off the base and break away the outer leaves and fronds. Cut into quarters or julienne strips or dice. Place in a shallow 1-quart casserole, cover with plastic wrap or the dish cover, and microwave on high for 7 to 8 minutes, or until the fennel is tender. Drain off the juices and add the butter or oil.

Fennel with Crumb Crust

1 fennel bulb, trimmed and cut into julienne strips

1 medium onion, chopped

2 garlic cloves, chopped

2 teaspoons olive oil

Salt and fresh ground pepper to taste

1 8-ounce can stewed tomatoes, drained and chopped

Topping

½ cup bread crumbs

¼ cup grated Parmesan cheese

1 teaspoon grated lemon peel

1 clove garlic, minced

Place all ingredients, except the tomatoes and topping ingredients, in a shallow 1-quart glass or ceramic casserole, cover with plastic wrap or the dish cover, and microwave on high for 8 to 10 minutes, or until the fennel is soft. Add the tomatoes, re-cover, and microwave 2 minutes. Mix the topping ingredients together, spread over the top, and place under your broiler for about 2 minutes, or until browned.

Garlic

Roasting garlic in a conventional oven takes about 45 minutes to 1 hour. In your microwave oven it only takes a few minutes. I like the flavor of oven-roasted garlic more but my wife prefers the microwaved variety. Compare for yourself.

Break heads of garlic into individual cloves and soak in water for 2 minutes. Remove from water and wrap 8 to 10 cloves in plastic wrap. Microwave on high about 10 seconds per clove, or until soft. Peel or squeeze the garlic from its skin and spread on bread or mash with a little olive oil and use as a spread.

Greens

Beet greens, collard greens, dandelion greens, kale, mustard greens, and turnip greens—these are all a little tougher than spinach, so they require the addition of water and longer cooking. For example, for my taste, 1 pound collard greens need about 1 ½ cups water and must cook for about 20 minutes to become tender. Kale cooks in about 10 minutes, with only ½ cup water. The remaining greens above cook in about 7 minutes, each with ½ cup water. So, you have to discover what works best for you. Generally, always add at least ½ cup water and cook, covered, on high 7 minutes, then test.

Kohlrabi

1 pound kohlrabi

Cut off the leaves and stem and peel off the outside skin. Dice or slice and place in a 1-quart casserole with ½ cup water. Cover with plastic wrap or the dish cover and microwave on high for 7 to 10 minutes, or until tender. Drain off the juices and add butter or margarine and salt and pepper to taste.

Leeks

1 pound leeks

Cut off the green tops and about 1 inch into the whites. Cut off the root ends. Slice halfway into the leek lengthwise, spread the leaves apart, and wash well under running water. Cook whole or cut into rings. Place leeks in a 1-quart shallow casserole, cover with plastic wrap or the dish cover, and microwave on high for about 7 minutes, or until tender. Serve with melted butter or margarine and lemon juice. Also, serve with the crumb topping for fennel (page 200).

Mushrooms

1 pound mushrooms

2 to 4 tablespoons butter or margarine

Several tablespoons Worcestershire sauce

Wipe mushrooms clean and cut off ends of stems. Slice or quarter the mushrooms. Place in a 2-quart casserole and microwave on high, uncovered, so the moisture can escape, for 5 minutes. Press them, using a can or jar, and drain off the juices. Add the butter or margarine and continue cooking for about 5 more minutes. Or, put the mushrooms in a dish towel and twist them into a ball. Place on a plate and microwave on high for 5 minutes. Twist the towel to remove the juices and place the mushrooms in a 1-quart casserole with the butter or margarine. Cook 5 minutes more, uncovered. Add Worcestershire sauce if desired.

Mushroom Medley

1 pound mixed whole mushrooms, such as white button, Shiitake, brown, and so on; include some reconstituted dried varieties also. (If you can get enokis, add them raw after the dish has been cooked.)

4 tablespoons butter, margarine, or oil

1 small onion, minced

2 tablespoons minced garlic

2 teaspoons minced parsley

Place all ingredients in a 2-quart microwave dish and micro-wave on high, uncovered, for 7 to 10 minutes. Stir once while cooking.

Mushrooms, Dried Fruit, and Rice

A nice side dish that requires little effort to make.

½ pound raw mushrooms, sliced

2 ounces mixed dried fruit, chopped

½ cup long-grain rice

1¼ cups water or broth

Place all ingredients in a 2-quart microwave dish, cover with plastic wrap or the dish cover, and microwave on high for 3 minutes and medium, 50%, for 10 to 15 minutes, or until the rice is tender.

Paprika Mushrooms

1 pound mushrooms, sliced

2 scallions, sliced

1 tablespoon paprika

1 tablespoon flour

½ cup plain yogurt

Place all ingredients, except the yogurt, in a 2-quart microwave dish and microwave, uncovered, on high for 7 to 10 minutes, stirring once. Add yogurt and microwave 1 minute more.

Okra

1 pound okra

I don't know of many people who like okra plain unless it's fried in batter. Since you can't fry worth a diddle in your microwave, always cook okra in soups or gumbo or with other vegetables, as directed in the following recipes.

Okra and Corn

½ pound raw okra, ends removed

1 14-ounce can creamed corn

½ teaspoon cayenne pepper

Place the okra in a 1-quart microwave dish, cover with plastic wrap or the dish cover, and microwave on high for 5 minutes. Add the corn and pepper, stir, and microwave on high, uncovered, 5 minutes.

Okra and Tomatoes

If you can find diced Rotel tomatoes, use them. They add a nice zing to the recipe.

½ **pound raw okra**

1 **14½-ounce can stewed tomatoes, drained, or 1 10-ounce can stewed tomatoes flavored with chile peppers**

Trim the ends off the okra and slice into 1-inch pieces. Place pieces in a shallow 1-quart casserole and add the stewed tomatoes. Microwave on high, uncovered, so the moisture can escape for 10 to 12 minutes, or until the okra is soft.

Onions

I usually use onions for flavoring stews, casseroles, pot roasts, braised meats, soups, and so on. I always loved them raw in salads, salsas, and soups, but I never thought they'd be as delicious as they are when microwaved. My wife loves to serve creamed onions at Thanksgiving, so one year I decided to prepare them with raw, pearl onions. They cooked beautifully and tasted great, but after peeling all of those little onions I vowed to use canned from then on.

Onions with Butter and Brown Sugar

2 medium yellow onions,
   peeled and cut in half

4 tablespoons margarine or
   butter

4 tablespoons brown sugar,
   chutney, or maple syrup

Place the onions in a shallow 1-quart microwave dish and place equal amounts of margarine and sugar on top of each. Cover with plastic wrap or the dish cover and microwave on high for about 8 minutes, or until the onions are soft.

Onions Microwaved in Their Skins

4 medium yellow onions,
   unskinned but washed and
   ¼ of stem end on each
   cut off

Butter, margarine, or oil

Salt and fresh ground pepper

Place the onions in a 1-quart microwave dish, cover with plastic wrap or the dish cover, and microwave on high for about 2 to 3 minutes per onion, or until soft. Squeeze the onions out of their skins and add the butter and salt and pepper.

Braised Scallions

Take 2 bunches (16 onions), about 4 each per serving, and cut off the root ends and about half of the green end. Turn half of the scallions around so you integrate the white ends with the green ends. (This is done so they cook evenly.) Place in an oblong serving dish and cover with plastic wrap. Microwave on high for about 4 to 5 minutes, or until soft. Serve with salt and fresh ground pepper.

Parsnips

Parsnips are shaped like carrots and have to be microwaved the same way or they will shrivel and dry out. I like them because they are a little different and add variety to one's diet. Use also in stews and soups.

1 pound parsnips

Trim and peel the parsnips and cut into 1-inch rounds. Place in a 4-cup measuring cup or similar bowl and cover with water. Cover with plastic wrap and microwave on high for 8 to 10 minutes, or until the parsnips are soft. Serve as you would carrots.

Peas

When I was a little boy growing up in Wisconsin, I remember walking along country roads and finding clumps of pea vines that had fallen off the trucks that were taking the peas from the fields to the canning factories. We would eat those raw peas all the way to our destination and were they delicious! I still love them raw right from the pod. However, I don't think it's worth the price and effort to shuck peas for cooking. I prefer using frozen ones. I think peas become three distinctly different vegetables when they are raw compared to frozen compared to canned. You agree? Raw peas are a great snack when you're trying to lose a few pounds. It takes time and effort to eat them and they are so low in calories.

Edible-Pod Peas

1 pound peas

These peas you eat pod and all. There are two types—snow peas and sugar snap peas—and both are tasty and so easy to cook by microwave. Just trim off the stem ends and cook covered with plastic wrap or dish cover on high for 4 to 5 minutes. Don't overcook because they should be tender and crispy. Add a little oil before cooking and they take on a nice sheen.

Use edible-pod peas for dipping. They can also be filled with soft cheese and caviar and other fillings and served as appetizers.

Oriental Vegetables

⅓ pound snow peas

⅓ pound bean sprouts

⅓ pound mushrooms, sliced

1 tablespoon oil

1 tablespoon cornstarch

1 tablespoon soy sauce

In a 1-quart casserole, combine the vegetables, cover with plastic wrap, and microwave on high for 4 to 5 minutes. Drain off the water. Mix with the oil and dissolve the cornstarch in the soy sauce. Stir into the vegetables and microwave 1 to 2 minutes, or until the sauce thickens.

Peppers

There is no more beautiful sight than a platter full of multicolored peppers cooked in the microwave. The colors burst forth like an Impressionist painting. When pimientos are in season, add them to the recipe.

1 each of green, red, and yellow bell pepper, cored and sliced or diced

1 medium yellow onion, sliced

4 cloves garlic, minced

4 tablespoons olive oil

Place all ingredients, except the oil, in a 2-quart casserole. Cover with plastic wrap or the dish cover and microwave on high for 8 to 10 minutes, or until the peppers are done to your satisfaction. Stir once during the cooking. Drain off the juices and add the oil. Stir to coat with oil and serve.

Platter of Hot Peppers Add 1 seeded jalapeño pepper, minced, or 1 teaspoon crushed dried red pepper to the above recipe.

Pickled Hot Peppers Add ½ cup white vinegar and ½ cup sugar to a Platter of Hot Peppers recipe and stir into the juices.

Paprika Peppers Add 2 tablespoons Hungarian paprika and 1 large ripe tomato, diced, to the basic pepper recipe above.

Plantains

Even though plantains are a fruit, I'm including them here because they are usually served as a vegetable. Allow one plantain per serving.

1 whole plantain	**Salt and fresh ground pepper**
Butter	

Slit the skin lengthwise but leave on the fruit. Microwave on high for about 4 to 6 minutes per plantain, or until soft. Peel off the skin, cut up or mash the flesh, and serve with the butter and salt and pepper.

Cheesy Plantains

1 whole plantain per serving	**Fresh ground pepper**
4 tablespoons butter or margarine	**Grated Parmesan cheese**

Cut the ends off the plantains and cut the plantains in half. Make lengthwise slits in the skin and peel off. Slice plantains into ½-inch rounds and place in a 1-quart microwave casserole. Add the butter or margarine. Cover with plastic wrap and microwave on high for about 4 minutes per plantain, or until soft. Serve with the pepper and Parmesan cheese.

Potatoes

Probably more microwave ovens have been purchased to cook potatoes than for any other reason. And why not, when you realize that you can cook a potato between 4 and 12 minutes, depending upon the size, instead of 1 hour in a conventional oven. Add to this the fact that potatoes are one of the best and most versatile foods that you can eat. They are low in calories and high in fiber and vitamins and minerals.

I still find, however, that some people complain that the skin doesn't get crispy as it does when the potato is baked in a hot conventional oven. I say that the skin from a microwaved potato is more palatable than the dried-out woody skin of a conventionally baked one. Also some people will complain that microwaved potatoes are too moist, like a boiled potato. Here I think their prejudice is showing; I've done numerous blind taste tests and people can't tell the difference or prefer the microwave potato over the conventionally baked one. Try it yourself. Bake a potato in your hot oven and during the last 10 minutes microwave a potato. Serve both to your family, without telling which is which, and ask if they can tell the difference and which one they like the best.

Incidentally, you may have read or heard that you should poke or pierce potatoes before you microwave or, for that matter, bake them in your conventional oven. This is supposed to prevent them from exploding. I have never poked a potato and have never had one explode. Don't worry about poking your potatoes and only do it when you need a release from stress or tension.

Here are some general rules for microwaving potatoes:

1. Always try to use the finest available, usually graded #1.

2. All types of potato microwave well, but I like to use Russets, those with the thick rough skin, for baked, oven baked, French fried, mashed, and twice baked. The round red and whites and the long whites are best for potato salads and boiled potatoes.

3. Microwave on high and allow about 1 minute per ounce for a room temperature (70 degrees) potato. That amounts to 4 minutes for an average-size potato and 8 to 9 minutes for a large one; and 12 to 15 for a jumbo. When you microwave several potatoes at one time allow slightly less time per potato. For example, microwave 2 average potatoes only 7 minutes, instead of 4 minutes each. And, of course, you must figure the correct times for your oven in your house. It may be a little different from the ovens in my house. If you have an instant read thermometer, microwave the potatoes to a temperature of 200 degrees or use your temperature probe set at 200 degrees.

4. To boil potatoes, use thin-skinned red or whites. Place them in a microwave container or a plastic cooking bag and add about ½ cup water to keep them moist. Cover with the dish cover or plastic wrap and microwave on high for about 12 to 15 minutes per pound. Smaller ones cook faster.

5. With some ovens, you may have to turn the potatoes over halfway through the cooking to ensure even cooking. Also, if your oven has hot spots, use a cooking bag and the contained heat will cook them evenly and thoroughly.

6. Use a microwave muffin pan when cooking more than one large potato. It keeps multiple potatoes separated for even energy absorption, and it's easy to handle because the pan doesn't get hot.

Microwave Baked Potatoes

1 potato per serving

Microwave about 1 minute per ounce. When cooked, slit open the top and push in the ends to open a pocket in the potato. Add butter, margarine, sour cream, yogurt, chopped scallions, bacon bits, shredded cheese, canned navy beans, cooked lentils, or whatever.

If you must have a dried-out skin, microwave the potatoes until soft and place in a preheated 400 degree oven for 15 to 20 minutes. You still save half the time of a conventionally baked potato. For a drier texture, after microwaving, break up and fluff the potato pulp and microwave, uncovered, for another minute or so.

ZAP TIP: Use Worcestershire sauce and/or low-fat yogurt for a good, tasty, satisfying, low-calorie diet potato.

Stuffed Potatoes

½ potato per serving

Microwave 1 minute per ounce of potatoes and dash the potatoes in cold water to cool so they are easy to handle. Cut in half lengthwise and scoop out the flesh with a tablespoon. Leave about ⅛ on an inch of potato in the shell. Mash the potato with shredded cheese, chopped scallions or chives, watercress, bacon bits, butter, sour cream, cream cheese, or whatever, and enough milk to make the filling smooth. Stuff back into the potato skin. Microwave, uncovered, on high about 1 minute per serving, or place under your broiler for a couple minutes until the top browns.

ZAP TIP: To make a dry, crisp shell, remove the potato pulp from the skin, place the skins, open side down on a plate, and microwave, uncovered, on high for 2 to 3 minutes per skin, or until they brown and get crisp.

Mashed Potatoes

4 medium Russet potatoes,
about 1½ pounds

4 tablespoons butter or
margarine

½ cup milk or cream

Salt and pepper to taste

Place the potatoes in a 3-quart microwave container, cover with plastic wrap or the dish cover, and microwave on high, 100%, power for about 20 minutes or until they are done. Peel (optional) and mash or pass through a ricer. Stir in the butter or margarine and milk or cream. Season with salt and pepper to taste. Don't mash the potatoes with a food processor; it tends to make them sticky.

Garlic Mashed Potatoes

Place 10 cloves (5 tablespoons) minced garlic and 3 tablespoons butter or margarine in a measuring cup and microwave on high for 2 to 3 minutes, or until the garlic is soft. Mash or process and stir into Mashed Potatoes. Enough for 4 servings.

Fried Potatoes

Peel (optional) and slice 4 medium potatoes ½ inch thick and lay in a single layer on a large platter. Drizzle ½ tablespoon oil or butter or margarine on each potato. Cover with plastic wrap and microwave on high for about 1 minute per slice. After microwaving, slide the potato slices into a preheated skillet and fry on medium heat until brown and crisp on both sides. Microwave another platter of potatoes while frying the first batch. Continue until all are fried. Hold completed potatoes in a 300 degree oven until all are done.

Oven-Browned Potatoes

Peel (optional) and cut 4 medium potatoes into quarters lengthwise. Grease the bottom of a 9- × 13-inch baking pan with vegetable oil. Place the potatoes, skin side down, in the pan and microwave, uncovered, on high for about 15 minutes, or until the potatoes are barely done. Place in a preheated 400 degree oven for about 15 minutes, or until the potatoes are browned and crisp on the surface. Enough for 4 servings.

Whole Oven-Browned Potatoes

Peel 4 long white or 8 round red or white potatoes and place in an 8-inch-square Pyrex baking pan. Microwave, uncovered, on high for 8 to 10 minutes, or until the potatoes are done. Coat with vegetable oil and bake in a preheated 400 degree oven for about 15 minutes, or until the potatoes are brown and crisp. You may want to turn them over during the conventional oven bake. Enough for 4 servings.

French Fried Potatoes

Cut off the ends and sides of 4 medium Russet potatoes so they are rectangular in shape. Cut into ½-inch-square lengths and place in a 2-quart microwave casserole or ring pan. Coat with vegetable oil, cover with plastic wrap or the dish cover, and microwave on high for 12 to 15 minutes, or until the potatoes are cooked. Remove the cover and place casserole in your refrigerator overnight. This is important because the potatoes tend to dehydrate slightly, which makes for a crisper fry.

When ready to fry, heat 4 to 5 cups vegetable oil (peanut is best) in a deep straight-sided metal pot to 375 degrees, and, if using a basket, make sure you heat it with the oil. A cold basket will lower the oil temperature and the fries will absorb oil and become soggy. Fry a handful at a time until the potatoes brown and float to the top of the oil. Hold in a 300 degree oven until all are fried. Enough for 4 servings.

Scalloped Potatoes

A 2-quart microwave ring pan works best for this recipe, but you can use a glass loaf pan or an 8-inch-square glass baking pan.

**4 medium Russet potatoes,
sliced into ¼-inch rounds**

Flour

Butter or margarine

Salt and fresh ground pepper

Milk

Make a layer of potato slices on the bottom of the pan. Sprinkle with flour and add a few pats of butter. Lightly salt and pepper. Continue layering until all of the potatoes have been used. Add milk to just below the top layer of potatoes. Cover with plastic wrap or the dish cover and microwave on medium-high, 80%, power for 15 to 20 minutes, or until the potatoes in the center are very soft. If you use a glass container you can brown the top under your broiler.

Variations: Add sliced onions, shredded cheese, or my favorite—anchovies—to the basic recipe. Canned condensed cream of mushroom, celery, or potato soup added to the milk gives a richer flavor and texture.

Pretty Platter of Potatoes, Peppers, and Onions

2 medium Russet potatoes, cut
    in half lengthwise, (peeled
    optional)

2 bell peppers, cored, seeded,
    and cut in half

2 medium yellow onions,
    peeled and cut in half

Butter or margarine

Arrange the vegetables, alternating them, on a glass pizza pan or 9- × 13-inch glass baking pan with the potatoes cut side up and the peppers cut side down. Cover with plastic wrap and microwave on high for about 10 to 12 minutes, or until the potatoes are done. Remove the plastic wrap and dot the tops of the potatoes and onions with butter. Place under your broiler for a few minutes, or until the vegetables start to brown.

Potato Salad

2 pounds round red or white
    potatoes

2 bunches of scallions,
    trimmed and sliced

1 large stalk celery, chopped

1 cup lite mayonnaise

1 tablespoon sweet prepared
    mustard

1 tablespoon dried dillweed

Place the potatoes and ½ cup water in a 2-quart microwave casserole or ring pan, cover with plastic wrap or the dish cover, and microwave on high for 15 to 20 minutes, or until the potatoes are tender. Stir once if not using a ring pan. Drain off the cooking water and fill the pot with cold water. Allow the potatoes to cool and cut into 1-inch dice. Mix with the remaining ingredients and allow to sit for about 1 hour before serving.

Potatoes Italiano

2 large Russet potatoes, sliced
   ½ inch thick lengthwise

1 cup prepared spaghetti
   sauce

1½ cups shredded Fontina
   cheese

Place the potato slices in an oiled 9- × 13-inch glass baking pan. Cover with plastic wrap and microwave on high for 12 to 15 minutes, or until soft. Add sauce and cheese to each piece and place under a preheated broiler until the cheese melts and starts to brown.

Sweet Potatoes and Yams

1 potato per serving

I always forget which is which. Sweet potatoes have a yellowish hue and are usually fatter and more uniform in shape. Yams have a reddish hue and are longer and slimmer. Microwave the potatoes whole, exactly as you would Russet potatoes. Microwave on high for about 1 minute per ounce, or until soft, about 4 to 5 minutes for a medium one. If you experience hard spots, wrap in plastic wrap before cooking the next time. Sometimes the thin ends will overcook and become dry and hard. Just cut them off and enjoy the rest of the potato.

Stuffed Liquored Sweet Potatoes

4 medium sweet potatoes or
   yams

3 tablespoons butter or
   margarine

2 tablespoons liqueur, such as
   Drambuie, triple sec,
   Cointreau, and so on

2 tablespoons cream or milk

Place the potatoes in a shallow 1-quart casserole dish or an 8-inch-square glass baking pan, and microwave about 16 minutes on high, or until soft. Slit the tops and scoop out the pulp. Mix with the remaining ingredients and stuff back into the skins. Microwave 4 minutes before serving.

Fried Yam Cakes

4 yams, about 1 pound total

1 small onion, minced

2 tablespoons minced parsley

2 egg whites

2 tablespoons cooking oil

Microwave the yams on high about 15 minutes, or until soft. Scoop out the pulp and mix with the onion, parsley, and egg whites. Form into 4 patties.

Heat the oil in a frying pan and fry the cakes until crisp on both sides. Serve with maple syrup.

Stuffed Sweet Potatoes with Pineapple

4 medium sweet potatoes or
    yams

1 8-ounce can crushed
    pineapple with heavy syrup

Microwave the potatoes on high for 12 to 15 minutes, or until soft. Scoop out the pulp and mix with the pineapple. Stuff into the skins or serve in a bowl without skins.

ZAP TIP: If you like crispy potato skins, remove the pulp and place the skins, cut sides down, on a plate. Microwave on high, uncovered, 2 or 3 minutes per skin, or until they brown and get crisp.

Variations: Add mini-marshmallows and/or chopped nuts or raw apples to the basic stuffed potato for more variety.

Potato Chips

Making potato chips in the microwave got more audience response than any other recipe when I made guest appearances on radio and television shows. Even though it is not practical to make huge amounts of chips by microwave, you can do it without any fat or oil and it's a fun thing to do. I love to use this recipe to teach children how to cook with a microwave. They can see the process as it occurs and get a feel for timing and testing for doneness and finally tasting something that is good for them. It also demonstrates browning and crisping and most important, overcooking, which can ruin most recipes.

Making potato chips is a good exercise for learning how fast and evenly your oven cooks. Make up a basketful for your next party and listen to the accolades from your guests.

The process is very simple, just slice a large Russet potato very thin. You should be able to read newsprint through the slices. Use the slicing blade on your food processor and just let the weight of the potato feed it through the blade. Or, use a very sharp French knife and slice very thin. Fat slices tend to burn and get hard rather than crisp. Apply nonstick spray to a microwave roasting rack or the inside of a plastic colander and lay the potato slices close together but not touching. Sprinkle with seasoned salt or herbs and microwave on high, uncovered, about 40 to 50 seconds per chip.

Sesame Chips: Sprinkle with sesame seeds before microwaving.

Garlic Chips: Sprinkle with dried minced garlic chips.

Onion Chips: Sprinkle with dried minced onion chips.

Parmesan Chips: Sprinkle with grated Parmesan cheese.

Vegemite Chips: There is a product from Australia called Vegemite. It tastes salty but is quite low in sodium. Brush it on microwaved chips for a taste treat. Anyway, I think it's a treat.

Chocolate Chips: Melt chocolate chips and dip unseasoned chips into it. Cool on wax paper in your refrigerator.

Rutabagas

Rutabaga raw is a wonderful vegetable for dipping; cooked, it makes a great alternative to potatoes.

1 pound rutabagas	**Fresh ground pepper**
2 to 4 tablespoons butter or margarine	

Peel off the wax and skin and cut the rutabaga into 1-inch dice. Place in a 1-quart microwave dish, add ½ cup water, and cover with the dish cover or plastic wrap. Microwave on high for about 8 to 10 minutes, or until soft. Stir once during the cooking. Drain off the liquid and mash or process until smooth. Add butter or margarine and fresh ground pepper and serve.

Rutabagas with Orange and Ginger

1 pound rutabagas	1 teaspoon ground ginger
4 tablespoons frozen orange juice concentrate	

Prepare and cook the rutabagas as directed above. Drain off the cooking water and add the orange juice concentrate and ginger. Mash or process until smooth.

ZAP TIP: You can remove excess water from mashed vegetables by microwaving them, uncovered, for 5 to 10 minutes, or until they thicken to your specifications.

Spinach

This is a really easy one.

1 pound spinach

Wash in a large pot or sinkful of water. Shake off the excess water and place spinach in a microwave cooking pot. Cover with the lid and microwave on high for about 5 minutes. Place in a colander and press out excess water.

Creamed Spinach

1 pound spinach

3 ounces cream cheese or
herb and garlic cheese
spread, softened

Prepare the spinach as directed above and add the cream cheese or herb and garlic cheese spread. Stir or process until blended.

Pesto Spinach

1 pound spinach, washed and
chopped

1 medium onion, chopped

4 tablespoons *pesto* sauce

Grated Parmesan cheese
(optional)

Place spinach and onion in a 2-quart microwave dish, cover with the dish cover, and microwave on high for 5 minutes. Press out water and stir in the *pesto*. Add the Parmesan if desired.

Simple Acorn Squash

2 acorn squash

2 teaspoons butter

2 tablespoons brown sugar or
molasses

Pierce the shell with a pick or thin-bladed knife and microwave on high for 8 to 10 minutes, or until soft. Turn over halfway through the cooking. Scrape out the seeds and strings and add the butter and brown sugar or molasses.

Summer Squash

This group of soft-skinned squash includes zucchini, crookneck, pattypan, sunburst, and the lesser-known scallopini. They all cook beautifully by microwave and are usually served alone with the simplest of seasonings.

1 pound summer squash

Just trim the squash and cut into uniform 1-inch pieces. Microwave in a covered microwave pot for about 5 to 7 minutes per pound, or until tender crispy. Drain off the excess water and serve with a little butter or oil and maybe a little grated cheese.

Winter Squash

The most common squash in this hard-shell category is the acorn squash. Others are butternut, pumpkin, sweet dumpling, banana, and Hubbard. The small ones are best cooked whole because you cook them in their own container—the shell—and you don't need a cooking pot. And they are much easier to cut open after they are cooked and become soft. The large Hubbard, banana, and pumpkin should be cut into pieces and cooked, covered, in a pot. When microwaving them whole be sure you pierce them with a pick or thin-bladed knife. Unlike potatoes, winter squash will burst when pressure builds up within them. Microwave on high about 10 minutes per pound or until they are soft.

Acorn Squash with Sherbet

Try it, you'll like it. Nutty ice cream works well also.

1 large (2-pound) acorn squash   **Orange or lemon sherbet**

Cut the squash in half lengthwise and scrape out the seeds and strings. Place in a casserole. Put a large scoop of the sherbet in each half and cover. Microwave on high for about 10 to 12 minutes, or until the squash is soft.

Butternut Squash

Do yourself a favor and microwave a butternut squash. You have never tasted squash this good. Just plain it is almost as sweet as candy. Stab a 2-pound squash a couple of times with a thin-bladed knife and microwave on high for about 10 minutes, or until soft. Scoop out the seeds and enjoy!

Pumpkin for Pie

Cut up a small pumpkin and scrape off the seeds and strings. Separate the seeds and save for drying in your microwave. Place the pumpkin pieces in a large microwave container and cover. Microwave on high about 10 minutes per pound, or until soft. Scrape or cut the pulp off of the shell and mash, rice, or blend in your food processor until smooth. Place the pulp back in the cooking container and microwave on high, uncovered, until the excess moisture evaporates and the pumpkin thickens, about 10 to 20 minutes. Stir often while microwaving.

ZAP TIP: To make toasted pumpkin seeds. clean, wash, and drain 1 cup of seeds. Place in a glass bowl or measuring cup and microwave on high uncovered for about 3 minutes. Stir several times.

Pumpkin Pie

2 cups pumpkin as prepared above	3 eggs
¾ cup sugar	1½ cups evaporated milk or light cream
1 tablespoon pumpkin pie spice blend	1 9-inch pie crust, conventionally baked in a glass pie pan
1 tablespoon cornstarch	

Mix all pie filling ingredients thoroughly and pour into the pie crust. Cover with wax paper and microwave on medium, 50%, power for 12 to 15 minutes, or until set. Or, bake in your conventional oven at 350 degrees for 50 to 60 minutes.

This recipe is quite laborious, but if you have the time, try it. When I make a pumpkin pie I use canned pumpkin filling. It's very good and so easy.

ZAP TIP: I think pie crusts bake better in a hot conventional oven than in a microwave. However, graham cracker and chocolate crumb crusts work beautifully in a microwave oven.

Spaghetti Squash

I love demonstrating how to microwave this unusual squash. It's very dramatic and really shows the advantage of cooking by microwave instead of conventionally. An average-size squash takes about 15 minutes in a microwave compared with over an hour conventionally.

1 medium spaghetti squash	**Butter or margarine**
Tomato sauce (optional)	**Salt and fresh ground pepper**

Stab the spaghetti squash with a paring or other thin short-bladed knife. Place in your microwave, no dish is necessary, and microwave on high for 12 to 15 minutes, or until soft. Turn over once during the cooking. Cut in half lengthwise and scrape out the seeds. Scrape the strands of squash into a serving bowl and top with tomato sauce or just butter or margarine and salt and pepper.

Spaghetti Squash Primavera

1 spaghetti squash, prepared
  as directed above

1 cup broccoli flowerets

1 cup cauliflower flowerets

1 cup frozen peas

3 stalks raw asparagus, cut
  into 1-inch pieces

5 mushrooms, quartered

6 cherry tomatoes, quartered

4 tablespoons *pesto* sauce
  (optional)

½ cup pine nuts

¼ cup olive oil

½ cup grated Parmesan
  cheese

Place all vegetables, except the cooked squash and tomatoes in a 2-quart microwave dish or ring pan, cover with plastic wrap or the dish cover, and microwave on high for 5 to 7 minutes, or until tender. Drain off the water and add the tomatoes, *pesto,* nuts, oil, and cheese. Stir into the cooked squash.

Swiss Chard

1 pound chard

Wash and chop stems and leaves. Shake off excess water and place in a 2-quart microwave dish. Cover with the dish cover or plastic wrap and microwave on high for about 4 to 5 minutes. Drain off water and serve with butter, oil, and or grated Parmesan cheese.

Tomatoes

I use only canned tomatoes for cooking. They are far superior in taste and texture to the things that they call tomatoes that are sold at markets. The only good raw tomatoes that I've had in the last twenty years have come from home gardens. They are so good that I eat them raw rather than cook them. Now and then you can find a cherry tomato that tastes like a tomato, but I still prefer to use canned ones for cooking. Why, oh why, do restaurants still add tasteless, hard, or pulpy tomatoes to salads? If it's only for color, I suggest that they use red bell peppers or apples instead or maybe dye some zucchini red. Almost anything would be better.

Marinated Tomatoes with Fresh Basil

My wife, Doris, before I met her, lived in Italy, where you can still buy ripe tomatoes, and there learned the following recipe, which is one of my favorites.

2 large RIPE tomatoes from your garden, sliced ½ inch thick

½ cup chopped fresh basil

Lemon juice

Olive oil

4 cloves garlic, minced

Fresh ground pepper

Arrange the tomatoes on a large platter and sprinkle the remaining ingredients over them. Cover with plastic wrap for about 1 hour and serve at room temperature.

Cheesy Stewed Tomatoes

1 14½-ounce can stewed tomatoes

1 cup seasoned bread crumbs

1 cup shredded Mozzarella cheese

Place the tomatoes in a 1-quart microwave dish, add the crumbs and then the cheese. Microwave, uncovered, on high for 5 to 7 minutes, or until the cheese is melted.

Vegetarian Chili

The blend of spices in this recipe makes it a robust and very satisfying meal. It is especially good if you're watching your cholesterol intake and the combination of beans, nuts, and cheese gives you a complete protein. Because you don't have to be concerned with cooking any meat until it becomes tender, this recipe can be made very quickly.

1 medium onion, chopped

1 stalk celery, chopped

1 large carrot, chopped

3 tablespoons chopped garlic

2 tablespoons chili powder

1 tablespoon ground cumin

2 14½-ounce cans stewed tomatoes, drained

1 15-ounce can red kidney beans or garbanzo beans

1 cup unsalted peanuts

½ cup shredded Cheddar cheese or cottage cheese

1 4-ounce can diced green chili peppers with juice

Place first 6 ingredients in a 2-quart casserole, cover with plastic wrap or the dish cover, and microwave on high for 5 minutes. Add tomatoes, beans, and nuts and microwave on high for 10 minutes. Add cheese and stir to blend. Serve bottled hot sauce with the chili peppers so folks can add them according to their own taste.

Rice, Legumes, and Grains

Picture this scenario. You want to serve brown or wild rice for dinner and your schedule for the day is really tight. No problem, because you've got a microwave oven. In the morning, you simply set it and forget it and when you return from work or play you know your rice will be cooked perfectly. You didn't have to worry about burning the rice because you know that the microwave turns off automatically and the pot doesn't get hot as it does when you cook rice on top of your stove. You won't save a lot of time when you cook rice with your microwave compared to cooking on your stove top because rice and grains need to be cooked with a lot of water and microwave ovens become very inefficient when a lot of free water is used. But because of the above reasons, the microwave is the ideal tool for cooking rice and grains.

People in Hawaii always argue with me that they can cook rice perfectly with their rice cookers. Rice cookers are great, but if you use your microwave you don't have another appliance cluttering your countertop.

I get a lot of letters from new microwavers complaining that whenever they microwave rice it boils over and makes a mess in their ovens. Well, what would you do if rice were boiling over on your stove top? Turn down the energy. Do the same with your microwave. Or next time use a bigger pot. It's all a matter of common sense.

Long-Grain Rice

MICROWAVE ONLY

ENERGY LEVEL:
high, 100%, and medium, 50%

SERVINGS:
4

COMPLETE RECIPE TIME:
about 20 minutes

COOKING TIME:
about 20 minutes

MICROWAVE COOKWARE:
deep 4-quart plastic or glass container

COVERING:
plastic wrap or the dish cover

This is the most popular rice used in the United States. You can buy it plain, enriched, or enriched converted. The converted cooks a little better by microwave but all are very simple to make. The enriched and converted have more nutritional value than plain white rice.

There are many ways to cook rice by microwave. I'm going to suggest a couple and hope you experiment to determine the best way to cook rice using your oven.

1 cup long-grain rice	**Salt and butter (optional)**
2 cups water	

Place rice and water in a 4-quart microwave dish or ring pan, cover with plastic wrap or the dish cover, and microwave on high for 5 minutes and medium, 50%, for 12 to 15 minutes, or until the water is absorbed and the rice tender. Let sit for a few minutes, fluff, and serve.

It is advisable not to rinse rice before or after cooking. However, a very famous New York food writer cooks his rice in a lot of water and then drains it, which is the same as rinsing it. The rice comes out perfectly and the grains don't stick at all. For aesthetic reasons, you may want to serve it cooked this way. Just cook 1 cup rice with 4 cups water about 25 minutes on medium, 50%, and drain it.

ZAP TIP: Microwave big batches of rice and freeze individual portions in plastic bags. When you need rice, just microwave portions of it on high, until hot, usually 2 to 3 minutes.

Rapid Red Beans and Rice

MICROWAVE ONLY

ENERGY LEVEL:
high, 100%, and medium, 50%

SERVINGS:
4

COMPLETE RECIPE TIME:
about 30 minutes

COOKING TIME:
about 25 minutes

MICROWAVE COOKWARE:
4-quart glass or plastic container

COVERING:
plastic wrap or the dish cover

I'm including this recipe here because you cook the rice and used canned beans instead of cooking dry beans.

1 pound picnic ham meat only, diced, or 4 smoked ham hocks

1 cup chopped celery

6 scallions, chopped

1 medium green bell pepper, chopped

4 cloves garlic, minced

1 cup long-grain rice

2 cups water

1 16-ounce can red beans

Bottled hot sauce

Place ham, celery, scallions, pepper, and garlic in a 4-quart microwave dish or ring pan, cover with plastic wrap or the dish cover, and microwave on high for 4 to 5 minutes, or until the vegetables are tender. Add the rice and water, re-cover, and microwave on high for 5 minutes and medium, 50%, for about 15 minutes, or until the rice is tender. Stir in the beans with their liquid and microwave for 5 minutes. Serve with the hot sauce.

Note: You may substitute brown rice if you add 1 more cup of water and cook the recipe about 15 minutes longer or until rice is tender.

Vegetarian Red Beans and Rice

MICROWAVE ONLY

ENERGY LEVEL:
high, 100%, and medium, 50%

SERVINGS:
4

COMPLETE RECIPE TIME:
about 30 minutes

COOKING TIME:
about 25 minutes

MICROWAVE COOKWARE:
3- to 4-quart glass or plastic container

COVERING:
plastic wrap or the dish cover

I'm always trying to find things that will make vegetarian meals taste as good or better than meat dishes. Try using *miso* paste available at health food stores. It is low in sodium but has a salty meaty flavor that really enhances this recipe.

Substitute 4 tablespoons of *miso* paste for the ham in Rapid Red Beans and Rice and add 4 tablespoons olive oil. Cook as directed.

Variations: Add 1 tablespoon ground cumin and a few sprigs chopped coriander to the above recipe.

Or, reduce the water to 1½ cups and add 1 can Cajun-style stewed tomatoes or stewed tomatoes flavored with chile peppers.

Black Beans and Rice

MICROWAVE ONLY

ENERGY LEVEL:
high, 100%, and medium, 50%

SERVINGS:
4

COMPLETE RECIPE TIME:
about 30 minutes

COOKING TIME:
about 28 minutes

MICROWAVE COOKWARE:
3- to 4-quart glass or plastic container

COVERING:
plastic wrap or the dish cover

Black beans have a slightly different flavor from red beans and can be substituted for variety in the previous recipes or used in this spicy recipe. You can substitute all of these recipes for meat dishes and still get complete protein in your diet.

1 medium onion, chopped

4 cloves garlic, minced

1 jalapeño pepper, seeded and chopped

2 tablespoons cooking oil of choice

1 cup long-grain rice

1 cup water

1 14-ounce can stewed tomatoes

1 tablespoon ground cumin

1 16-ounce can black beans, rinsed

½ cup chopped coriander (cilantro)

Bottled hot sauce to taste

Place the onion, garlic, pepper, and oil in a 3- to 4-quart microwave dish or ring pan, cover with plastic wrap or the lid, and microwave on high for 3 minutes. Add the rice, water, tomatoes, and cumin. Re-cover and microwave on high for 5 minutes and medium, 50%, power for 15 minutes, or until the rice is tender. Stir in the beans and microwave on high for 5 minutes, or until heated through. Garnish with the coriander and serve with the hot sauce.

Note: You may substitute brown rice in the above recipe. Just add another cup of water and cook 15 minutes longer or until the rice is tender.

Asian Rice with Tofu

MICROWAVE ONLY

ENERGY LEVEL:
high, 100%, and medium, 50%

SERVINGS:
4

COMPLETE RECIPE TIME:
about 30 minutes

COOKING TIME:
about 25 minutes

MICROWAVE COOKWARE:
3- to 4-quart glass or plastic container

COVERING:
plastic wrap or the dish cover

You can find baked tofu in health food stores or you can make it yourself by coating ½-inch-thick slices of tofu with a paste of brewer's yeast and soy sauce and microwaving the slices, uncovered, on high for about 2 to 3 minutes per slice. Baked tofu gives a real meaty taste to this recipe.

1 cup long-grain rice

2 cups water

4 scallions, thinly sliced

1 4-ounce can sliced water chestnuts, drained

1 4-ounce can pineapple chunks, drained

8 ounces baked tofu, diced (see above)

2 tablespoons soy sauce

1 tablespoon sesame chili oil

1 cup bean sprouts

4 medium mushrooms, sliced

Place the rice and water in a 3- to 4-quart microwave dish or ring pan, cover with plastic wrap or the dish cover, and microwave on high for 5 minutes and medium, 50%, power for 15 minutes. Add the remaining ingredients, stir to mix, re-cover, and microwave on high for 5 minutes, or until the rice is tender.

Fried Rice

Here are two versions of this recipe, one with meat and eggs and the other cholesterol free. Fried rice can be made many different ways and if you don't like these recipes I hope you experiment and find one that suits you.

8 slices bacon	4 eggs
1 cup long-grain rice	8 scallions, thinly sliced
2 cups water	4 tablespoons soy sauce

Place the bacon on a roasting rack and cover with a paper towel or place it between paper towels and microwave on high for 8 to 10 minutes, or until crisp. Allow to cool and crumble. Place the rice and water in a 3- to 4-quart microwave dish or ring pan, cover with plastic wrap or the dish cover, and microwave on high for 5 minutes and medium, 50%, power for 15 minutes, or until tender. Place the eggs in a bowl and beat until blended. Microwave 2 to 3 minutes, or until solid. Chop the eggs and add to the rice with the bacon and remaining ingredients. Mix thoroughly.

Note: You may substitute brown rice in the above recipe. Just add another cup of water and cook about 15 minutes longer.

Variations: Add to or substitute in the basic recipe chopped spinach, chopped celery, cooked shrimp, chopped baked ham, pickled gingerroot, leftover meat, or vegetables.

Vegetarian Fried Rice

In the fried rice recipe, substitute 1 cup imitation bacon bits or baked tofu for the bacon and use egg substitute for the eggs.

Rice and Cabbage

Here's an Italian recipe that can be used as a side dish or for a light meatless lunch. Serve either hot or chilled.

½ cup long-grain rice

1 cup water

2 cups chopped cabbage

1 teaspoon dried sage

1 16-ounce can red kidney beans, drained

½ cup grated Parmesan cheese

Place the rice, water, and cabbage in a 3-quart microwave dish or ring pan, cover with plastic wrap or the dish cover, and microwave on high for 5 minutes and medium, 50%, for 5 to 7 minutes, or until the rice is tender. Add the sage and beans and microwave on high for 3 minutes. Stir in the cheese and serve.

Note: You may substitute brown rice if you add another ½ water and cook the recipe 10 minutes longer.

MICROWAVE ONLY

ENERGY LEVEL:
high, 100%, medium, 50%

SERVINGS:
4

COMPLETE RECIPE TIME:
about 20 minutes

COOKING TIME:
about 15 minutes

MICROWAVE COOKWARE:
3-quart glass or plastic container or ring pan

COVERING:
plastic wrap or the dish cover

Rice and Peas

MICROWAVE ONLY

ENERGY LEVEL:
high, 100%

SERVINGS:
4

COMPLETE RECIPE TIME:
about 15 minutes

COOKING TIME:
about 10 minutes

MICROWAVE COOKWARE:
3- to 4-quart glass or plastic
container or ring pan

COVERING:
plastic wrap or the dish cover

This traditional Italian recipe is called *risi e bisi*. If you have children, just having them say the name will make them want to try it.

3 cups cooked rice, white or brown	1 10-ounce package frozen peas
1 cup bacon bits, real or imitation	¾ cup grated Parmesan cheese
3 scallions, thinly sliced	½ cup chopped parsley

Place all ingredients except the cheese and parsley, in a 3-quart microwave dish, cover with plastic wrap or the dish cover, and microwave on high for 8 to 10 minutes, or until the peas are hot. Stir in the cheese and sprinkle on the parsley.

Garlic Rice

MICROWAVE ONLY

ENERGY LEVEL:
high, 100%, medium, 50%

SERVINGS:
4

COMPLETE RECIPE TIME:
about 30 minutes

COOKING TIME:
about 20 minutes

MICROWAVE COOKWARE:
3- to 4-quart glass or plastic container or ring pan

COVERING:
plastic wrap or the dish cover

A great side dish for all meats and stews. Pungent and pleasurable.

1 cup long-grain rice

2 cups chicken broth

8 cloves garlic, smashed

1 medium onion, chopped

1 medium bell pepper, chopped

2 tablespoons minced lemon zest

½ cup grated Parmesan cheese

½ cup chopped parsley

Place the rice, broth, garlic, onion, and pepper in a 3-quart microwave dish, cover with plastic wrap or the dish cover, and microwave on high for 5 minutes and medium, 50%, power for 15 minutes, or until the water is absorbed and the rice is tender. Stir in the lemon zest, cheese, and parsley and serve.

Brown Rice

MICROWAVE ONLY

ENERGY LEVEL:
high, 100%, medium, 50%

SERVINGS:
4

COMPLETE SERVING TIME:
about 40 minutes

COOKING TIME:
about 38 minutes

MICROWAVE COOKWARE:
4-quart glass or plastic container or ring pan

COVERING:
plastic wrap or the dish cover

Brown rice retains the nutritious germ and layer of fiber on the grain. You have to cook it a long time for that fiber to become tender and palatable. Also, because of the long cooking time required you must use more water. If you cook it by microwave, you will save about one third of the cooking time, but again, the reason you cook rice by microwave is not for the time saved—it's for the convenience of being able to set it and forget it and not worry about it burning and sticking to the pot.

1 cup brown rice	Salt to taste
3 cups water	

Place all ingredients in a 4-quart microwave dish or ring pan, cover with plastic wrap or the dish cover, and microwave on high for 8 minutes and medium, 50%, power for 25 to 30 minutes, or until the water is absorbed and the rice is tender.

ZAP TIP: Microwave large batches or rice and freeze serving portions of it in plastic bags. When you need rice, just microwave it on high for a few minutes until hot.

Brown Rice Ratatouille

MICROWAVE ONLY

ENERGY LEVEL:
high, 100%, medium, 50%

SERVINGS:
4

COMPLETE RECIPE TIME:
about 50 minutes

COOKING TIME:
about 45 minutes

MICROWAVE COOKWARE:
4-quart glass or plastic container
or ring pan

COVERING:
plastic wrap or the dish cover

You can make this recipe from scratch, as indicated below, but it's a great way to use leftover cooked rice. Just microwave the vegetables, add cooked rice, and microwave until heated through.

½ cup brown rice

1 cup beef broth

1 14-ounce can stewed
tomatoes

1 medium onion, chopped

½ medium bell pepper,
chopped

4 cloves garlic, chopped

2 tablespoons olive oil

¼ medium unskinned eggplant,
diced (about 2 cups)

1 medium zucchini, sliced

1 cup shredded Romano
cheese

Place the rice, broth, tomatoes, onion, pepper, garlic, and oil in a 4-quart microwave dish or ring pan, cover with plastic wrap or the dish cover, and microwave on high for 15 minutes. Add the eggplant and zucchini and microwave, uncovered, on medium, 50%, power for about 30 minutes, or until the rice is tender and the vegetables are soft. Serve with the cheese.

Dirty Brown Rice

MICROWAVE ONLY

ENERGY LEVEL:
high, 100%, medium, 50%

SERVINGS:
4

COMPLETE RECIPE TIME:
about 45 minutes

COOKING TIME:
about 38 minutes

MICROWAVE COOKWARE:
4-quart glass or plastic container
or ring pan

COVERING:
plastic wrap or the dish cover

Normally dirty rice has chicken livers and gizzards in it. Nowadays everyone is frightened to near death by anything that has cholesterol in it, so I've made this recipe cholesterol free. It still looks dirty.

1 cup brown rice

3 cups water or vegetable broth

1 medium green pepper, chopped

1 medium yellow onion, chopped

1 large stalk celery, chopped

1 tablespoon poultry seasoning

½ cup dried lentils

1 4-ounce can chopped black olives

Place all ingredients in a 4-quart microwave dish or ring pan, cover with plastic wrap or the dish cover, and microwave on high for 8 minutes and medium, 50%, power for 25 to 30 minutes, or until the rice is tender.

Wild Rice

Wild rice is actually a grain, but because we call it rice I'm including it in this category. It is quite expensive. The next time you cook it, therefore, be sure you do it in your microwave so you don't have to worry about burning or scorching it. You almost can't ruin it when you cook it by microwave.

¾ cup wild rice   3 cups water

Place the rice and water in a 4-quart microwave dish or ring pan, cover with plastic wrap or the dish cover, and microwave on high for 8 minutes and medium, 50%, power for about 35 to 40 minutes more, or until it is chewy tender. There will be some water left after cooking even though the rice is tender. Just drain it off or save it for making soups and stews.

MICROWAVE ONLY

ENERGY LEVEL:
high, 100%, medium, 50%

SERVINGS:
4

COMPLETE RECIPE TIME:
about 45 minutes

COOKING TIME:
about 45 minutes

MICROWAVE COOKWARE:
4-quart glass or plastic container or ring pan

COVERING:
plastic wrap or the dish cover

Wild Rice and Mushrooms

These two foods seem to have a natural affinity for each other. Cook them together and enjoy!

2½ cups wild rice

2 ounces dried mushrooms of
     choice, whole or chopped

3 cups water

4 scallions, thinly sliced

4 tablespoons butter or
     margarine

Place the rice, mushrooms, and water in a 4-quart microwave dish, cover with plastic wrap or the dish cover, and microwave on high for 8 minutes and on medium, 50%, power 35 to 40 minutes or until the rice is tender. Drain off any excess water and stir in the scallions and butter.

MICROWAVE ONLY

ENERGY LEVEL:
high, 100%, medium, 50%

SERVINGS:
4

COMPLETE RECIPE TIME:
about 50 minutes

COOKING TIME:
about 48 minutes

MICROWAVE COOKWARE:
4-quart glass or plastic container or ring pan

COVERING:
plastic wrap or the dish cover

Microwaved Chestnuts

Chestnuts cooked by microwave taste the same as those roasted on an open fire or in your conventional oven, but are much easier and faster to make.

12 chestnuts   Salt to taste
1 tablespoon olive oil

Cut an X in the rounded top of each nut and place everything in a 1-quart casserole. Cover and shake to coat the nuts with the oil and salt. Microwave on high for about 30 seconds per nut or until the shells have peeled back. Remove hard outer shell and soft, dark inner peel before eating.

Wild Rice with Chestnuts

MICROWAVE ONLY

ENERGY LEVEL:
high, 100%, medium, 50%

SERVINGS:
4

COMPLETE RECIPE TIME:
about 60 minutes, including preparing chestnuts

COOKING TIME:
about 45 minutes

MICROWAVE COOKWARE:
4-quart glass or plastic container or ring pan

COVERING:
plastic wrap or the dish cover

¾ cup wild rice   2 cups (12 to 15) shelled and
3 cups water   quartered cooked
                                 chestnuts
                             ½ teaspoon grated nutmeg

Place all ingredients in a 4-quart microwave dish or ring pan, cover with plastic wrap or the dish cover, and microwave on high for 8 minutes and medium, 50%, power for 35 to 40 minutes, or until the rice is tender. Drain off any excess water and serve.

Wild Rice with Dried Fruit and Nuts

This recipe makes a dandy side dish served with any kind of poultry. Also use it as a bed for microwaved or grilled chicken, pork, or lamb.

¾ cup wild rice

3 cups water

4 ounces mixed dried fruit, chopped

1 cup nuts of choice, pecans, walnuts, almonds, and so on, chopped

Place rice, water, and fruit in a 4-quart microwave dish or ring pan, cover with plastic wrap or the dish cover, and microwave on high for 8 minutes and medium, 50%, power for 35 to 40 minutes, or until the rice is tender. Drain off any excess water and stir in the nuts.

MICROWAVE ONLY

ENERGY LEVEL:
high, 100%, medium, 50%

SERVINGS:
4

COMPLETE RECIPE TIME:
about 50 minutes

COOKING TIME:
about 50 minutes

MICROWAVE COOKWARE:
4-quart glass or plastic container or ring pan

COVERING:
plastic wrap or the dish cover

Wild Rice and Bell Peppers

The variety of colors in this recipe will brighten your table. Also good cold for lunch or for a picnic.

¾ cup wild rice

2½ cups water

½ red bell pepper, diced

½ yellow bell pepper, diced

½ green bell pepper, diced

½ small red onion, chopped

1 cup ranch-style salad dressing (optional)

Place all ingredients, except the dressing, in a 4-quart microwave dish or ring pan, cover with plastic wrap or the dish cover, and microwave on high for 8 minutes and medium, 50%, power for 35 to 40 minutes, or until the rice is tender. Drain off any excess water and mix in the salad dressing if desired.

MICROWAVE ONLY

ENERGY LEVEL:
high, 100%, medium, 50%

SERVINGS:
4

COMPLETE RECIPE TIME:
about 55 minutes

COOKING TIME:
about 48 minutes

MICROWAVE COOKWARE:
4-quart glass or plastic container or ring pan

COVERING:
plastic wrap or the dish cover

Rice Salads | Use white, brown, or wild rice as a base for all sorts of salads. Use your imagination and creativity to compose dishes that use foods that are in season or on sale or left over from other meals. If you freeze rice, you'll have it on hand whenever you want to make a quickie meal for yourself or unexpected guests.

Oriental Rice Salad

SERVINGS:
4

COMPLETE RECIPE TIME:
about 25 minutes

COOKING TIME:
none

MICROWAVE COOKWARE:
4-quart glass or plastic mixing bowl

3 cups cooked rice

2 cups chopped bok choy

1 cup bean sprouts

1 8-ounce can crushed
   pineapple with juice

16 sugar peas, trimmed

1 cup peanuts

4 tablespoons chopped pickled
   gingerroot

½ cup soy sauce

1 tablespoon sesame oil

4 tablespoons sesame seeds

Mix all ingredients and let set for 15 minutes. Serve on lettuce leaves.

Rice and Yogurt Salad

An excellent low-fat lunch or even breakfast dish. It provides good protein without the addition of any meat product.

- 3 cups cooked rice, white or brown
- 1 6-ounce can crushed pineapple with juice
- 1 large orange, peeled and cut into bite-size pieces
- 1 cup peanuts
- 1 stalk celery, chopped
- 1 cup plain yogurt
- 3 cups chopped Romaine lettuce

SERVINGS:
4

COMPLETE RECIPE TIME:
about 10 minutes

COOKING TIME:
none

COOKWARE:
4-quart mixing bowl

Mix all ingredients, except the lettuce. Place 1 cup of lettuce on each plate and top with equal amounts of the salad.

Variations: Add 1 cup shredded coconut or 1 tablespoon curry powder to the recipe.

Mexican Rice Salad

Another simple recipe that provides good protein without any animal product.

- ½ head of lettuce, shredded
- 3 cups cooked rice
- 1 16-ounce can canned chili beans, drained
- 1 cup prepared salsa
- 1 medium green bell pepper, chopped
- 1 small onion, chopped
- 1 stalk celery, chopped
- ½ cup chopped coriander (cilantro)
- 1 tablespoon chili powder

SERVINGS:
4

COMPLETE RECIPE TIME:
about 10 minutes

COOKING TIME:
none

COOKWARE:
4-quart mixing bowl

Divide the lettuce among 4 plates. Mix remaining ingredients and place equal amounts on the lettuce.

Risotto | Risotto is rice cooked Italian style. It normally uses Arborio rice, which is an oval, plump grain rice grown in Italy. It is quite expensive and cooks very well by microwave. But I've found that if you use pearl rice, which is inexpensive, it will turn out just great and I'll bet nobody can tell the difference in a blind taste test. Another option is to use Japanese sweet rice. It has a glutinous quality that lends itself to risotto. Traditionally, risotto is made by sautéing onions, butter, and rice and then adding stock gradually until the rice is tender and plump. This technique takes 30 to 40 minutes and requires constant attention and stirring. When you make risotto by microwave you can set it, forget it, and relax. The best container to use is a microwave ring pan.

Basic Risotto

MICROWAVE ONLY

ENERGY LEVEL:
high, 100%, medium-low, 30 to 40%

SERVING:
4

COMPLETE RECIPE TIME:
about 35 minutes

COOKING TIME:
about 33 minutes

MICROWAVE COOKWARE:
2-quart glass or plastic container or ring pan

COVERING:
plastic wrap or the dish cover

1 medium onion, chopped

4 tablespoons butter or margarine

¾ cup Arborio, pearl, or medium-grain rice

2½ cups chicken broth

½ cup dry white wine

½ cup grated Parmesan cheese

Place the onion, half the butter, and the rice in a 2-quart ring pan or other microwave dish and microwave on high for 3 minutes, or until the onion is soft. Add the broth and wine, cover with plastic wrap or the dish cover, and microwave on high for 5 minutes and medium-low 30 to 40%, power for about 25 minutes, or until the rice is tender. It should have a puddinglike consistency. Stir in the rest of the butter and the cheese and serve immediately.

Risotto à la Milanese: Soak 10 threads of saffron in the wine for 10 minutes before adding to the basic recipe.

Risotto with Spicy Tomatoes: To the basic recipe add 1 10-ounce can stewed tomatoes flavored with chile peppers or 1 14-ounce can Cajun-style stewed tomatoes plus ¼ teaspoon cayenne pepper and reduce the broth to 2 cups.

Risotto with Mushrooms: To the basic recipe add 8 ounces dried mushrooms, not reconstituted.

Legumes | This group of foods includes beans, peas, and lentils. Some cook well by microwave but others, particularly dried beans, can perhaps be cooked better on your stove top. All require a lot of water, so the efficiency of the microwave oven is diminished. The only advantage of cooking dried beans in your microwave oven is the fact that the cooking container doesn't get hot so you can't burn or scorch the beans. I once had a beautiful steel pot that I used to cook dried beans. I became involved in another activity and forgot about the beans cooking on the stove. When I returned from the tennis courts, I was immediately aware of the overwhelming smell of burned beans. I didn't even try to scrape the charcoal residue of the beans off the bottom of that pot; I knew it would be a futile task. The pot, to this day, is soaking on the back porch and is used reluctantly by my dogs as a water dish.

You may have noticed in other chapters of this book that I prefer to use canned beans in my recipes. It's so much easier and I think they taste as good as, or better than, dried beans. One argument given me, especially by natural-food people, against using canned beans is that they contain some sodium. These same people usually add salt to their dried bean recipes.

Dried peas and lentils cook very nicely by microwave. Just be aware that they will take almost as long as they do to cook on the stove top.

Red, Navy, Garbanzo, or Black Beans

1 pound dried beans   **Water**

Place the beans in a 3-quart glass or plastic container or ring pan and cover with water. Cover with plastic wrap or the dish cover and microwave 10 minutes. Let soak for 1 hour. Remove any beans that float to the top of the water and drain. Add 2 quarts hot tap water, re-cover, and microwave on high for 15 minutes and medium-low, 30 to 40% power for about 2 to 2½ hours, or until the beans are tender.

MICROWAVE ONLY

ENERGY LEVEL:
high, 100%, medium-low, 30 to 40%

SERVINGS:
4

COMPLETE RECIPE TIME:
about 2½ to 3 hours

COOKING TIME:
about 2½ to 3 hours

MICROWAVE COOKWARE:
4-quart glass or plastic container or ring pan

COVERING:
plastic wrap or the dish cover

Dried Peas or Lentils

1 cup peas or lentils   **3 cups water**

Place both ingredients in a 2-quart microwave dish or ring pan. Cover with plastic wrap or the dish cover and microwave on medium, 50%, power for 25 to 30 minutes, or until the legumes are tender.

MICROWAVE ONLY

ENERGY LEVEL:
medium, 50%

SERVINGS:
4

COMPLETE RECIPE TIME:
about 23 minutes

COOKING TIME:
about 23 minutes

MICROWAVE COOKWARE:
2-quart glass or plastic container or ring pan

COVERING:
plastic wrap or the dish cover

Grains (Kasha, Kashi, Bulgur Wheat, Couscous)

The easiest way to cook grains by microwave is to follow the instructions on the package. The manufacturers of these foods seem to be way ahead of others in this category and realize the saturation of microwave ovens in American homes and the desire of microwavers to use their ovens for everything possible.

All grains cook beautifully by microwave. I'm not including oatmeal, cream of wheat, and other breakfast cereals because even though they cook well by microwave, they are so mundane that there is no excitement in it. But I must admit that being able to make a bowl of oatmeal right in the dish that you are going to eat from is really convenient. I still remember scouring out the pot in which my mother made oatmeal. It always seemed to stick on the bottom more securely than any other food.

Kasha

MICROWAVE ONLY

ENERGY LEVEL:
high, 100%, medium, 50%

SERVINGS:
4

COMPLETE RECIPE TIME:
about 22 minutes

COOKING TIME:
about 20 minutes

MICROWAVE COOKWARE:
1-quart glass or plastic measuring cup

COVERING:
plastic wrap or the dish cover

The conventional instructions on the box suggest that you coat the buckwheat groats with beaten egg before you cook them to render them light and fluffy. Well, this doesn't work worth a groat when you do it by microwave. If you want the fluffiest kasha that you've ever eaten, cook it plain in your microwave oven.

½ cup buckwheat groats (kasha)   1½ cups water

2 tablespoons oil

Mix the buckwheat groats with the oil in a 1-quart measuring cup and microwave, uncovered, on high for 2 minutes. Add the water, cover with plastic wrap or the dish cover, and microwave on high for 5 minutes and medium, 50%, power for 12 to 15 minutes.

Kashi

Kashi is a blend of grains plus sesame seeds. I really like this product because it provides a complete protein from only vegetable ingredients and is easy to cook and to reheat. You can use it combined with a myriad of other foods to make interesting vegetarian meals.

1 cup kashi	**2 cups water or broth**

Place both ingredients in a 2-quart microwave dish or ring pan, cover with plastic wrap or the dish cover, and microwave on high for 5 minutes and medium, 50%, power for about 20 minutes, or until the water is absorbed and the kashi is tender.

Variations: Add ½ cup each of raisins or other dried fruit and nuts to the recipe before cooking.

MICROWAVE ONLY

ENERGY LEVEL:
high, 100%, medium, 50%

SERVINGS:
4

COMPLETE RECIPE TIME:
about 30 minutes

COOKING TIME:
about 25 minutes

MICROWAVE COOKWARE:
2-quart glass or plastic container or ring pan

COVERING:
plastic wrap or the dish cover

Bulgur Wheat

MICROWAVE ONLY

ENERGY LEVEL:
high, 100%

SERVINGS:
4

COMPLETE RECIPE TIME:
about 35 minutes

COOKING TIME:
about 5 minutes

MICROWAVE COOKWARE:
2-quart glass or plastic container
or ring pan

COVERING:
plastic wrap or the dish cover

The easiest way to find bulgur wheat at your market is to look for a product called Ala. It is cracked bulgur wheat, just under a different name.

1 cup Ala   **2 cups water or broth**

Place both ingredients in a 2-quart microwave dish or ring pan, cover with plastic wrap or the dish cover, and microwave on high for 5 minutes. Let stand until the water is absorbed and the bulgur wheat is tender.

Tabouli Salad

SERVINGS:
4

COMPLETE RECIPE TIME:
about 10 minutes

COOKING TIME:
none

MICROWAVE COOKWARE:
large mixing bowl

I served tabouli at my restaurants before anyone but an Arab knew what it was. It became very popular because it's so light and nutritious. Traditionally it is made with bulgur wheat, but you can use any of the grains mentioned in this chapter.

2 cups cooked bulgur wheat,   **1 cup chopped parsley or**
  kasha, kashi, or couscous   **coriander (cilantro)**

1 large ripe tomato, diced   **2 tablespoons lemon juice**

1 medium onion, chopped   **2 tablespoons oil (optional)**

Mix all ingredients and serve on lettuce.

Variations: Add to the basic recipe chopped dates or figs, chopped nuts, chopped cucumber, chopped olives, capers, chopped mint, grated cheese, or whatever suits your fancy.

Pilaf

MICROWAVE ONLY

ENERGY LEVEL:
high, 100%, medium, 50%

SERVINGS:
4

COMPLETE RECIPE TIME:
about 30 minutes

COOKING TIME:
about 25 minutes

MICROWAVE COOKWARE:
3-quart glass or plastic container or ring pan

COVERING:
plastic wrap or the dish cover

1 cup bulgur wheat or kashi

2 cups broth, chicken or vegetable

1 stalk celery, chopped

2 medium onion, chopped

1 medium carrot, chopped

2 cloves garlic, minced

4 ounces dried or raw mushrooms, sliced

Place all ingredients in a 3-quart microwave dish or ring pan, cover with plastic wrap or the dish cover, and microwave on high for 5 minutes and medium, 50%, power for 15 to 20 minutes, or until the vegetables are soft and the grain tender.

Couscous

MICROWAVE ONLY

ENERGY LEVEL:
high, 100%

SERVINGS:
4

COMPLETE RECIPE TIME:
about 10 minutes

COOKING TIME:
about 5 minutes

MICROWAVE COOKWARE:
2-quart glass or plastic container
or ring pan

COVERING:
plastic wrap or the dish cover

Use instead of rice, potatoes, or noodles.

1 cup water or broth	**4 tablespoons butter or oil**
1 cup couscous	**(optional)**

Place all ingredients in a 2-quart microwave dish or ring pan, cover with plastic wrap or the dish cover, and microwave on high for 5 minutes. Let stand for 2 to 3 minutes, or until the water is absorbed and the couscous is tender.

Couscous Pilaf

MICROWAVE ONLY

ENERGY LEVEL:
high, 100%

SERVINGS:
4

COMPLETE RECIPE TIME:
about 10 minutes

COOKING TIME:
about 5 minutes

MICROWAVE COOKWARE:
3-quart glass or plastic container

COVERING:
plastic wrap or the dish cover

1 stalk celery, chopped	**½ cup nuts, chopped**
1 medium onion, chopped	**3 cups cooked couscous**
1 carrot, chopped	**½ cup chopped parsley**
½ cup raisins	

Place the celery, onion, carrot, raisins, and nuts in a 3-quart microwave dish, cover with plastic wrap or the dish cover, and microwave on high for 4 to 5 minutes, or until the vegetables are tender. Stir in the couscous and parsley and serve hot or chilled.

Grits

Until I lived in the South, I thought grits was a one-syllable word. There I learned that it has two syllables, and is pronounced "gree its." I first ate grits while serving in the army, where I was stationed in Virginia. I thought it was cream of wheat and wondered why it was served with butter and pepper instead of sugar and milk. Actually grits have little flavor; you can eat them mixed with almost anything.

1 cup quick, not instant, grits   3 cups water

Place ingredients in a 3-quart microwave dish or ring pan and microwave on high, uncovered, for 10 to 12 minutes, or until thickened. Stir a couple of times during the cooking.

MICROWAVE ONLY

ENERGY LEVEL:
high, 100%

SERVINGS:
4

COMPLETE RECIPE TIME:
about 15 minutes

COOKING TIME:
about 10 to 12 minutes

MICROWAVE COOKWARE:
3-quart glass or plastic container or ring pan

Glamorous Grits

1 bell pepper, cored and diced

1 medium onion, chopped

1 cup diced baked ham

1 14-ounce can tomato
   wedges, drained

1 cup quick, not instant, grits

3 cups chicken broth

1 cup shredded Swiss cheese

Place the pepper and onion in a 3-quart microwave dish or ring pan, cover with plastic wrap or the dish cover, and microwave on high for 4 to 5 minutes, or until vegetables are soft. Add the ham, tomatoes, grits, and broth. Microwave on high, uncovered, for 10 to 12 minutes, or until thickened. Stir in the cheese and serve.

MICROWAVE ONLY

ENERGY LEVEL:
high, 100%

SERVINGS:
4

COMPLETE RECIPE TIME:
about 25 minutes

COOKING TIME:
about 17 minutes

MICROWAVE COOKWARE:
3-quart glass or plastic container or ring pan

COVERING:
plastic wrap or the dish cover

Polenta

MICROWAVE ONLY

ENERGY LEVEL:
high, 100%

SERVINGS:
4 to 6

COMPLETE RECIPE TIME:
about 20 minutes

COOKING TIME:
about 13 to 15 minutes

MICROWAVE COOKWARE:
glass or plastic bread loaf pan,
8 ½ × 3 ½ × 2½

Polenta is simply cornmeal mush. You can make it with coarse-ground cornmeal or regular white or yellow cornmeal. You can make it thin, like pudding, or firm, like moist corn bread—in other words, anyway you like it. It is similar to grits in that it has little flavor. Use it with flavorful toppings or just add butter and/or cheese. Polenta makes a great side dish. And, it is much easier to make by microwave than on top of your stove.

1 cup cornmeal   **3 cups water**

Place both ingredients in a bread loaf pan 8½ × 3½ × 2½ inches and stir. Microwave, uncovered, on high about 13 to 15 minutes. Stir once or twice during the cooking. Allow to cool and become firm. Unmold, slice, and serve with butter, cheese, tomato sauce, gravy, or whatever. Or, fry or grill and top with meat sauce or tomato sauce or puréed vegetables.

Pasta and Pasta Sauces

Pasta should be cooked only on your stove top. You need a lot of rapidly boiling water to cook noodles properly and water never boils well when heated by microwave. All sauces and toppings for pasta dishes, however, cook beautifully by microwave, so I'm going to include some here. After one of my cooking classes, where I made a spaghetti sauce in about one hour, a young woman of Italian ancestry commented to me that if she ever cooked a spaghetti sauce in less than seven hours her grandmother would turn over in her grave. You have to realize that when her grandmother cooked sauces she was using raw tomatoes and it took a long time over low heat to cook them so that the water would evaporate and the sauce would thicken. Nowadays, we use canned tomatoes and tomato paste and tomato sauce that have already been reduced.

Basic Meat Sauce

This is a no-fail recipe that you can put together and cook in your microwave while you take off and indulge in other activities.

1 pound ground beef

½ pound bulk Italian sausage or 2 links, casings removed

1 medium yellow onion, chopped

4 large cloves garlic, minced

1 small carrot, minced

1 28-ounce can Italian-style tomatoes, chopped

1 8-ounce can tomato sauce

2 tablespoons dried spaghetti sauce seasoning

2 bay leaves

1 cup dry red wine

2 tablespoons anchovy paste (optional)

MICROWAVE ONLY

ENERGY LEVEL:
high, 100%

YIELD:
about 1 ½ quarts

COMPLETE RECIPE TIME:
about 60 minutes

COOKING TIME:
about 60 minutes

MICROWAVE COOKWARE:
3–4-quart glass or plastic container or ring pan

COVERING:
paper towel, wax paper, or other nonstick cooking paper

Place the meat and vegetables in a 3-quart microwave dish or ring pan, cover with plastic wrap or the dish cover, and microwave on high for 5 to 6 minutes, or until the meat loses its pink color. Drain off the fat and crumble the meat. Add the remaining ingredients, stir, and cover with a paper towel. Microwave on high for 30 minutes, stir, and microwave 15 to 30 minutes longer, or until it thickens to your specifications.

Marinara Sauce: Omit the meat in the above recipe.

Fresh Tomato Sauce

If you can get nice RIPE tomatoes, make this recipe. Otherwise forget it.

4 large ripe tomatoes, chopped and drained

4 scallions, thinly sliced

2 large cloves garlic, minced

2 tablespoons olive oil

2 tablespoons minced fresh basil

Mix together and serve raw with pasta. Or microwave, uncovered, on high for 4 to 5 minutes, or just enough to blend the flavors.

Parsley Tomato Sauce

MICROWAVE ONLY

ENERGY LEVEL:
high, 100%

YIELD:
about 1 quart

COMPLETE RECIPE TIME:
about 35 minutes

COOKING TIME:
about 30 minutes

MICROWAVE COOKWARE:
2-quart glass or plastic container or ring pan

COVERING:
paper towel, wax paper, or other nonstick cooking paper

1 28-ounce can, crushed tomatoes

1 cup chopped parsley

2 tablespoons lemon juice

4 cloves garlic, minced

4 tablespoons olive oil

Place all ingredients in a 2-quart microwave dish or ring pan, cover with a paper towel, and microwave on high for 30 minutes, stirring once or twice.

Chicken Sauce

This is a delicious, simple to make sauce. It also can be made using leftover chicken or turkey.

1 medium onion, chopped

4 tablespoons butter or margarine

2 tablespoons olive oil

4 chicken breast halves, sliced into ¼-inch strips

½ cup dry red wine

½ cup milk

4 tablespoons tomato paste

1 tablespoon cornstarch

Salt and fresh ground pepper

½ cup grated Parmesan cheese

MICROWAVE ONLY

ENERGY LEVEL:
high, 100%

YIELD:
about 1 quart

COMPLETE RECIPE TIME:
about 30 minutes

COOKING TIME:
about 20 minutes

MICROWAVE COOKWARE:
3-quart glass or plastic container or ring pan

COVERING:
plastic wrap or the dish cover

Place the onion, butter, and oil in a 3-quart microwave dish or ring pan, cover with plastic wrap or the dish cover, and microwave on high for 3 to 4 minutes, or until the onion is soft. Add the chicken, re-cover, and microwave on high for about 10 minutes, or until the chicken is cooked. Stir in the remaining ingredients, except the cheese, and microwave, uncovered, for 5 minutes, or until thickened. Stir in the cheese and serve.

Simple Red Clam Sauce

MICROWAVE ONLY

ENERGY LEVEL:
high, 100%

YIELD:
about 1 quart

COMPLETE RECIPE TIME:
about 20 minutes

COOKING TIME:
about 18 minutes

MICROWAVE COOKWARE:
2-quart glass or plastic measuring cup

COVERING:
plastic wrap or the dish cover and a paper towel

1 medium onion, minced

4 cloves garlic, minced

1 10-ounce can minced clams and juice

1 28-ounce can crushed tomatoes

2 tablespoons dried Italian herbs

Tabasco to taste (optional)

Place the onion and garlic in a 2-quart measuring container, cover with plastic wrap, and microwave on high 3 minutes. Add the remaining ingredients, cover with a paper towel, and microwave on high for 10 to 15 minutes.

Mussel Sauce

MICROWAVE ONLY

ENERGY LEVEL:
high, 100%

YIELD:
1 quart

COMPLETE RECIPE TIME:
about 20 minutes

COOKING TIME:
about 15 minutes

MICROWAVE COOKWARE:
4-quart glass or plastic container
or ring pan

COVERING:
plastic wrap or the dish cover

1 14-ounce can stewed tomatoes

4 tablespoons olive oil

½ teaspoon Tabasco

2 pounds raw mussels, soaked in water to remove grit

4 tablespoons minced parsley

Place the tomatoes, oil, and Tabasco in a 4-quart microwave dish or ring pan, cover with plastic wrap or the dish cover, and microwave on high for 5 minutes.

In the meantime, wash the mussels and remove beards. Discard any that don't close when tapped. Add the mussels to the tomatoes, re-cover, and microwave on high for 10 minutes. Shake the pan several times during the cooking but don't open the container. Serve with mussels in the shell or remove the shells, leaving the mussels in the sauce. Stir in the parsley.

Hot Sausage and Mushroom Sauce

MICROWAVE ONLY

ENERGY LEVEL:
high, 100%

SERVINGS:
4

COMPLETE RECIPE TIME:
about 15 minutes

COOKING TIME:
about 10 minutes

MICROWAVE COOKWARE:
2-quart glass or plastic container
or ring pan

COVERING:
plastic wrap or the dish cover

3 hot Italian sausages, about ¾ pound, casing removed and cut into ½-inch slices

8 ounces raw *porcini* or *shiitake* mushrooms, sliced

2 tablespoons olive oil

1 medium onion, chopped

2 cloves garlic, minced

½ cup grated Parmesan cheese

4 tablespoons chopped parsley

Place all ingredients, except the cheese and parsley, in a 2-quart microwave dish, cover with plastic wrap or the dish cover, and microwave on high for 8 to 10 minutes. Stir in the cheese and parsley.

Artichoke and Olive Sauce

MICROWAVE ONLY

ENERGY LEVEL:
high, 100%

SERVINGS:
4

COMPLETE RECIPE TIME:
about 10 minutes

COOKING TIME:
about 8 minutes

MICROWAVE COOKWARE:
2-quart glass or plastic container
or ring pan

COVERING:
plastic wrap or the dish cover

1 small onion, minced

4 tablespoons butter or margarine

3 tablespoons olive oil

1 6-ounce jar marinated artichokes with oil

1 7-ounce can ripe green or black olives, pitted and halved, drained

½ cup grated Parmesan cheese

Place the onion, butter, and oil in a 2-quart microwave dish, cover with plastic wrap or the dish cover, and microwave on high for 3 to 4 minutes, or until the onion is soft. Add the artichokes and olives and re-cover and microwave on high for 3 to 4 minutes, or until heated through. Stir in the cheese.

Tuna Sauce

MICROWAVE ONLY

ENERGY LEVEL:
high, 100%

SERVINGS:
4

COMPLETE RECIPE TIME:
about 10 minutes

COOKING TIME:
about 6 minutes

MICROWAVE COOKWARE:
1-quart glass or plastic measuring
container

2 tablespoons flour

2 tablespoons margarine

1 cup clam juice or fish broth

1 6½-ounce can tuna in oil

¼ cup grated Parmesan cheese

Fresh ground pepper to taste

Place the flour and margarine in a 1-quart measuring cup and microwave, uncovered, on high for 2 minutes. Stir to blend and gradually stir in the clam juice. Microwave, uncovered, on high for 4 minutes. Stir in the tuna and cheese and pepper.

Broccoli and Anchovy Sauce

4 flat anchovy fillets with oil or
    4 tablespoons anchovy
    paste

2 cloves garlic, minced

4 tablespoons olive oil

4 cups broccoli flowerets

Mash together the anchovies, garlic, and oil. Wash the broccoli and place in a 2-quart microwave dish. Stir in the anchovy mash. Cover with plastic wrap or the dish cover and microwave on high for 5 to 6 minutes, or until the broccoli is al dente.

MICROWAVE ONLY

ENERGY LEVEL:
high, 100%

SERVINGS:
4

COMPLETE RECIPE TIME:
about 10 minutes

COOKING TIME:
about 6 minutes

MICROWAVE COOKWARE:
2-quart glass or plastic container or ring pan

COVERING:
plastic wrap or the dish cover

Gorgonzola Sauce

MICROWAVE ONLY

ENERGY LEVEL:
high, 100%

SERVINGS:
4

COMPLETE RECIPE TIME:
about 10 minutes

COOKING TIME:
about 6 minutes

MICROWAVE COOKWARE:
1½-quart glass or plastic container or measuring cup

COVERING:
plastic wrap or the dish cover

2 cups light cream or
    condensed milk

6 ounces gorgonzola cheese or
    other blue cheese

White pepper to taste

Place all ingredients in a 1½-quart measuring cup. Cover with plastic wrap or the dish cover and microwave on high for 5 to 6 minutes, or until the cheese is melted and the sauce is smooth. Stir with a whisk to blend.

Ham with Onion and Pea Sauce

MICROWAVE ONLY

ENERGY LEVEL:
high, 100%

SERVINGS:
4

COMPLETE RECIPE TIME:
about 15 minutes

COOKING TIME:
about 10 minutes

MICROWAVE COOKWARE:
2-quart glass or plastic container measuring cup

2 tablespoons flour

2 tablespoons margarine

1 cup milk

½ pound baked ham, diced

1 10-ounce package frozen
    peas and onions, defrosted

½ cup grated Parmesan or
    Romano cheese

Place the flour and margarine in a 2-quart measuring cup and microwave, uncovered, on high for 2 minutes. Stir to blend and add the milk, ham, and peas and onions. Microwave on high, uncovered, for 5 to 7 minutes, or until thickened and heated through.

Gardiniera Sauce

1 red bell pepper, cored and
diced

1 cup broccoli flowerets

4 ounces raw mushrooms,
sliced

4 ounces sugar peas

1 14-ounce can tomato wedges
or stewed tomatoes,
chopped and drained

2 scallions, thinly sliced

2 cloves garlic, minced

4 tablespoons olive oil

2 tablespoons dried Italian
herbs

MICROWAVE ONLY

ENERGY LEVEL:
high, 100%

SERVINGS:
4

COMPLETE RECIPE TIME:
about 20 minutes

COOKING TIME:
about 10 minutes

MICROWAVE COOKWARE:
3-quart glass or plastic container
or ring pan

COVERING:
plastic wrap or the dish cover

Place all ingredients in a 3-quart microwave dish or ring pan,
cover with plastic wrap or the dish cover, and microwave on
high for 8 to 10 minutes, or until the broccoli is al dente.

Egg Dishes

Some egg dishes cook very well by microwave and others are better done conventionally. Use your own judgment as to the best and easiest way to cook egg recipes.

Fried Eggs

Use your stove top. It's easier, faster, and better.

Melt 1 tablespoon butter or margarine in a skillet on the stove. Add 2 to 4 eggs and fry until the bottoms are set and the edges start to brown. Add 1 teaspoon water and cover quickly with the lid. Continue frying for about 20 to 30 seconds, or until the white on top of the yolk becomes translucent.

Scrambled Eggs

Microwaved scrambled eggs are very light and easy to make. You can also eliminate all cooking oil if you're cutting back on calories. However, the residue tends to stick to the cooking container, so I recommend you use some nonstick vegetable oil spray.

1 tablespoon butter or margarine (optional)   **2 eggs, beaten**

Melt the butter in a glass bowl or 4-cup measuring cup and add the eggs. Microwave, uncovered, on high for 1 to 2 minutes, stirring every 30 seconds. Stop cooking when the eggs are still very moist. Let them sit for a little until they set.

Omelets

Omelets are easy to make in a skillet and are always perfect if you use this recipe.

1 tablespoon butter or
    margarine

cheese, cooked vegetables,
    and ham or bacon

2 eggs, whipped until just
    blended, or equivalent egg
    substitute

Melt butter in an 8-inch skillet. Add the eggs and cook until the edges set. Push the cooked edges to the center so the uncooked egg on top flows onto the surface of the frying pan. Add the other ingredients and cook until the eggs are almost completely cooked. Slide the omelet halfway onto a heated plate and fold the half still in the skillet over the top.

ZAP TIP: To serve a number of omelets at one time, make them conventionally as directed above and store them on a platter, covered with plastic wrap, in your refrigerator until you want to serve them. Then microwave about 1 minute per omelet or until heated through.

Omelets in Pepper Cups

MICROWAVE ONLY

ENERGY LEVEL:
high, 100%

SERVINGS:
4

COMPLETE RECIPE TIME:
about 25 minutes

COOKING TIME:
about 14 minutes

MICROWAVE COOKWARE:
3-quart glass or plastic casserole
or ring pan

COVERING:
plastic wrap or the dish cover

This is a unique presentation of an egg dish that is beautiful and can be made only by microwave.

4 green, yellow, or red bell peppers (or a combination)	4 tablespoons cooked chopped onions
4 ounces shredded cheese (Cheddar, Swiss, Gouda)	10 eggs
	Salt and fresh ground pepper
4 ounces boiled ham, diced	Tomato or cheese sauce

Use peppers that have even bottoms so they will stand upright. With the peppers standing upright, cut off the tops so they are parallel to the cutting surface. Remove the seeds and membrane and place the peppers in a three-quart microwave dish or ring pan. Cover with plastic wrap and microwave on high for 4 minutes. Add ¼ of each ingredient, except the eggs, to each pepper. Mix the eggs with a fork and fill the peppers equally. Re-cover the dish and microwave on high for 8 to 10 minutes, or until the eggs have set. After cooking, poke into the omelets with a fork to be sure the eggs are not still liquid. Cook longer if necessary. Serve with a tomato or cheese sauce.

Note: If you can't get peppers with even bottoms, lay the peppers on their sides and cut off the top side. Proceed as directed above.

Puff Omelet

This is what I call a microwave omelet. The best container to use is a large coffee mug. If you are having a breakfast for a lot of people, you can make five or six at once and not spend all your time slaving over your stove.

1 tablespoon butter or margarine per omelet

2 eggs per omelet or equivalent egg substitute

shredded cheese, cooked vegetables, and/or cooked meat

Salsa or tomato sauce (optional)

Melt butter in each coffee mug or in a small bowl. Add the eggs and beat with a fork until blended. Add the remaining ingredients and microwave on high, uncovered, for about 1½ to 2 minutes, or until the eggs puff over the top of the mug. Transfer to a heated plate and serve plain or with the sauce.

Poached Eggs

I think it's easy and better to poach eggs by microwave because it takes less time and you use less water. Because the yolk and white cook at such a different rate by microwave, you have to use water to balance out the cooking rate. Use custard cups or similar size and shaped bowls.

In each cup, microwave ½ cup water about 1 minute, or until it boils. Add 1 refrigerated egg (room temperature eggs will cook in about 15 seconds) per cup and microwave on high for about 30 seconds, or until the white is cooked. Drain on a slotted spoon and transfer to a serving plate.

Hard-Cooked Eggs

If you are going to chop hard-cooked eggs for egg salad you can cook the eggs in your microwave very quickly and easily. Crack them into a glass bowl, poke the yolks with a fork, cover with plastic wrap, and microwave on high for about 40 seconds per egg, or until they are just hard. Let them sit for a couple of minutes and chop and mix them. If you are going to use the eggs as deviled eggs or to eat whole you are better off to cook them in boiling water for 10 to 15 minutes on the stove top.

If you want to cook them in the microwave, wrap the eggs individually or all together in foil and place them in enough water just to cover them. Microwave on high for about 15 minutes, or until they are hard. The only advantage to cooking them this way is that you don't have to watch them and take them off the heat when they are done. The microwave will turn off automatically.

Do not cook eggs in the shell in your microwave. They will almost certainly explode and you will spend a lot of time cleaning the residue from the inside of your oven.

Quiche

I introduced quiche to the San Francisco Bay area before anyone, besides the French and gourmet professionals, knew what it was. My wife, Doris, made one for dinner one night and I couldn't get over how delicious it was. This was before the fear of cholesterol had enveloped the nation and you could eat eggs, cheese, and cream and not worry about dropping dead the next moment. I was so impressed that I started a wholesale quiche business, catering to most of the delicatessens and supermarkets around San Francisco. The name of the product was "French Quiche," which many people confused with an amorous embrace.

You can make quiche in your microwave but if you are going to make more than one it is easier and more efficient to do so in your conventional oven. The biggest problem with making quiche by microwave is that the edges cook a lot faster than the center, so by the time the center is cooked the edges have dried out and toughened. You can overcome that problem by microwaving the quiche ingredients in a large measuring cup and then transferring them to a prebaked crust and completing the cooking in your microwave. Sometimes people don't like the beautiful golden color of a microwaved quiche because they are used to the browned color of a conventionally baked one. You can enhance a microwaved quiche by garnishing the top with bell pepper rings, tomato wedges, fresh herb leaves, or even edible flowers.

You can also make cholesterol-free quiches by using egg substitutes, soy-based cheeses, and powdered milk. They are not as tasty, but they still make a nice meal.

Quiche Lorraine

MICROWAVE ONLY

4 large eggs

1 cup cream or milk

1 cup shredded Swiss cheese coated with 1 tablespoon cornstarch

1 9-inch pie crust, baked conventionally in a glass pie plate

1 cup cooked bacon, crumbled, or diced cooked ham

Bell pepper rings, raw ripe seeded tomato slices, or zucchini or nasturtium flowers for garnish

ENERGY LEVEL:
high, 100%

SERVINGS:
4

COMPLETE RECIPE TIME:
about 25 minutes

COOKING TIME:
about 18 minutes

MICROWAVE COOKWARE:
2-quart glass or plastic batter bowl

ACCESSORY EQUIPMENT:
9-inch glass pie plate

Beat the eggs and mix with the cream and cheese in a 2-quart batter bowl or similar container. Microwave on high for about 6 minutes, or until the mixture has thickened. Stir to blend. Cover the pie crust with the bacon and pour the egg mixture on top, Microwave the pie on high for about 10 to 12 minutes, or until the custard has set. Allow to cool and garnish the top.

Vegetarian Quiche: Substitute cooked vegetables for the bacon or ham in the above recipe.

Quiche in Pepper Cups

MICROWAVE ONLY

ENERGY LEVEL:
high, 100%

SERVINGS:
4

COMPLETE RECIPE TIME:
about 26 minutes

COOKING TIME:
about 12 to 16 minutes

MICROWAVE COOKWARE:
3-quart glass or plastic casserole
or ring pan

COVERING:
plastic wrap or the dish cover

This recipe is similar to Omelets in Pepper Cups (page 274), but it uses cream. It takes longer to cook until the custard sets, though, so it isn't necessary to precook the peppers as you do in the omelet recipe.

4 bell peppers with even
    bottoms

4 large eggs or equivalent egg
    substitute

1 cup cream or milk

1 cup shredded Swiss cheese
    coated with 1 tablespoon
    cornstarch

4 ounces cooked bacon or ham
    or vegetables

1 cup salsa or tomato sauce

Cut the tops off of the peppers parallel to the cutting surface and remove the membrane and seeds. Add an equal amount of cheese and cooked meat and/or vegetables to each pepper cup. Mix the eggs and cream and fill each pepper. Place in a three-quart microwave dish or ring pan and cover with plastic wrap. Microwave on high for about 12 to 16 minutes, or until the custard has set. Check doneness by inserting a fork into the center of the custard. Serve topped with salsa or tomato sauce.

Variations: Use cooked rice or kashi instead of the bacon or ham.

Terrines and Pâtés

Most terrines and pâtés are cooked in a water bath. Since this is not necessary when you cook with the microwave oven, it is the ideal appliance for this grouping.

These recipes are a little elaborate but the beauty of the finished product is worth the trouble. Terrines are the ideal dish to serve at a buffet or to take to a potluck dinner. After you look at these recipes I know that you will be able to convert your own favorite conventional ones and realize the beauty of quick, quality cooking by microwave.

Vegetable Terrine

MICROWAVE ONLY

ENERGY LEVEL:
high, 100%

SERVINGS:
about 8 to 16

COMPLETE RECIPE TIME:
about 30 minutes plus 8 hours for
chilling

COOKING TIME:
about 10 minutes

MICROWAVE COOKWARE:
8½ × 3½ × 2½-inch glass or
plastic bread loaf pan and large
measuring cup

ACCESSORY EQUIPMENT:
5-pound bag of flour or sugar

COVERING:
plastic wrap

1 6-inch zucchini, ends
   removed

1 yellow squash, ends removed

1 small unpeeled eggplant,
   ends removed

6 asparagus spears, tough
   ends cut off

1 medium red bell pepper or
   pimiento, skin removed
   with a vegetable peeler,
   cored, and cut into thin
   strips

6 mushrooms, sliced

1 tablespoon minced garlic

1 cup Chicken Stock, canned
   or homemade (page 150)

2 envelopes plain gelatin

1 14-ounce can tomato
   wedges, drained and sliced
   lengthwise

1 cup chopped coriander or
   parsley leaves

2 tablespoons Shilling
   Vegetable Delight
   Seasoning

Slice the zucchini, yellow squash, and eggplant lengthwise into thin strips and place with the asparagus, pepper, mushrooms, and garlic in a glass loaf pan. Cover with plastic wrap and microwave on high for 5 to 8 minutes, or until cooked al dente. Gently press the vegetables and drain off the juices into a 4-cup measuring cup. Mix the juices with the chicken stock and the gelatin and microwave on high for 1 minute or so until the gelatin dissolves. Add the coriander and seasoning to the gelatin.

Remove the vegetables from the loaf pan and line the pan with plastic wrap with enough hanging over the sides to cover the top of the terrine. Return the vegetables to the loaf pan and pour the gelatin over them. Using two forks seperate the vegetables and arrange them so that the colors are blended evenly. Fold the plastic wrap over the top of the terrine and weight the top with a 5-pound bag of flour or sugar to compress it. Refrigerate overnight or at least 8 hours. Unmold, remove the plastic wrap, and slice into ¾-inch-thick slabs.

Chicken Terrine

2 whole boneless chicken
  breasts, about 1 pound,
  skin removed

1 cup chicken broth

2 leeks, thinly sliced
  lengthwise and washed

6 asparagus spears, tough
  ends cut off

2 envelopes plain gelatin

2 tablespoons Dijon mustard

1 tablespoon dried *fines
  herbes*

1 10-ounce package chopped
  spinach, microwaved 7
  minutes and squeezed dry

1 14½-ounce can stewed
  tomatoes, drained, plus 1
  teaspoon Tabasco

MICROWAVE ONLY

ENERGY LEVEL:
high, 100%

SERVINGS:
8 to 16

COMPLETE RECIPE TIME:
about 40 minutes plus 8 hours for
chilling

COOKING TIME:
about 22 minutes

MICROWAVE COOKWARE:
8½ × 3½ × 2½-inch glass or
plastic bread loaf pan

ACCESSORY EQUIPMENT:
5-pound bag of flour or sugar

COVERING:
plastic wrap

Place the chicken, broth, leeks, and asparagus in a glass loaf pan, cover with plastic wrap, and microwave on high for about 15 minutes, or until the chicken is done and the vegetables are tender. Pour the juices into a 1-quart measuring container and mix with the gelatin, mustard, and *herbes*. Stir to dissolve the gelatin. Mix the spinach with the tomatoes. Remove the chicken and vegetables from the loaf pan and cut the chicken across the grain into ¼-inch slices. Line the loaf pan with plastic wrap with enough hanging over to cover the top. Pour a little gelatin mixture over the bottom of the pan and add a layer of the spinach-tomato mixture and then a layer of chicken and vegetables. Continue layering until all of the ingredients are used. Fold the plastic wrap over the top of the terrine. Place a 5-pound bag of sugar or flour on top to compress it. Refrigerate 8 hours or overnight. Unmold, remove the plastic wrap, and slice into 1-inch slices.

Fish Mousse Mold

MICROWAVE ONLY

ENERGY LEVEL:
medium, 50%

SERVINGS:
8 to 16

COMPLETE RECIPE TIME:
about 22 minutes plus about 4
hours for chilling

COOKING TIME:
about 12 minutes

MICROWAVE COOKWARE:
glass or plastic bread loaf pan

ACCESSORY EQUIPMENT:
food processor, serving platter,
5-pound bag of flour or sugar

COVERING:
plastic wrap or the dish cover

¾ pound raw boneless salmon,
diced

¾ pound white fish, cod,
catfish, halibut, and so on,
diced

2 eggs or equivalent egg
substitute

1½ cups light cream

1 tablespoon dried or fresh
dillweed

Salt and fresh ground pepper
to taste

Lemon slices

Dill or parsley sprigs

Process half of each fish with the eggs and cream until smooth. Stir in the remaining fish and the seasonings. Line an 8½ x 3½ x 2½-inch glass loaf pan with plastic wrap and pour in the fish mixture. Microwave on medium, 50%, power for 10 to 12 minutes, or until the center has set. Place a 5-pound bag of flour or sugar on top to compress it. Refrigerate at least 4 hours. Unmold on a serving platter, remove plastic wrap, and garnish with the lemon slices and dill or parsley sprigs.

Variation: Microwave ½ cup each of chopped red and green bell pepper for 3 minutes, or until soft, and add to the fish mixture.

Corned Beef and Cabbage Terrine

You can make this with leftover corned beef and cabbage or from scratch, using canned corned beef.

1 1-pound can corned beef

2 cups chopped cabbage

1 large Russet potato, diced (peeled optional)

1 carrot, diced

1½ cups beef broth

2 tablespoons cream-style horseradish

2 tablespoons coarse-ground mustard

2 envelopes plain gelatin

MICROWAVE ONLY

ENERGY LEVEL:
high, 100%

SERVINGS:
about 8 to 16

COMPLETE RECIPE TIME:
about 33 minutes

COOKING TIME:
about 23 minutes

MICROWAVE COOKWARE:
dinner plate, 2-quart glass or plastic container, large measuring cup, and glass or plastic bread loaf pan

ACCESSORY EQUIPMENT:
5-pound bag of flour or sugar

COVERING:
plastic wrap or the dish cover

Microwave the corned beef on high on a plate for 4 to 5 minutes and press out the fat. Place the cabbage, potato, and carrot in a 2-quart microwave dish, cover with plastic wrap or the dish cover, and microwave on high for about 15 minutes, or until the potato is tender. Drain the juices into a 4-cup measuring cup and add the broth. Add the horseradish and mustard and gelatin and microwave on high 2 to 3 minutes, or until the gelatin is dissolved. Combine the beef, vegetables, and broth-gelatin mixture and pour into a glass 8½ × 3½ × 2½-inch loaf pan lined with plastic wrap. Place a 5-pound bag of flour or sugar on top to compress it. Refrigerate 8 hours or overnight until firm. Unmold on a serving platter, remove the plastic wrap, and cut into 1-inch slices.

ZAP TIP: You can elevate leftovers to new heights by using them in terrines as described in the previous recipes. Just cut into dice or process and set in a mold with the gelatin. Shredded leftover pot roast makes a great terrine.

Herbed Turkey Pâté

MICROWAVE ONLY

ENERGY LEVEL:
high, 100%

SERVINGS:
8 to 16

COMPLETE RECIPE TIME:
about 30 minutes plus 1 hour for chilling

COOKING TIME:
about 20 minutes

MICROWAVE COOKWARE:
2-quart glass or plastic batter bowl and a glass or plastic bread loaf pan

ACCESSORY EQUIPMENT:
serving platter, 5-pound bag of flour or sugar

COVERING:
plastic wrap

1 large onion, chopped

3 cloves garlic, minced

1 bunch spinach (about ½ pound), stems removed, washed, and chopped

1½ pounds ground turkey

1 egg or equivalent egg substitute

3 tablespoons Italian herbs or 2 tablespoons each of chopped fresh basil and rosemary

Salt and fresh ground pepper

½ pound Italian sausage links, casings removed

Place the onion, garlic, and spinach in a 2-quart glass or plastic batter bowl and microwave on high, uncovered, for 4 to 5 minutes, or until the onion is soft. Drain and press out the juices. Mix onion-garlic-spinach mixture with the turkey, egg, herbs, and seasonings. Lay half of the mixture in the bottom on a 8½ × 3½ × 2½-inch glass loaf pan and lay the sausages in the center. Add the remaining turkey mixture and press and compress the mold. Cover with plastic wrap and microwave on medium, 50%, power for about 15 minutes, or until the pâté is cooked. The internal temperature should be about 170 degrees. Place a 5-pound bag of sugar or flour on the top and chill for at least 1 hour. Remove the plastic wrap and unmold on a serving platter. Slice into ½- to ¾-inch slices.

Variation: Substitute hard-cooked eggs for the sausage in the center portion.

Sauces

Here again I have to tout the advantages of making something in the microwave. When you make some sauces on top of your stove you have to use a water bath or stir constantly to avoid scorching. With your microwave, the container doesn't get hot. You stir once or twice and that's all there is to it.

Roux

Roux is a flour and butter or oil mixture that is used to thicken sauces. Because the flour is first cooked with the oil the floury taste sometimes detected when flour alone is used for thickening is eliminated. Cooking the flour first also hastens the thickening process.

Light Roux

4 tablespoons butter,
  margarine, or oil

¼ cup flour

Place the ingredients in a 1-quart Pyrex batter bowl and stir to blend. Microwave on high 2 to 3 minutes and stir with a whisk.

Dark Roux

MICROWAVE ONLY

ENERGY LEVEL:
high, 100%

YIELD:
½ to 1 cup

COMPLETE RECIPE TIME:
about 10 minutes

COOKING TIME:
about 7 to 10 minutes

MICROWAVE COOKWARE:
2-quart Pyrex batter bowl

Y ou must use oil for this *roux,* because it has to cook for a long time to brown the flour and develop the flavor. If you used butter it would burn before the results were obtained. When you make this type of *roux* on top of the stove you must cook it over low heat and stir constantly. Some Cajun cooks make it over high heat while whipping the devil out of it and it comes out just fine. I'm not talented enough to whip hot oil without endangering the whole kitchen, so I use my microwave and hopefully you will also.

½ cup oil

½ cup flour

Place both ingredients in a 2-quart Pyrex batter bowl or other heatproof glass or ceramic dish of the same size. Microwave on high, uncovered, for 5 minutes and stir with a whisk. Continue microwaving and stirring in 1-minute increments until the desired color is reached. Between 7 and 10 minutes it goes from tan to dark brown. The darker it gets the more intense the flavor. Be careful when you handle the bowl because even the handle will be hot. Use this *roux* for gumbos and stews.

Béchamel Sauce

This sauce should be called a ballet sauce because of all the two twos.

2 tablespoons butter or oil   **1 cup milk**

2 tablespoons flour

Mix the butter and flour in a 4-cup measuring cup and microwave, uncovered, on high for 2 minutes. Stir to blend and add the milk. Microwave 2 minutes and stir. Microwave 2 minutes, or until thickened, and stir again. Season with salt and pepper to taste. The sauce as it is now can be used for soufflés and casseroles like moussaka.

Buttery Sauce: Stir 1 tablespoon butter into the Béchamel and use the sauce on cooked vegetables.

Cream Sauce: Gradually stir ¼ to ½ cup whipping cream into the Béchamel for a very rich sauce that can be used to enhance most dishes or as a topping for preparations that you want to brown under the broiler, like gratinéed asparagus.

Tomato Sauce: Stir 2 to 4 tablespoons tomato or dried tomato paste into the Béchamel.

Herb Sauce: Stir 2 tablespoons dried *fines herbes* into the Béchamel. If you have fresh herbs use minced tarragon or chervil.

Curry Sauce: Stir 2 tablespoons curry powder and 1 tablespoon lemon juice into the Béchamel. Use with chicken and light meats.

Anchovy Sauce: Stir 2 to 4 tablespoons anchovy paste into the Béchamel.

Mornay Sauce: Add ¼ to ½ cup shredded Swiss cheese to the Béchamel after it has thickened and stir until the cheese is completely melted and blended. Season with salt and pepper, a pinch of nutmeg, and/or a little Tabasco.

Velouté Sauce

MICROWAVE ONLY

ENERGY LEVEL:
high, 100%

YIELD:
1 to 1½ cups

COMPLETE RECIPE TIME:
about 10 minutes

COOKING TIME:
about 8 minutes

MICROWAVE COOKWARE:
4-cup glass or plastic measuring container

This is a white sauce made with broth rather than milk as in béchamel.

2 tablespoons butter, margarine, or oil	1 cup chicken broth of fish stock or bottled clam juice
2 tablespoons flour	

Mix the butter and flour in a 4-cup measuring cup and microwave, uncovered, on high for 2 minutes. Stir and add the broth and microwave on high for 4 minutes, or until thickened. Stir after 2 minutes and after the sauce has thickened.

Note: All of the flavorings suggested in the béchamel section can also be used with velouté sauce.

Simple Brown Sauce

MICROWAVE ONLY

ENERGY LEVEL:
high, 100%

YIELD:
about 1 cup

COMPLETE RECIPE TIME:
about 12 minutes

COOKING TIME:
about 8 minutes

MICROWAVE COOKWARE:
1-quart glass or plastic measuring container

Use the Beef Stock described in the stew section of this book or substitute canned beef broth or beef extracts like Bovril as a base for this sauce.

2 tablespoons butter, margarine, or oil	1 cup Beef Stock (page 151), or canned beef broth or 1 cup of water mixed with 1 tablespoon Bovril or other beef extract
2 tablespoons flour	

Mix the butter and flour in a 4-cup Pyrex measuring cup and microwave on high, uncovered, for 2 minutes. Stir and blend in the stock and microwave on high, uncovered, for 4 to 6 minutes, or until thickened.

You can enhance the flavor of basic brown sauce by adding tomato paste and/or onion paste, available also in tubes.

Vegetarian Brown Sauce: Use 1 tablespoon Vegemite or Savorex flavoring (available at health food stores) with 1 cup water instead of beef stock. Cook as directed above. Use on rice, beans, and fried vegetables.

Spicy Brown Sauce: Add 1 tablespoon chili-garlic paste to the basic recipe. Use on chicken, turkey, or other light meats.

Brown Mustard Sauce: Add 2 tablespoons Dijon or other good mustard to the basic recipe.

Brown Mushroom Sauce: Add ½ cup *Duxelles* (page 291) to the basic recipe.

Brown Sauce with Wine: Reduce ½ cup fortified wine—port or Madeira—by half in a skillet and add it to the brown sauce.

Note: Liquids reduce much faster in a skillet than in your microwave oven.

Hollandaise Sauce

You can make hollandaise in a saucepan, a double boiler, and even in a blender, but there's not an easier way than in your microwave. You only have to use one dish and actually you could make right it in your serving bowl and not have any other dish to wash.

During these days of cholesterol conscientiousness, people swoon at the idea of consuming any hollandaise. However, a little now and then isn't going to hurt if you have a healthy body and there is nothing that tastes as wonderful. So enjoy once in a while!

MICROWAVE ONLY

ENERGY LEVEL:
high, 100%

YIELD:
about ¾ cup

COMPLETE RECIPE TIME:
about 5 minutes

COOKING TIME:
about 1½ to 2 minutes

MICROWAVE COOKWARE:
1-quart glass or plastic measuring cup

3 large egg yolks

¼ pound butter or margarine, cut into 4 pieces

Lemon juice to taste

Salt and white pepper to taste

Tabasco to taste (optional)

Place the yolks and butter in a 1-quart measuring cup or bowl and stir a bit to break up the yolks. Microwave on high, uncovered, for 1½ to 2 minutes, stirring with a fork every 15 seconds or so until the sauce has thickened. Add the lemon juice and the seasonings and serve. You can store in the refrigerator and reheat by microwave when needed. Do so slowly and stir often. Now that you've made hollandaise sauce, don't you just love your microwave?

Béarnaise Sauce

¼ cup dry white wine

¼ cup wine vinegar

1 tablespoon minced shallots

½ teaspoon dried tarragon or 1 tablespoon minced fresh tarragon

Salt and pepper

Place all ingredients in a skillet and reduce to about 3 tablespoons. Add to hollandaise sauce in place of the lemon juice.

Hollandaise with Whipped Cream: Fold 1 cup whipped cream into hollandaise sauce. The cream makes the sauce a little lighter and is great on fish and green vegetables.

Orange-Flavored Hollandaise Sauce: Melt 2 tablespoons frozen orange juice concentrate and stir into hollandaise sauce.

Vegetable Flavoring Mixtures

These blends of vegetables are used to enhance the flavor of sauces, gravies, soups, stews, and anything else that you want to have taste a little richer. Conventionally they are simmered on the stove until they become soft and the flavors blend. You are always advised to be careful not to allow them to brown because that will alter the flavor. When you use your microwave you can cook them almost forever without any browning so it again is the perfect tool to make these recipes.

Duxelles

MICROWAVE ONLY

ENERGY LEVEL:
high, 100%

YIELD:
about 1 cup

COMPLETE RECIPE TIME:
about 15 minutes

COOKING TIME:
about 9 minutes

MICROWAVE COOKWARE:
1-quart glass or plastic measuring container

ACCESSORY EQUIPMENT:
kitchen towel

½ pound mushrooms, minced

2 tablespoons minced shallots

2 tablespoons butter or
  margarine

1 tablespoon oil

Salt and fresh ground pepper
  to taste

Pinch of nutmeg (optional)

Place the mushrooms in a dish towel, twist to close, and microwave on high for 4 minutes. Press and twist out as much water as possible. Place the mushrooms and the remaining ingredients in a small glass bowl or measuring cup and microwave on high, uncovered, for 3 to 5 minutes, or until all of the oil is absorbed by the mushrooms. Or place everything in a 1-quart microwave dish and cook on high, 100% (uncovered), for 15 minutes. Season to taste.

Mirepoix

MICROWAVE ONLY

ENERGY LEVEL:
high, 100%

YIELD:
about 1 cup

COMPLETE RECIPE TIME:
about 12 minutes

COOKING TIME:
about 10 minutes

MICROWAVE COOKWARE:
1-quart glass or plastic measuring cup

Making a *mirepoix* on the stove top would take about 20 to 30 minutes with constant attention to stirring. In your microwave it takes about 10 minutes and you only have to stir once if at all.

1 small onion, minced (about
  ½ cup)

1 stalk celery, minced (about
  ½ cup)

1 carrot, minced (about ½ cup)

1 tablespoon butter or
  margarine

1 tablespoon minced ham or
  bacon (optional)

Place all ingredients in a 1-quart measuring cup and microwave on high uncovered, for 7 to 10 minutes, or until the vegetables are very soft.

Sofrito

MICROWAVE ONLY

ENERGY LEVEL:
high, 100%

YIELD:
about 1½ cups

COMPLETE RECIPE TIME:
about 35 minutes

COOKING TIME:
about 20 to 30 minutes

MICROWAVE COOKWARE:
1-quart glass or plastic measuring cup

COVERING:
paper towel

When you make this recipe, everyone who enters your kitchen will exclaim, "What on Earth smells so good!"

1 medium onion, chopped	2 tablespoons oil
4 cloves garlic, minced	1 14-ounce can stewed tomatoes

Place all ingredients in a large glass bowl or measuring container and cover with a paper towel. Microwave on high for 20 to 30 minutes, or until the sauce is very thick. Stir once during the cooking if necessary.

Desserts

I love eating desserts but I'm not wild about making them. That's why I think that the microwave is the ideal tool for making sweet things. It's easier and faster, so you don't have to wait long to taste the end result. Use your microwave judiciously and only for those things that it does well. Don't microwave things that should be light and flaky, like pastries and crusts, or for meringues and things that should turn out stiff and browned.

Microwave ovens are great for pie fillings, custards, poached fruit, sauces, and anything that requires a double boiler. I used to advise that you not bake cakes with your microwave because I was concerned that new microwavers would have problems and become discouraged and not pursue real cooking by microwave. Actually, cakes are easy to microwave and they turn out beautifully moist and delicious. Just be sure you don't cook them too long and always use a ring pan to be sure they cook evenly.

Cakes

You can make them from scratch if you just follow the conventional recipe up to the point of baking and then use a microwave ring pan and microwave on medium power for about 12 to 15 minutes, or until a skewer inserted comes out clean. It helps if you cover with wax paper or other nonstick cooking paper to hold in enough of the heat to assure even cooking. Layer cakes are more difficult, especially if you have a microwave with an uneven cooking pattern. If you have to turn the pan a lot it's not worth the effort and since you can do only one layer at a time it takes just as long as if you baked the cakes in your conventional oven.

The cake mixes available today are superb and almost foolproof. I especially like the "pudding in the mix" type. I'm amazed that the manufacturers don't put microwave instructions on the package. Never fear, just follow the instructions for mixing and then microwave in a ring pan on medium power for 12 to 15 minutes, or until the batter is cooked. Invert on a wire rack and allow the cake to cool, frost it, and enjoy! Incidentally, if the cake is not completely cooked when you unmold it, just put it back into the ring pan and microwave it a little longer.

Pies

If you like, make your own crusts but bake them in your conventional oven. In the microwave they don't get brown unless you burn them and they don't cook as evenly as in a hot oven. I am not a good crust maker so I buy the ready-made frozen ones or cracker crusts. They are better than anything I can make and so much easier and mess free. By making the crust in your conventional oven and the filling in your microwave, you will find that the crust stays flakier for a longer time since you didn't bake it with the moist filling.

Apple Pie

MICROWAVE ONLY

ENERGY LEVEL:
high, 100%

SERVINGS:
8

COMPLETE RECIPE TIME:
about 25 minutes plus cooling time

COOKING TIME:
about 15 minutes

MICROWAVE COOKWARE:
2-quart glass or plastic bowl or mixing bowl

COVERING:
plastic wrap or the dish cover

1 9-inch prepared pie crust

8 cups apples, cored (definitely) and peeled (optional)

1 to 1½ cups sugar, depending on the sweetness of the apples

5 tablespoons cornstarch or instant tapioca

1 teaspoon apple pie spice

Bake the crust according to the package instructions. Place remaining ingredients in a 2-quart batter or mixing bowl. Cover with plastic wrap and microwave on high for about 15 minutes, or until the apples are cooked. Stir once during the cooking. Pour into the pie crust and allow to cool or chill in your refrigerator.

Blueberry or Other Berry Pie

MICROWAVE ONLY

ENERGY LEVEL:
high, 100%

SERVINGS:
8

COMPLETE RECIPE TIME:
about 15 minutes

COOKING TIME:
about 10 minutes

MICROWAVE COOKWARE:
2-quart glass or plastic batter bowl or mixing bowl

COVERING:
plastic wrap

1 9-inch prepared pie crust

6 cups berries, washed and all stems removed

1½ cups sugar

5 tablespoons cornstarch

1 tablespoon lemon juice

Bake the crust as directed on the package. Mix remaining ingredients in a 2-quart batter or mixing bowl. Cover with plastic wrap and microwave on high for 8 to 10 minutes, or until thickened. Pour into pie crust and chill.

Strawberry Pie

MICROWAVE ONLY

ENERGY LEVEL:
high, 100%

SERVINGS:
8

COMPLETE RECIPE TIME:
about 20 minutes

COOKING TIME:
about 8 to 10 minutes

MICROWAVE COOKWARE:
2-quart glass or plastic batter bowl
or mixing bowl

4 cups strawberries, hulls removed

4 tablespoons cornstarch

4 drops red food color

1 cup sugar

1 9-inch prebaked pie crust or graham cracker crust

Whipped cream

Mash or process 2 cups of berries, the cornstarch, food color, and sugar. Place in a 2-quart batter bowl or mixing bowl and microwave, uncovered, on high for 8 to 10 minutes, or until very thick. Add the remaining berries and stir together. Pour into the pie crust and chill. Serve plain or with the whipped cream.

Strawberry-Rhubarb Pie

MICROWAVE ONLY

ENERGY LEVEL:
high, 100%

SERVINGS:
8

COMPLETE RECIPE TIME:
about 25 minutes

COOKING TIME:
about 12 to 15 minutes

MICROWAVE COOKWARE:
2-quart glass or plastic batter bowl
or mixing bowl

1 9-inch prepared pie crust or graham cracker crust

2 cups strawberries, hulled and cut in half

2 cups rhubarb, trimmed and cut into ½-inch pieces

4 tablespoons cornstarch

1½ to 2 cups sugar

2 tablespoons lemon juice

4 drops red food color (optional)

Whipped cream

Bake the crust according to package directions. Place the berries, rhubarb, cornstarch, sugar, lemon juice, and food color in a 2-quart batter or mixing bowl and stir together. Microwave on high, uncovered, for 12 to 15 minutes, or until the rhubarb turns to sauce and the juices thicken. Stir after 5 and 10 minutes. Pour into the pie crust and chill. Serve topped with the whipped cream.

Rhubarb Sauce: 1 pound rhubarb, ends trimmed and cut into 1-inch pieces. ½–1 cup sugar. Place rhubarb and sugar in a 1-quart casserole and microwave on high, 100%, power, uncovered for about 10 minutes, or until it dissolves into a sauce. Stir once during cooking.

Cranberry Sauce: Although cranberry sauce is not thought of as a dessert, I'm including it here because there's no other place to fit it. 1-pound raw cranberries, washed. 1 cup sugar. 1 medium orange, peeled, sectioned, seeded. Place everything in a 1-quart microwave dish, stir and microwave on high, 100%, power for about 7 minutes. Stir once during cooking.

Peach Pie

5 cups peaches, peeled, pitted and sliced

1 cup Muesli-type cereal (optional)

3 tablespoons cornstarch if using cereal; 5 tablespoons if not

1 cup sugar, white or brown

1 9-inch prebaked pie crust or graham cracker crust

MICROWAVE ONLY

ENERGY LEVEL:
high, 100%

SERVINGS:
8

COMPLETE RECIPE TIME:
about 25 minutes

COOKING TIME:
about 10 to 12 minutes

MICROWAVE COOKWARE:
2-quart glass or plastic batter bowl or mixing bowl

Mix all filling ingredients in a 2-quart batter or mixing bowl and microwave on high, uncovered, for 10 to 12 minutes, or until the peaches are soft and the juices have thickened. Stir once during the cooking. Pour into the pie crust and chill.

Cream Pies

MICROWAVE ONLY

ENERGY LEVEL:
high, 100%

SERVINGS:
8

COMPLETE RECIPE TIME:
about 10 minutes

COOKING TIME:
about 7 minutes

MICROWAVE COOKWARE:
2-quart glass or plastic batter bowl
or mixing bowl

Making a custard on your stove top is a real chore. You have to stir the ingredients constantly in a double boiler to prevent scorching from direct heat. When you use your microwave, you stir only once and, since the container never gets hot, you don't have to worry about scorching.

⅔ cup sugar

3 tablespoons cornstarch

2 cups milk, skim or whole

2 teaspoons vanilla

2 tablespoons butter or margarine

1 9-inch prebaked pie crust or graham cracker crust

Mix the sugar, cornstarch, and milk in a 2-quart batter or mixing bowl. Microwave on high, uncovered, for about 7 minutes, or until thick. Add the vanilla and butter, stir until the butter melts, and pour into the baked pie crust or custard cups. Chill until firm.

Banana Cream Pie: Line the pie crust with ripe banana slices before pouring in the custard.

Coconut Cream Pie: Mix 1 cup sweetened shredded coconut into the custard when adding the vanilla and butter.

Ultimate Fruit Cream Pie: Combine the banana and coconut recipe and place sliced strawberries over the top. In a measuring cup microwave 3 tablespoons strawberry jam for 30 to 40 seconds, or until thoroughly melted, and paint it over the top of the pie. Chill and serve.

Grape Nut Tart

There's no cooking involved in this recipe, but it shows the convenience of having a microwave oven.

8 ounces lite cream cheese

7 ounces condensed milk

1 cup broken nuts, such as walnuts, pecans, and so on

1 ounce sweet liqueur, such as Cointreau

1 9-inch graham cracker crust

3 cups red seedless grapes, cut in half

3 tablespoons grape jelly

Place the cheese and milk in a 1-quart measuring container and microwave on high 1 minute. Mix with a whisk until smooth and stir in the nuts and liqueur. Spread over the pie crust. Place the grapes, cut side down, over the cheese mixture. Microwave the jelly on high in a measuring cup for 30 to 40 seconds and paint over the top of the tart. Chill until firm.

MICROWAVE ONLY

ENERGY LEVEL:
high, 100%

SERVINGS:
8

COMPLETE RECIPE TIME:
about 12 minutes plus chilling time

COOKING TIME:
about 2 minutes

MICROWAVE COOKWARE:
2-quart glass or plastic batter bowl or mixing bowl

Whole Lemon Custard Tarts

MICROWAVE ONLY

ENERGY LEVEL:
high, 100%

SERVINGS:
8

COMPLETE RECIPE TIME:
about 10 minutes

COOKING TIME:
about 6 minutes

MICROWAVE COOKWARE:
1-quart glass or plastic batter bowl
or mixing bowl

ACCESSORY EQUIPMENT:
blender or food processor

Everything you read these days suggests that you consume more fiber. With that in mind I made up this recipe using the whole lemon instead of just the juice. There is also no cholesterol.

2 large lemons	¼ pound margarine
8 ounces egg substitute	6 prebaked tart shells or 1 9-inch graham cracker crust
1 cup sugar	

Cut the peel, including the white pulp, off of the lemons. Remove the seeds and cut the lemon flesh into pieces. In the food processor blend until smooth. Place the processed lemon in a 1-quart measuring bowl with the egg substitute and sugar.

Microwave the margarine in a measuring cup about 1 minute and add to the mixture. Stir to blend and microwave, uncovered, on high for 5 minutes, or until thickened. Stir often after 2 minutes. Pour into tart shells or Graham cracker crust. Chill until firm.

Cutsie Cups: Cut the lemons in half and run a tablespoon around the lemon between the fruit and the pulp. Scoop out the lemon flesh and cook as directed above. Slice just enough off of the ends of the lemon halves so they stand upright. After the lemon custard is cooked, pour into the lemon cups. Leftover custard can be placed in custard cups. Chill until firm. Makes 4.

Yeast breads do not bake well by microwave, therefore I'm not going to even suggest that you try them. Quick breads, such as banana bread, do just fine because they should stay moist and don't necessarily need a crust.

However, when baking bread conventionally there are a few tasks that can be performed with your microwave that complement bread baking.

Raising Dough: After you've made the dough you can halve the rising time by placing the dough in a plastic or glass bowl, covering it with a towel, and microwaving it for 10 minutes on the warm cycle, or 10% power, of your microwave. Let the dough sit in your microwave and it will double in size in about 20 minutes. If you don't have a warm setting, give it 1 minute on defrost and let it sit in the oven for 30 minutes, or until double in size.

Scalding Milk: Because the container doesn't get hot in microwave cooking, you can scald milk and not worry about scorching or burning. Just microwave 1 cup milk, uncovered, about 2 to 3 minutes on high.

Softening Cheese: When a recipe calls for cheese to be blended in, microwave it for a few minutes, until it becomes soft and easy to incorporate.

Melting Butter: Just microwave the quantity of butter until it melts.

Melting Chocolate: For 1 cup chocolate chips or chocolate bark, microwave on high for 1 minute and stir. Continue microwaving in 20-second increments until the chocolate is melted and smooth.

Softening Frostings: Microwave prepared frostings until they are soft enough to spread.

Browning Coconut: Place the shredded coconut in a measuring cup or bowl and microwave on high in 1-minute increments, stirring after each increment, until the coconut is as brown as you want.

Toasting Nuts: Do the same as with coconut.

Baking Breads in the Microwave

Caramelizing Sugar: Just dampen the sugar with water in a heatproof Pyrex measuring container and microwave it on high until it reaches the degree of caramelization you desire. One cup sugar plus 3 tablespoons water takes about 7 minutes to become dark brown.

All of the above techniques must be practiced and noted until you learn the times appropriate to your particular oven. There are so many variables that exact times cannot be stated.

Quick Breads

These breads are easy to prepare and stay nice and moist when you make them with the microwave oven. I especially enjoy making toast with them. The addition of the cereal gives you a lot more nutritional value than just using flour.

Banana Cereal Bread

MICROWAVE ONLY

ENERGY LEVEL:
high, 100%

SERVINGS:
8 to 12

COMPLETE RECIPE TIME:
about 20 minutes

COOKING TIME:
about 10 to 12 minutes

MICROWAVE COOKWARE:
2-quart glass or plastic batter bowl or mixing bowl and a glass or plastic bread loaf pan

COVERING:
wax paper or other nonstick cooking paper

1 very ripe banana, dark brown and mushy

4 ounces egg substitute or 2 large eggs

½ cup sugar

1 cup breakfast cereal of choice, high fiber and fortified

1 cup flour, white or whole wheat

2 teaspoons baking powder

Mix all ingredients and place in an 8½- x 3½- x 2½-inch glass loaf pan coated with nonstick spray. Cover with wax paper or other nonstick cooking paper and microwave on medium, 50%, power for 10 to 12 minutes, or until a pick inserted comes out clean or to an internal temperature of 200 degrees. Invert the loaf on a plate and microwave for 2 minutes on medium power to dry the bottom. Allow to cool.

Cranberry-Banana Bread: To the above recipe add 1 16-ounce can, whole berry cranberry sauce or 2 cups homemade cranberry sauce.

Rhubarb-Banana Bread: To Banana Cereal Bread add 2 cups rhubarb sauce.

Cheesecake

MICROWAVE ONLY

ENERGY LEVEL:
high, 100%, and medium, 50%

SERVINGS:
8

COMPLETE RECIPE TIME:
about 30 minutes

COOKING TIME:
about 20 minutes

MICROWAVE COOKWARE:
2-quart glass or plastic batter bowl or mixing bowl, a 9-inch glass pie dish

ACCESSORY EQUIPMENT:
food processor (optional)

COVERING:
wax paper or other nonstick cooking paper

Cheesecakes cook very well by microwave, but if you make them in a pie dish you must microwave slowly so the heat created around the edge of the dish can be conducted to the center without overcooking the edges. Sometimes the top tends to crack during the cooking. Therefore I like to top cheesecake with cherry or strawberry pie filling or fresh berries glazed with melted jelly.

7 ounces condensed milk

½ cup sugar

8 ounces cream cheese

3 eggs or 6 ounces egg substitute

1 cup cottage cheese

3 tablespoons lemon juice

1 9-inch prepared graham cracker pie crust in a glass pie dish

1 20-ounce can cherry or strawberry pie filling

Place the milk, sugar, and cream cheese in a mixing bowl and microwave on high for 1 to 2 minutes, or until the cheese is soft. Add the eggs, cottage cheese, and lemon juice and blend thoroughly or use your food processor. Pour the mixture into the crust and cover with wax paper. Microwave on medium, 50%, power for 18 to 20 minutes, or until the center has set. Chill until firm. Top with the pie filling before serving.

Crustless Cheesecake in a Ring Pan

MICROWAVE ONLY

ENERGY LEVEL:
high, 100%, medium, 50%

SERVINGS:
8

COMPLETE RECIPE TIME:
about 25 minutes

COOKING TIME:
about 15 minutes

MICROWAVE COOKWARE:
2-quart glass or plastic batter bowl or mixing bowl, a 2-quart plastic ring pan

COVERING:
wax paper or other nonstick cooking paper

Place a ring of wax paper on the bottom of a 2-quart ring pan. Spray the sides with nonstick spray. Prepare the ingredients as directed in the previous recipe and pour into the ring pan. Cover with wax paper and microwave on medium, 50%, power for 12 to 15 minutes, or until set. Chill until firm. Run a knife or spatula around the sides of the cake. Place a large platter over the ring pan and quickly invert the pan onto the platter. Remove the ring pan and carefully remove the wax paper. Top with pie filling and place fresh berries in the center hole.

Cereal Nut Crust

Instead of using a storebought crust, you might like to try this.

1 cup bran flakes (breakfast cereal)	4 tablespoons margarine
½ cup crushed pecans	

Place all ingredients in a small mixing bowl and microwave 1 to 2 minutes, or until the margarine is melted. Mix thoroughly and press into a 9-inch glass pie plate or on the bottom of a 2-quart ring pan.

Chocolate-Coated Strawberries

Coating berries with chocolate is a very easy task when you use your microwave. In most conventional recipes you are directed to use a double boiler to melt the chocolate. Whenever you see a reference to a double boiler, start thinking microwave. Because the containers do not get hot there is no need to protect the food within with a water barrier.

12 ounces chocolate chips or chocolate bark	Toothpicks
20 ripe strawberries, washed and hulled	

Place the chocolate in a measuring cup and microwave on high for 1 to 2 minutes, stirring several times after 1 minute, until the chocolate is melted and smooth. When it starts to melt, you don't have to microwave more because the accumulated energy will be enough to melt it completely.

Insert a toothpick into the stem end of each berry and dip it into the chocolate to completely coat it. Place on wax paper and chill until the chocolate has hardened.

Note: Get a chunk of 1-inch-thick Styrofoam from your building supply store and use it to hold the berries when chilling. Just invert the berry on the toothpick and stick the pick into the foam.

Chocolate-Coated Figs

MICROWAVE ONLY

ENERGY LEVEL:
high, 100%

SERVINGS:
20

COMPLETE RECIPE TIME:
about 10 minutes

COOKING TIME:
about 2 minutes

MICROWAVE COOKWARE:
1-cup measuring cup

ACCESSORY EQUIPMENT:
toothpicks

12 ounces chocolate chips or
    chocolate bark

20 peeled almonds

20 dried figs or pitted dates

Toothpicks

Place the chocolate in a measuring cup and microwave on high for 1 to 2 minutes, or until the chocolate is melted and smooth. Insert a nut into each fig and spear with a toothpick. Dip into the chocolate and swirl until the fig is completely coated. Place on wax paper and chill until the chocolate has hardened. Or use Styrofoam as directed in the previous recipe.

Zap Tips

Here are some more little tips to help you use your microwave more efficiently.

1. After you hollow out a loaf of bread, microwave it on high, uncovered, for 4 to 5 minutes and let it cool. It will harden and hold its shape when filled with a dip.

2. To reheat pizza using your microwave, place several pieces on a plate and microwave them about 1 minute per slice, or until the cheese starts bubbling. In the meantime, heat a skillet on your stove top. Take the pizza from the microwave, slide it onto the skillet, and heat it for 40 to 60 seconds, or until the crust is crisp.

3. Microwave raw sausage and pepperoni and pour off the fat before you add it to a pizza. You'll be amazed at how much fat you can eliminate from the pizza and still retain the flavor of the sausage.

4. Whole garlic cloves can be cooked in your microwave. Just break the heads into separate cloves and soak them in water for a couple of minutes. Wrap in plastic wrap and microwave on high for about 10 seconds per clove, or

until soft. Slip off the skins, mash with olive oil, and spread on French bread or add to pizza and other things.

5. To reduce liquids, use your stove top. It is faster and more efficient.

6. When making a sandwich with cold cuts or cooked sausage, microwave the meat for 30 to 40 seconds before you add it to the sandwich. You'll be amazed at how much more flavor is released.

7. Microwave lemons and limes 30 to 40 seconds before squeezing them; you'll get a lot more juice.

8. When microwaving whole fish, use less than full power. High power concentrates the energy in spots and tends to cause the fish to burst in spots.

9. When microwaving whole ears of corn, stick the little metal pronged holders into the cobs before you microwave them. It's easier than trying to stick them in when the corn is hot.

10. After microwaving Russet potatoes, cut them open and fluff the flesh with a fork. Microwave, uncovered, for 1 minute per potato. You'll get a dried potato just as if it had been baked in a hot oven.

11. If you want a dry, crisp shell for stuffed potatoes, remove the pulp from the skin and microwave the skins, open side down, for 2 to 3 minutes, or until crisp and brown.

12. Remove excess water from mashed potatoes by microwaving them, uncovered, for 5 to 10 minutes, or until they get as dry as you want them.

13. Microwave or cook conventionally large batches of rice and freeze small portions in plastic bags for use later. When needed, microwave a frozen serving for 2 to 3 minutes in the bag.

14. To separate fat from juices, insert a basting bulb under the fat and draw off the juices. Deposit into another container. Continue until only fat is left in the first container.

15. To make croutons in your microwave oven, dice French

bread or other bread and sprinkle with oil and seasonings. Place is a glass bowl or large measuring cup and microwave, uncovered, on high about 1 minute per cup of croutons. Stir and let set for a couple of minutes until they harden.

16. To toast sesame seeds in your microwave, place 3 tablespoons of seeds in a measuring cup and microwave, uncovered, on high for 4 to 5 minutes, or until they brown. Stir every minute or so.

17. To toast nuts in your microwave, microwave 1 cup raw nuts in a 1-cup measuring cup for 4 to 5 minutes, or until you smell them toasting. Let set for a couple minutes and test to see if they are dry enough.

18. To open oysters for stew or other cooked uses, microwave them, uncovered, for about 30 seconds each or until they open their lips a bit. Slip in your knife and cut them open.

19. To serve a number of omelets at one time, make them up conventionally, place on a serving platter, and cover with plastic wrap. When you want to serve them, microwave on high for about 1 minute per omelet, or until heated through.

20. To freshen cereal and crackers that have become stale, pour into a plastic colander and microwave, uncovered, for 2 to 3 minutes. Let stand for a couple of minutes, or until they become crisp. Replace in their box and seal tightly.

21. To bring out the flavor of refrigerated cheese, microwave for 10 to 20 seconds, or until the chill is gone.

22. Store leftover red wine in your refrigerator, it keeps better. Microwave a 6-ounce glass 10 to 20 seconds to bring it to proper drinking temperature—60 to 70 degrees is recommended.

23. To separate slices of refrigerated bacon, microwave the whole pound in its package for 20 to 30 seconds, or until it becomes soft.

24. Serve hot steaming towels to your guests by dampening cloth or high-quality finger towels and microwaving on a platter for about 1 minute for 6, or until they are hot.

25. Microwave rubbing alcohol before applying to avoid the shock of cold alcohol.

26. Microwave damp towels about 1 minute and use to ease the pain of muscle strains and arthritis.

27. Microwave hard ice cream 10 to 20 seconds, or until it just begins to soften so it's easier to scoop.

28. For fast, real, iced tea, place a tea bag in a cup and barely cover it with water. Microwave on high for 1 minute and add the bag and concentrated tea water to a glass of ice and fill with water. Squeeze the tea bag and discard.

29. Microwave tough cuts of meat like brisket and pot roast and shanks, covered, on high about 5 minutes per pound, or to an internal temperature of 120 degrees. Transfer to your conventional oven and cook until done and tender. By doing this you are quickly bringing the meat up to the temperature where it starts cooking and tenderizing by conventional cooking and you reduce the total cooking time by about half. The result is the same as if you had cooked it conventionally for the whole time.

30. Soften window putty before using to replace broken panes.

31. To heat serving plates, just place them under the food being microwaved during the last 5 minutes of cooking. Or place a damp towel on top of the plates and micro-wave the plates on high power for 2 to 3 minutes.

32. To make quick wishes, microwave chicken and turkey wishbones about 20 to 30 seconds and they will become dry and brittle so you can make a wish with your favorite person right after you've eaten the bird.

33. To make fat-free potato chips, slice large potatoes very thin, about 1/16 inch. Place on a microwave roasting rack or on the sides of a plastic colander and sprinkle with your favorite herbs or seasoned salt. Microwave 30 to 40 seconds, or until the chips turn brown and get crisp.

34. To make tasty, fat-free popcorn, place popped popcorn in a large microwave container and sprinkle with soy sauce, Worcestershire sauce, hot sauce, and so on. Microwave 1 to 2 minutes, uncovered, or until it gets crisp again.

35. To toast sunflower, pumpkin, or other squash seeds, clean, wash, and dry 1 cup of seeds. Place in a glass bowl or measuring cup and microwave on high, uncovered, for about 7 minutes, or until crisp. Stir several times.

Index